GREEN PSYCHOLOGY

GREEN PSYCHOLOGY

Transforming Our Relationship to the Earth

Ralph Metzner, Ph.D.

Park Street Press
Rochester, Vermont

Park Street Press
One Park Street
Rochester, Vermont 05767
www.InnerTraditions.com

Park Street Press is a division of Inner Traditions International

Library of Congress Cataloging-in-Publication Data

Metzner, Ralph.
    Green psychology : transforming our relationship to the
earth / Ralph Metzner.
      p. cm.
      Includes bibliographical references (p.   ) and index.
      ISBN 0-89281-798-4 (alk. paper)
      1. Nature—Psychological aspects. 2. Environmental psychology.
    3. Environmentalism—Psychological aspects. 4. Human ecology
—Religious aspects. 5. Psychology and religion. I. Title.
    BF353.5.N37M47   1999
    155.9'1—dc21   99-20490
                                                              CIP

Printed and bound in Canada

10 9 8 7 6 5 4 3 2

Text design and layout by Crystal Roberts
This book was typeset in Minion

The author acknowledges, with gratitude, the assistance of Padma Catell
and Jack Coddington in preparing the slides of the art work; and Alex Grey
for permission to reproduce his magnificent painting *Gaia,* which epitomizes
the central theme of this book.

This work is dedicated
to four elders
who have inspired me
with their wisdom and vision—
Hildegard von Bingen
Thomas Berry
Marija Gimbutas
Paul Shepard

Contents

Foreword

Cultures keep secrets; they illuminate some things and suppress others. Every culture conceals as much as it reveals; that is its style and its distinctive contribution. Cultures survive as long as they can maintain that style, which means as long as they can hide from themselves. There is a sense in which every culture is a conspiracy, a coordinated effort to open a few doors of perception and to close others.

The natural environment has been excluded from mainstream psychological theory so totally that it might very well be a deliberate conspiratorial act. How could so vast a flaw go unnoticed except by collusive negligence? Let me, in fact, put the case as strongly as possible. The environmental disconnection of modern psychology is indeed a conspiracy: a centuries-long collaboration among the best and most authoritative minds in our society to keep human nature as distant, different, and disengaged from nature as possible.

It is only during rare periods of disintegration or strenuous transition that courageously inquiring minds have the chance to see through the "official secret acts" of their culture and take a greater perspective into account. This is obviously such a period. Over the past two to three generations, for reasons both internal and external, Western culture has been showing more and more cracks in its intellectual defenses; the truths and beauties of other peoples have been showing through. Interestingly, the language in which we tend to describe this condition is frequently psychological. On a collective level, we speak of "repression" and "break-down." On the individual level, since the days of the Romantic artists, we have been fascinated with work and thought that walks the edges of sanity. Artists try to derange the sensibilities, seeking the madness that we sense is akin to genius. We have more and more looked to the mad but gifted few to reveal deep truths like the babbling oracles of ancient times. It sometimes seems that we take breakdown to be the signature of breakthrough—as R. D. Laing once phrased it. Unless we are in the presence of a mind that confabulates with the forbidden, that dares to look beyond the conventional reality, we feel we are not in the presence of depth and truth.

As of the late twentieth century, if one were to argue that the political tensions that crisscross family life play no part in determining the sanity of individuals, who would take such a diagnosis seriously? Yet it remains a defensible professional assumption that the sanity of individuals and of whole societies has no connection with the depletion of the ozone, the death of the seas, the devastation of the rain forests, the mass extinction of species, global warming, runaway population growth, resource exhaustion . . . in short, with behavior both individual and collective that now threatens to destroy the living planet. In the great debate over human survival, professional psychology has elected not to be a player.

Over the past decade, an increasing number of more adventurous psychologists have sought to create new, ecologically relevant forms of therapy. Their motivation is as much ethical as it is a matter of pure theoretical curiosity. Just as lawyers have elaborated the study of environmental law and teachers have introduced environmental curricula into our schools, so the psychologists are finally, if belatedly, responding to the influence of the environmental movement.

Ralph Metzner is among the pioneers in broadening psychological theory to include the world that lies beyond our social connections. His "green psychology" gracefully brings the fullness of the natural environment into the theory and practice of psychotherapy. He has taken us beyond the city limits of conventional psychology to see our deep emotional connection to the planet at large. In this timely and necessary project, he deserves to take his place among the major figures in modern psychological thought.

In *Green Psychology,* Metzner's work with myth is particularly brilliant. Where Freud and even Jung could see no greater meaning to myth than its role in the individuating process—a focus that remains wholly within the human unconscious—Metzner interprets the great myths as messages from Earth, which has been the greater nurturing presence in our evolutionary story. In his hands, the myths suddenly take on a depth they never had before. Another, greater voice than our own speaks through them.

Metzner argues that there is a sympathetic bond between our species and the planet that is every bit as tenacious as the sexual instincts Freud found in the depths of the psyche and every bit as powerful as our family ties. His green psychology begins with matters as familiar to all of us as the empathic rapport with the natural world that is reborn in every child and which survives in the work of nature poets and landscape painters. Where this sense of shared identity is experienced as we most often experience it between person and person, we call it love. More coolly and distantly felt between the human and nonhuman, it is called compassion. In either case, the result is spontaneous loyalty.

Saving the life of the planet is the biggest political cause human beings have yet taken on; it requires a vision of the human personality that is just as big. Blaming and shaming are bound to continue playing a major role in environmental politics; there is more than enough guilty conscience to be worked through and still plenty of environmental malefactors to be called to account. But once politics as usual has been given its due, perhaps it is the green psychologists who will help us understand the true emotional depths of the cause, asking what environmental responsibility connects with in people that is generous, joyous, freely given, and noble.

Theodore Roszak
Professor Emeritus of History,
California State University, Hayward
author of *The Voice of the Earth*

Introduction

No one can doubt that we live in a time of unprecedented ecological destruction. The fabric of life on this planet is being degraded at an ever accelerating pace, accompanied by massive loss of animal and plant diversity and escalating threats to human health and well-being. Evolutionary biologists tell us that there have been numerous episodes of worldwide extinction before, including five major "spasms" involving the loss of up to 90 percent of existing species—the last one being the cataclysm sixty-five million years ago that brought the Age of Dinosaurs to an end. What is unprecedented about the present situation is that it is the actions and technological productions of one species—the human being—that are bringing about this biosphere meltdown. Increasing numbers of people have therefore come to the conclusion that it is in the hearts and minds of human beings that the causes *and* cures of the ecocatastrophe are to be found.

This is the basic reason why a psychologist like me is concerning himself with the imbalance in the human-nature relationship and how it can be healed. If the imbalance exists because of certain mistaken or delusional attitudes, perceptions, and beliefs, then we can ask the psychological questions of how this came about and how it can be changed.

As a psychotherapist, I am a member of a profession that deals with psychic disturbance and pathology. Cannot what we have learned from working with troubled individuals and families help us deal with this collective psychopathology, this profound alienation of the human psyche from Earth? These are a few of the basic questions of "green psychology" that I wish to address in this book.

I prefer the term *green psychology* to *ecopsychology*, which is presently gaining considerable currency largely owing to Theodore Roszak's brilliant work in *The Voice of the Earth*. The reason is that those of us in this field (including Roszak) do not mean to advocate the creation of a new subdiscipline of psychology, to join clinical, social, developmental, and other forms. Rather we are talking about a fundamental re-envisioning of what psychology is, or what it should have been in the first place—a revision that would take the ecological context of human life into account. As Roszak says, "Psychology needs ecology, and ecology needs psychology." The absence of any consideration given to the ecological basis of human life in textbooks and theories of psychology is startling: it's as if we lived in a vacuum or a space capsule. Interestingly, some of the earliest and most profound contributions to an ecological psychology were made by nonpsychologists: the ecologist Paul Shepard (in *Nature and Madness*), the theologian Thomas Berry (in *The Dream of the Earth*), the philosopher Warwick Fox (in *Transpersonal Ecology*), and the historian Theodore Roszak (in *The Voice of the Earth*).

The kind of fundamental re-envisioning called for by ecologically minded, "green" psychologists parallels similar movements in other fields. Philosophers in the new field of environmental ethics have been working for twenty years on the philosophical and moral aspects of environmental problems and how ethical considerations can be brought into discussions of public policy. A small but growing number of ecological economists have been investigating the thorny problems involved in re-envisioning conventional economic theory to take the ecological basis of all economic activity into account. Unlikely as it may seem, even the field of religious studies has undergone significant soul-searching, under the stimulus of devastating critiques by environmental philosophers. Conferences have been held in which representatives of the major organized religions have examined their traditions in response to a call for religious consideration of ecological issues. Together with major paradigm shifts in the natural sciences—primarily from the mechanistic, atomistic framework to a systems view of nature and the cosmos—these re-envisionings amount to the beginnings of an ecological or systems worldview.

Ecology has been called the "subversive science" because by making relationships and interdependencies the central focus of its concerns, it subverts the traditional academic tendencies to specialization and fragmentation. Ecopsychology within a systems worldview, therefore, of necessity, would have to consider questions traditionally dealt with by philosophers, economists, biologists, theologians, or historians from within their respective paradigms. As an educator, I have wrestled for twenty years with the problems involved in teaching ecological perspectives to students who do not see the relevance of these issues to their interests in the human psyche or in self-development. I can't say that I have found any certain answers to this educational dilemma, but the essays in this book point to possible approaches that I've found useful.

A new understanding of the role of the human in the biosphere is urgently needed. Philosophers dating back to the European Romantic movement and American Transcendentalism have identified the domination of nature by humans as the root pathology of Western civilization. In the twentieth century, as the pace of worldwide ecological destruction and the loss of species diversity has accelerated under the relentless onslaught of technological industrialism, such critiques have taken on a tone of urgency verging on desperation.

A distinction can be made between those environmental movements that focus on improved legislative control over pollution and waste and on scientific ecosystem management, on the one hand, and, on the other, those movements of "radical ecology" that challenge the very foundations of the modernist industrial worldview and the ideologies of domination associated with it. Radical ecology movements include deep ecology, ecofeminism, social ecology, socialist ecology, ecojustice, bioregionalism—and perhaps ecopsychology, if considered from a holistic or systems perspective.

The radical ecology movements emphasize one or another form of domination as the core of the interlocking systems of domination that characterize the modern world. The deep ecology movement has as its central focus the replacement of anthropocentric, exploitative attitudes toward nature by nondominating eco- or biocentric values and paradigms. Ecofeminism links the domination of nature with the patriachal domination of women. Social ecology critiques all forms of hierarchical order and domination, whether of class, ethnicity, or gender. For socialist ecology the crucial diagnosis is via the analysis of capital accumulation and the profit motive. The eco- or environmental justice movement focuses on the links between racism and the human domination of nature. Bioregionalism involves a critique of conventional political and economic approaches to places and regions. Green psychology, or ecopsychology, could also be considered "radical"—insofar as it posits a fundamental reorientation of human attitudes toward the totality of the "more-than-human world."

In addition to these radical re-envisionings of fundamental paradigms and value systems in the social sciences, philosophy, and religion, there has also been an increased openness and receptivity to indigenous and archaic forms of knowledge. As the environmental devastation wrought by the industrial model of development increases, the realization has grown that indigenous societies (those that have survived) have, in fact, often preserved practices of sustainability that we are now desperately trying to re-invent. As the generally negative or neglectful attitudes toward the environment enshrined in the major organized religions have become more obvious, many concerned individuals have found themselves turning toward the animistic, polytheistic religion of their "pagan" ancestors—the pre-Christian "country dwellers" who recognized and respected the spiritual intelligences inherent in nature. As the spiritual emptiness and moral shallowness in many religious and psychotherapeutic systems have become more and more evident, thousands of seekers have turned to shamanic practices—such as the shamanic journey, the vision quest, or the use of hallucinogenic visionary plants—to cultivate a more direct psychic, conscious connection with the natural world.

These are a few of the major themes in this work. In the first chapter, "The True, Original First World," I describe how a trip to the Lacandon Maya in Chiapas, Mexico, and my participation in a ceremony with their traditional intoxicant *balché* led to a radical paradigm shift in my thinking: the multinational industrial empire based on economic and military might cannot be considered the "First World." That appellation should belong to the historically oldest and primary layer of civilization—the world of the indigenous tribal peoples. In the next chapter, "Gaia's Alchemy: Ruin and Renewal of the Earth," I explore how the symbolic language of alchemy, the medieval science that concerned itself with the transformation of matter, can be used to understand the massive biospheric transformations taking place in our time. This essay is followed by an account of my participation in a traditional vision quest in the California desert. Through this experience, I came to a much deeper appreciation for the role of such earth-honoring rituals.

Chapter 4, "Mystical Greenness: The Visions of Hildegard von Bingen," discusses the astonishing ecological spirituality and nature mysticism of this twelfth-century Benedictine abbess and visionary prophet, a prime exponent of what some are calling the "creation spirituality" tradition within Christianity.

In the fifth chapter, I discuss the historical and potential future role of psychoactive plant medicines in systems of transformation, such as shamanism, alchemy, and yoga. In chapter 6, I review the diagnostic metaphors from psychopathology that have been proposed to account for the collective pathology of the human relationship to nature—concepts such as autism, amnesia, addiction, dissociation, and others. In the seventh chapter, I discuss some of the historical roots of the split between humans and nature, particularly its origins in the rise of mechanistic science and, further back, in the ascendancy of transcendental monotheism.

Chapter 8, "Sky Gods and Earth Deities," traces the split even further back into prehistory—into the long, drawn-out struggle between the invading nomadic Indo-Europeans, with their sky and warrior gods, and the aboriginal matricentric goddess cultures of Old Europe, with their Earth, animal, and feminine deities. In chapter 9, "The Black Goddess, the Green God, and the Wild Human," I explore the key mythic figures of our pagan ancestors—the gods and goddesses that personify our relationship to the Earth, to the plant realm, and to the world of animals. Chapter 10, "Reunification of the Sacred and the Natural," argues that the current revival of interest in the sacramental use of visionary plants can contribute to a healing of the split in our collective psyche.

With the last two chapters, I return to the present. The eleventh chapter, "Transition to an Ecological Worldview," summarizes, in as condensed a fashion as possible, the main distinguishing features of the ecosystems worldview, as it is emerging in many disciplines simultaneously out of the inadequacies of the modernist worldview with its associated techno-industrial excesses. Finally, in chapter 12, "The Place and the Story," I show how in such an ecological worldview, a new, yet ancient perspective on human identity can arise. Traditional people have a much closer relationship to place; we need to learn to understand ourselves in relationship to a place and to the story of that place—and, ultimately, to the story of the universe.

The True, Original
First World

My interests in shamanism, ethnopharmacology and indigenous cultures converged in a trip I made to the Lacandon Maya in the rain forest of Chiapas, Mexico. While there, I was able to sample the ceremonial intoxicant known as balché. This journey led me to the realization that our familiar conception of First, Third, and Fourth Worlds, based on economic power, is logically and historically flawed. The world of the indigenous tribal people is the true, original first world.[1]

In January of 1995, I had the opportunity to visit one of the villages of the Lacandon Maya, in the company of a fluent speaker of their native tongue—an anthropologist who had lived among them for more than two years. This visit occurred a few weeks before the crackdown by the Mexican army on indigenous villagers perceived as being supporters of the Zapatistas. We ourselves did not see any of the rebels, though they had been seen earlier by the villagers, before disappearing into the remote jungles and highlands of southern Chiapas. In the small town of Palenque, street vendors of indigenous crafts were offering Zapatista puppets, complete with black ski masks and rifles—images of revolution turned into commodities as folk art. Likewise, we did not see the army in action, although we had to pass through three roadblocks on the drive to the village and troops from a nearby army encampment did their daily exercise jog by our hotel, chanting training slogans and accompanied by armed guards in jeeps. We were told the young men passed their time in the camp playing cards and smoking pot and supplementing their meager salaries by dealing pot as well.

The occasion for the visit to the Lacandones was a seminar on the Ethnobotany and Chemistry of Psychoactive Plants organized by the Botanical Preservation Corps, a North American educational and research group dedicated to gathering and preserving traditional knowledge of medicinal and psychoactive plants, particularly from Central and South America.[2] My general approach to the topic of psychoactive (or entheogenic or hallucinogenic or psychedelic) plants is that I see the revival of interest in them as an aspect of the renewed respect for indigenous traditions of knowledge. They are forms of knowledge and practice that have preserved a relationship of mutuality and reciprocity with the natural world. The reemergence of a respectful and ceremonial approach to sacred visionary plants (*not* drugs, which is another story altogether) can be seen as an aspect of a grassroots paradigm shift toward more Gaian, holistic, and ecological thinking and values.

I would argue that at a time when the global techno-industrial culture is leading to massive erosion of biodiversity, worldwide ecosystem destruction, and profound social and economic disintegration, there are a number of cultural movements that are cautiously and purposively moving toward the articulation of an ecological worldview and a bioregional, sustainable lifestyle. Among movements with similar values and assumptions, I would include the revival of interest in herbal, homeopathic, and natural medicine; shamanic practices; bioregionalism; deep ecology; ecofeminism; social ecology; environmental ethics; ecopsychology; ecotheology; green economics; and the neopagan revival. The ecology movement was born out of the same 1960s cauldron of social transformations, along with the civil rights movement, the antiwar movement, the free-speech movement, the women's liberation "consciousness-raising" movement, and the so-called sexual revolution. All of these groups challenged the alienating and restrictive attitudes of earlier generations.

Even though corporate practices continue to degrade and pollute the environment and government policies to prevent or reduce these practices are woefully inadequate, public opinion surveys carried out in the United States over the past two decades have shown a persistent increase in general pro-environmental attitudes and concerns, to the point where 70 to 80 percent of Americans acknowledge environmental preservation as one of their highest-priority values.[3] With the 1990s has come increased public awareness of economic and technological globalization, which has vastly increased the scope and power of the multinational industrial corporations, with a concomitant increase in the scope and intensity of worldwide biosphere destruction, loss of species diversity, and massive social disruptions accompanied by poverty, famine, disease, violence, war, refugee migrations, and the like.[4]

A key theme in the political rhetoric and media punditry of the seventies and eighties was the cold war confrontation between what were called the "First World" and the "Second World." These two worlds were seen as competing for the political allegiance and economic alliance of the countries of the so-called Third World, which was seen as needing "development" in order to bring it to the levels of prosperity assumed (falsely) to be prevalent in the industrialized First and Second Worlds. During the nineties, this whole balance of power has collapsed. What we have now instead is one remaining military superpower, the United States, with its politically aligned yet economically competing trading partners, primarily Western Europe and Japan, constituting the so-called First World or the industrialized North. The former Second World is no more. Russia and its erstwhile client states, including Eastern Europe, are rapidly being turned into Third World countries, in which cheap labor and as yet unexploited natural resources can become fodder for the industrial growth machine of the Northern First World. This transformation is sometimes referred to as the "triumph of capitalism."

The East–West political dynamic, backed by military might and the threat of nuclear force, has been replaced by a North–South economic dynamic, also backed by the threat of military power. The continuing exploitation of the Southern Third World by the Northern and Western First World, which used to be called colonialism and is now called "development," is encountering growing resistance, however, particularly in the Southern countries, whose people can see more clearly the nature of the beast. In the industrialized Northern First World, the resistance can also be seen in the opposition (by various labor and environmental groups and some conservatives) to the passage of NAFTA, GATT, MAI, and similar instruments of economic globalization.[5]

A further aspect of this resistance has been the concept of the Fourth World: the world of indigenous societies politically encapsulated within larger nation-states, living by subsistence economies, and not participating voluntarily in the industrial development process but equally threatened by exploitation and extinction. Between two hundred and six hundred million of Earth's people belong to indigenous societies, making up as many as five thousand different language cultures. Environmentalists and conservationists working in various parts of the globe have increasingly come to the realization that indigenous societies provide models for the kind of sustainable stewardship of natural resources that the industrial world desperately needs to learn. Indigenous writers have pointed out that these people are the "miner's canary" of the human family: existing in direct dependence on nature, they are the first to suffer the effects of pollution, degradation, and exploitation.[6]

FROM THE INDUSTRIAL FIRST WORLD TO THE INDIGENOUS FOURTH WORLD

In the journey that we took to the Lacandones living in the rain forest of Chiapas, we traveled from the First World through the Third and into the Fourth, and in the process of doing so, I came to a new appreciation of the complex and precarious cultural dynamics that constitute the real present-day world order. Flying into Mexico City, a thick, poisonous, yellow-brown blanket of smog is visible over the city, and numerous smokestacks can be seen emitting huge plumes of even thicker smoke. With well over thirty million inhabitants and adding several hundred thousand more per year, Mexico City is the largest urban conglomeration in the world, containing vast masses of impoverished rural immigrants living in unimaginable squalor. At the same time, it is an outpost of the North's industrial and financial empire, where wealthy Mexican and multinational corporate elites, with their armies of managers, lawyers, accountants, and bankers, pursue ever increasing profit opportunities through intensified exploitation of natural resources, currency and financial speculations, and assorted marginally legal forms of trade, primarily involving drugs and arms.

When, on January 1, 1994, NAFTA was signed into law, the Zapatista Army of National Liberation occupied several towns and villages in Chiapas, demanding that the government recognize the Indians' rights to their lands, their culture, and their autonomy and equal participation in the democratic process. Whether the Indians will ultimately gain any of their demands as a result of this rebellion remains to be seen. A series of military and political moves and countermoves ensued, which have led directly to the unraveling of the seventy-year stranglehold of the ruling Mexican party, the collapse of the Mexican stock market and economy, the political disgrace of former President Carlos Salinas de Gortari, rampant inflation, and mass unemployment.

From Mexico City, we flew to Villahermosa, industrial capital of the state of Tabasco, where tens of thousands of protesters organized by the opposition party had occupied the plaza in front of the government building, demanding the resignation of the recently and fraudulently elected governor (a demand to which he ultimately acceded). The protests forced the government to move to other buildings and triggered sporadic army roadblocks and airport closures in retaliation. One can see these conflicts as expressions of the ongoing divisions between the ruling elites and the disenfranchised masses, between the centralized nation-state and the outlying rural populations, or more generally between First World centers (capital and industry) and Third World periphery (peasants and indigenous people).

From Villahermosa, a two-hour bus or taxi ride takes us to the small town of Palenque and a hotel beautifully situated near the ancient ruins. We immersed ourselves in the arcana of the chemistry, botany, and indigenous lore concerning visionary plants and fungi. We also visited the ruins of Palenque, a Classic Mayan ceremonial city abandoned one thousand years ago that the Lacandones still refer to as the "navel of the world." Here, in an immense complex of dozens of temples, more than a hundred thousand people—nobles and their families, priests, magicians, scribes, astronomers, stonemasons, sculptors, painters, artisans, as well as the traders and farmers who supported them—lived and died, performing elaborate ceremonies and celebrations, honoring the cycles of the sun and moon and planets and their earthly counterparts. The Mayan nobility referred to themselves as *halach uinic,* "the true, original humans," and also *zac uinic,* "the white (or radiant, or bright) people." On a night when the moon was full, when the Moon goddess, Ix'chel, also the goddess of beauty, love, healing, herbs and flowers, and women and children, bathed the bleached stones of the ancient temples in ethereal radiance, we were able to enter the complex and sit in quiet meditation on the steps of the central temple. While the fragrance of copal incense mingled with the smells of the tropical night, I wrote this poem:

We sit in silence on the steps
of the House of Our True Lord,
in the soothing silvery light
of the full moon, embraced by
the goddess Ix'chel.
And the spirits of the noble
Maya lords and ladies,
halach uinic, zac uinic,
the true humans, the bright ones,
who left this place a thousand years ago,
graced our presence in
a moment of unspeakable beauty,
and flowered again in our dreams.

According to our guide, the anthropologist Christian Rätsch, who has studied the ancient and modern Mayan languages, "flowering dreams" is the term used to describe the visions induced by certain plants, minerals, animals, or magical practices. Today we refer to such experiences as "altered states of consciousness" or "nonordinary realities." The ancient Maya and their modern descendants certainly were deeply familiar with a whole range of visionary states—traveling in other worlds and encountering beings that, to us, appear incomprehensible, nonordinary, magical, or even alien. Their visions were expressed with surpassing artistry in the bas-relief sculptures on the walls of the temples, which in ancient times were brightly painted, and in ceramic vases and sometimes frescoes. These show the figures of men and women in various ritual postures, dressed in animal skins, especially the jaguar, encoiled with serpents, toads, and monkeys and with outrageously fantastic feathered headdresses and ornaments on noses, ears, lips, and heads.

The Lacandon and other Mayan societies still surviving in Chiapas, Yucatan, and Guatemala have preserved many of the traditions and practices of their forebear. Until quite recent times, when the pressure of tourism stopped them, small groups of Lacandones used to regularly visit the ruins of Palenque and perform ceremonies in the temples, burning copal and singing invocations to their gods and goddesses. Worldwide, the indigenous peoples of the so-called Fourth World have preserved the spiritual practices as well as the ecological awareness of their ancestors. By contrast, in the industrialized, urban North, the increasing dominance of the materialist worldview, and the colonialist mentality that accompanied it, has led to severe alienation from the traditional sense of embeddedness in the cycles of the natural world. This represents a contraction of consciousness and perspective—what the Indian ecologist Vandana Shiva has aptly called "monocultures of the mind."[7]

Our little party of five people drove in a van the hundred or so kilometers from Palenque to the village of Naha, one of three remaining Lacandon settlements. On the drive there we had to pass through three army roadblocks, where solemn young men with machine guns questioned us about our destination, our origin, how much money we had, and so on. Laboriously, they wrote our names and passport numbers in a book—evidently under orders to track all movements of people in and out of the contested regions. The road became progressively narrow and eventually unpaved, winding through open fields and dense tropical rain forest. We seemed to be leaving the Third World urban environment and entering the indigenous Fourth World environment of small villages by lake- or streamside. We saw fewer and fewer cars and trucks, but the villages, including Naha, had an occasional satellite dish and color televisions—the long tentacles of the urban industrial center have reached here as well.

Most of the remaining five hundred Lacandones live in traditional villages; some of them live in towns like Palenque, like our driver, and make a living doing odd jobs there while still maintaining frequent contact with relatives. Christian Rätsch is an adopted relative of the Lacandones because of his previous long stays there, and he was therefore asked to don the ankle-length white cotton robe worn by all the men. When we arrived in Naha, several of the young men came out to greet him, maintaining a certain respectful distance but laughing and talking with great animation and obvious pleasure. Christian introduced us as relatives of his, and we were graciously welcomed also. All the men were barefoot, wearing white robes, and they had long, jet-black hair, which never turns gray or white with age. The women wore somewhat more colorful clothes, with necklaces of beads and multicolored sashes and dresses. The young boys also wore the "white" robes—though most boys and their clothing were incredibly filthy. Their speech is delightful to listen to, even though I didn't understand a word; it has a kind of rhythmic cadence, with many glottal stops and rich vowel sounds. I was content just to soak up the nonverbal ambience.

Although some of the Lacandones have watches, and some have television sets and radios, these artifacts of twentieth-century technology seem to play a marginal role in their lives. Like other indigenous people, they are still mostly connected to the natural cycles of sun and moon, of wind and rain, of growing crops and flowering plants. The Lacandones

Lacandon men conversing with Christian Rätsch, on right, in the village of Naha. (Photo by Ralph Metzner)

do not make decisions about when to plant or harvest, when to go on a hunt, or when to hold a ceremony on the basis of complex calendrical calculations, as did their ancestors, who lived in the ceremonial centers of Palenque and Yaxchilan. Rather, they let the natural occurrences of the seasons and the needs of the community determine the timing of such events.

We spent the afternoon visiting several families, including that of old Chan K'in, who is said to be between 107 and 110 years old (he does not know himself, nor does he care). He has had four wives, dozens of children, and innumerable grandchildren. Two of his wives are still living—one in her seventies and a younger one in her forties. The younger one was carrying around a two-year old child of the old man. He is not a chief—the anarchic Lacandones have no chiefs. Perhaps "elder" would be an appropriate term. He is obviously respected, even revered, and has a reputation far beyond his village for his extensive knowledge of

Old Chan K'in, 110-year-old village elder. (Photo by Ralph Metzner)

traditional lore, chants, incantations, and magical practices. We found him sitting on a pile of blankets on a cot in the middle of his hut, which, like all the huts in the village, had plain wooden board walls and an earthen floor, with a few simple pieces of wooden furniture. His very mobile, expressive face was kind, with large, sparkling, round eyes. Christian told us that the Lacandones have no way of saying "hello" or "goodbye"; when they meet they just start talking, and when they depart they just walk away. It's as if the bonds of family and friendship are not disconnected by distance and therefore do not need to be reestablished.

The Lacandones farm the surrounding land, growing corn, beans, chili, and squash using the traditional slash-and-burn technique; their diet is supplemented by occasional hunting expeditions (formerly with bows and arrows, now with rifles) for monkeys, tapirs, parrots, and other game. The old Chan K'in has always worked on his part of the communal land; later, we saw him walking, slowly, carefully placing his feet, assisted by a long wooden staff. I was reminded of Lao-tzu's description of the Taoist sage: "He walks carefully, like a fox crossing a frozen river." Christian tells me that when he lived here, he once contracted amebic dysentery and lay at death's door for three days; none of the Western medicines was working, and he wrote a farewell letter to his parents. Finally, old Chan K'in came and chanted magical songs for several hours—this led to a full recovery. Although the Lacandones have extensive knowledge of edible and healing plants of the forest, they seem to rely for most healing primarily on chants and incantations. There are no "shamans," or healers. Everyone learns to heal through singing, just as everyone learns to plant and to harvest, to hunt and to prepare food.

A *BALCHÉ* CEREMONY

Balché is the ceremonial intoxicant of the Lacandones. The preparation of the drink normally takes two or three days, but in honor of our coming one of Christian's adopted relatives, a man in his seventies who looked to be in his forties, had already prepared the drink for us, and the following morning, after a freezing night, we assembled in the "god-house" for the ceremony. The drink is made in a large dugout canoe from the strips of bark of the *balché* tree *(Lonchocarpus violaceus)* soaked in water and fermented with honey. Hour-long incantations are sung by the

The god-house, with balché ceremony in process, seen from the forest. (Photo by Ralph Metzner)

one who prepares the drink: numerous gods and spirits of the forest are invoked, especially the spirits of various poisonous plants, mushrooms, and insects. They are asked to enter into the drink, to make it strong and healthy. The Lacandones say the balché makes them strong and helps them live long. Perhaps the invocation of poisonous ingredients is a kind of spiritual immunization; the drink with those spirits in it fortifies the drinker against those poisons.[8]

The god-house is a thatched-roof structure with open sides. Only the men assemble for the ceremony; women, if they participate at all (rarely, though it is not prohibited), sit in a separate structure about twenty-five feet to the side. Inside the god-house are rows of blackened god-pots—ceramic pots for holding the copal incense, each one carved with the face of a deity. Part of the way through the ceremony, the master of ceremonies lights the chunks of copal resin, which burn brightly and send up great clouds of black smoke. He also takes a gourd bowl of the drink and offers each of the god-faces a little bit of the drink with a leaf—all the while chanting and praying softly. The master takes a quantity of the drink from the canoe that is nearby and fills a large gourd; from this

Master of the balché ceremony lighting the copal-filled god-pots. (Photo by Ralph Metzner)

large gourd he then fills the smaller gourds and gives each participant one to drink from. One is expected to drink large quantities, we are told—several liters every hour—and the ceremony continues for several hours. Balché is an intoxicant, emetic, and purgative; from time to time, the men go into the nearby forest to urinate, vomit, or defecate. Afterward you feel cleansed, lightened, hungry. As visitors, no one put pressure on us to drink—we were told just to take as much as we wanted.

The three Western men in the group sat on low stools in the god-house along with about a dozen Lacandones, who came and went quite informally. The group included, from time to time, young boys, who also drink the balché. Two visiting women sat in the nearby women's house and were also given balché to drink. The mood was festive, respectful but joyous, with much laughter and mutual kidding and teasing. Only when the balché master sang his songs to the gods did everyone become quiet and attentive. At the beginning, in a nervous mishap, I spilled my just-filled gourd on the leg, foot, and robe of the master, who was sitting close by. He looked at me and laughed—there was not the slightest hint of reproach. The Lacandones' approach to the ceremony was very casual; there was much animated conversation (including political discussions—I heard the Zapatistas mentioned) and almost constant smiling and laughter.

The drink tasted slightly bitter and tart in a pleasant way. After drinking about three or four gourds, I began to feel a warmth in my chest, accompanied by mild distress in the abdomen. My head felt light and almost transparent, without any hint of alcoholic wooziness. Indeed, measurements confirm that the alcohol content of the drink is only about 2 percent. The feelings that gradually developed over the next couple of hours were not unlike those with which I am familiar from therapeutic work with "empathogenic" substances, such as MDMA (commonly known as Ecstasy). There were no perceptual changes or inner visions, as with the classic hallucinogens.[9] The effect of the balché seemed similar to what I have heard about the Polynesian drink kava: a nonalcoholic euphoric intoxicant that induces strong feelings of interpersonal affection and functions to bond community members.

I noted that I was feeling a profound affection and admiration toward these people, whom I don't know and can't even understand. I also felt affection emanating from them toward me and toward each other. Those not participating in the ceremony were also included in this empathic web, as were the creatures and plants of the forest all around us— indeed, the whole world of sky and earth, rain and sunlight, wind and rocks, and trees. It seemed that by not understanding the words being said, I could concentrate totally on the waves of positive feeling that were washing through the group. Someone began to laugh, and the rhythmic sounds of laughter rippled and resonated until all of us were laughing in synchrony. Deep black eyes were shining in dark, bronze-skinned faces. And then one or another of the men, leaning up against one of the supporting poles, fell silent and looked to a faraway place of dreams.

My capacity to take the drink is quite limited compared with that of the Lacandones, who down five or six liters every hour. After three or four hours, the ceremony comes to a close. The master stops filling the gourds, and the people disperse back to their respective houses or work projects, carrying benevolent and cooperative feelings with them. The cycles of life continue. Such ceremonies are not conducted on fixed days, as are worship on Sundays or the Sabbath; rather they are held when someone requests a healing, or when the weather has destroyed crops, or when someone is being honored, or when there is a crisis or conflict of some kind in the community. The balché ceremony can be used as a way of resolving conflicts. Christian told us of ceremonies he's participated in where the master has given two men angry with each other enormous quantities of the drink, until the two antagonists are no longer able to hold on to their enmity. From our Western point of view, this must be considered a truly innovative method of conflict resolution.

THE TRUE, ORIGINAL FIRST WORLD

Gradually, it dawned on me: we have it backward in our conventional view. The world of the indigenous people, like these Lacandones, is the real First World, because it has been here the longest and it was here first. The so-called First World of the industrialized North is first only in capital wealth and military force. Those cultures that were superimposed later in time on the enduring world of the aboriginal inhabitants are the ones that should be called Second, Third, or Fourth Worlds. We can understand why some North American "Indians" have begun to refer to themselves as "First Americans" or "First Nations"—after all, the term Native American would logically apply to anyone born in America. "First Nations" or "First World" puts it in the correct historical context.

I realize, too, that the lifestyle of these "true, original humans" is much the same as that of my Germanic and Celtic and pre–Indo-European ancestors in the neolithic village cultures of Old Europe—a mixed subsistence economy of farming and gardening, supplemented by hunting and fishing to add meat protein. Everyone was attuned to the recurring cycles of nature, revering nature and all the gods and goddesses that animate the world of visible living beings and that connect us to the invisible realms of spirits, of the ancestors, and of dreams.[10] A few such cultures have survived more or less intact to this day. Cultivating social bonds through shared food and drink and ceremonies of empathic intoxication, such as the balché, is a widespread practice; one example is the Polynesian kava ceremony. The old Norse Eddas tell of rituals of reconciliation between previously warring rival clans of gods that involve a shared "mead of inspiration."

To consistently use the term "First World" in a manner that reflects the realities of historical development, rather than the realpolitik of military and economic dominance, would have a consciousness-raising effect on our thinking, I believe. The mixed farming-gardening village communities that began to be formed concomitantly with the rise of grain cultivation about ten thousand years ago in Europe, the Near East, Southeast Asia, and the Americas represented the form of social organization that evolved with the so-called neolithic revolution, also known as "domestication." It was truly the first, original form of human settlement, and in a large, though diminishing, number of areas around the world, this form still survives and thrives. The Lacandones, for example, are not in any real sense of the word "underdeveloped." They have an economy and culture that is sustainably adapted to existing ecological conditions.

It is, of course, true that preceding the neolithic village culture, there was an even more original, primal world—the world of the nomadic bands of paleolithic gatherer-hunters, which existed for hundreds of thousands of years. Before the domestication of Homo sapiens—the only animal species ever known to have domesticated itself, our ancestors lived in the "wild" state, even more dependent upon and hence attuned to the ever changing cycles of nature than the settled villagers. Remnants of paleolithic hunter-gatherer societies also survive, in such areas as Australia and the Kalahari Desert. The Lacandon Mayan economy combines elements from both layers, since they both farm and hunt. Perhaps we should say that the real, or original, First World is the combined world of indigenous people, made up of seminomadic gatherer-hunters and small gardening and farming villages. The historic (and prehistoric) developmental sequence—gathering-hunting economies, followed by farming-herding with some elements of hunting and gathering preserved—can be observed to this day in the layering of different strata of society, superimposed one upon the other or blended together like a photographic multiple exposure.

Actually, we should say that this aboriginal, indigenous First World, with its mixed farming, gardening, and hunting economies, is preceded by an even older, primordial world—the world of nonhuman, or prehuman, nature. The temporal precedence of ecosystem to human culture includes the animals, since Homo sapiens is decidedly the neophyte on the evolutionary stage. In both the ecological and the evolutionary sense, the world of nature—of animals, plants, land, water, air, biotic communities—provides interdependent support for every living being. This is not so much an earlier culture preceding the aboriginal First World as it is the ecological substrate, the niche or habitat, to which the cultures have developed more or less successful adaptations. We could say that the indigenous or aboriginal cultures constitute the First (human) World, keeping in mind that without the ecological substrate, this world would literally have no place to exist.

In this alternate historic-developmental schema, what then are the Second, Third, and Fourth Worlds? I suggest that they are the world of cities and towns (second), the world of the nation-state (third), and the world of the global capitalist industrial economy (fourth). Historically, each of these worlds was superimposed on the cultures that preceded it, and today they coexist as interpenetrating layers of varying density and concentration. In an ecological sense, the relationship of the later, larger systems is parasitical to the earlier, indigenous cultures: the flow of resources, including raw materials and food, is primarily from the indigenous world to the urban, national, and capitalist-industrial worlds, and military-political control is exerted in the opposite direction. This analysis corresponds to what some call the dynamic beween center (capital concentrations) and periphery (labor and resource pools).[11]

In our journey to the land of the Lacandon Maya, we had traversed these different worlds, traveling backward in time, as it were, to an earlier, pre-industrial, pre-urban culture and sharing for a moment in their way of life, which is primarily First World but interpenetrated in complex ways by Second, Third, and Fourth World culture. The *Second World of cities*, descended from the city-states of ancient times, is distinguishable from the First World by the presence of specialized workers, producing goods and services; traders; and administrative hierarchies (priests in ancient times, bureaucrats in modern days). The Lacandones participate in the life of the cities by going to trade there, or to buy furniture and supplies, or to work at part-time jobs; they also receive municipal water supply and electricity. Occasional visits from city-based police or bureaucrats maintain the lines of administrative control.

We encountered the *nation-state Third World* system on our journey when we passed through the Mexican federal army's roadblocks; they controlled the movements into and through the territories occupied by the indigenous peasants using military force. The relationship of the

centralized nation-state to the indigenous populations living in peripheral, rural areas is purely exploitative and parasitical. There is nothing
that being part of the Mexican nation in reality contributes to the wel-
fare and survival of the Lacandones and other Indian peasant groups.
On the contrary, ever since the arrival of the Europeans in the Americas
and continuing to this day, the indigenous First World people have been
consistently marginalized or exterminated, while their landholdings are
expropriated to form the cattle ranches of wealthy Mexicans. The ex-
propriation of Indian lands is supported by the military force of the
Mexican central government. Indian and peasant groups who protest
this takeover of their ancestral lands, like the Zapatistas and their prede-
cessor revolutionaries Emiliano Zapata and Pancho Villa, are branded
as "rebels" and criminalized.

Shortly after President Ernesto Zedillo's aggressive crackdown on the
Zapatistas, North American newspapers reported on a leaked memo from
the Chase Manhattan Bank in New York to the Mexican government.
The memo gave Zedillo an ultimatum: neutralize the Zapatistas or international investors would pull out of Mexico completely, dooming its
economy. This message made explicit what many have long suggested
was going on behind the scenes.[12] It represents the global power of the
multinational financial and industrial corporations to control the political and economic affairs of nation-states. The *multinational corporate Fourth World,* which is erroneously referred to as "First World" in
current political discourse, essentially supports and extends the para-
sitic, exploitative reach of the nation-state Third World. So-called free-
trade agreements, such as GATT, provide the legal framework for the
free movement of capital to areas of lowest labor costs and easiest access
to natural resources, thus maximizing profit returns.

All over the world, the multinational, capitalist-industrial Fourth
World extends its reach, searching for trees, animals, minerals, or fossil
fuels that can be converted to profitable commodities. In exchange, the
products of this global economic system are sold to ever larger masses of
"consumers" in all corners of the globe. The production-consumption
tentacles of this Fourth World industrial growth monster had even
reached into the Lacandon village, in the form of satellite dishes and
color television sets. It was strange to see these TV sets in mud-floored
houses in the rain forest and barefoot children watching atrociously

vulgar Mexican television gameshows. The Lacandon Maya have been lucky thus far—industrial corporate scouts have not found anything yet in their bioregion that they want to exploit. Indigenous societies in other areas of the Americas have been devastated and destroyed if they live in the path of land-hungry cattle ranchers or the prospectors for oil, gold, or uranium. The most likely threat to the Lacandones will come from logging companies looking for increasingly scarce tropical hardwoods, such as mahogany.

The Lacandones have a prophecy about the end of the world, our anthropologist friend Christian told us. According to their lineage of prophets, of which old Chan K'in is the last representative, the world will be destroyed when the last mahogany tree is gone. In the ecologists' language, we would say the mahogany is the "indicator species" for the Central American rain forest. Its health or death is indicative of the health or death of the entire ecosystem. It is true; when deforestation has proceeded to the degree that there are no mahogany trees left, the forest, and thus the habitat, or world, of the Maya will be destroyed. The prophecy tells that the burning eyes of the One True Lord, Hachak Yum, will consume the forest in flames. The smoke from the burning of tropical rain forests can already be seen from satellites miles above Earth.

The indigenous people of the true, original First World are preparing themselves for the final struggle. Many have nothing left to lose, only the remaining trees and land, and their children, to fight for. And so we are told, in one of the first declarations of the Zapatistas, coming out of the Lacandon jungle: "We are the dead, rising to die again so our people can live once more."

Gaia's Alchemy:
Ruin and Renewal
of the Earth

The degradation of the biosphere occurring under the impact of industrialism can be described using the symbolic language of alchemy—the medieval science that concerned itself with the transformations of matter. According to the Gaia theory of Lovelock and Margulis, the entire planet is one vast living organism. Can we apply the principles of psychology and alchemy to understand the massive global transformations taking place in our time?[1]

The Hermetic axiom "As above, so below" encapsulates the ancient idea that there is an analogy, a pattern correspondence, between the macrocosm and the human microcosm. It was said that the human being is a "little world," and the "great world," or universe as we would call it, was given names such as *archanthropos* by the Gnostics, or *Adam Kadmon* in Kabala, or *purushottama* ("ultimate person") in the Upanishads. The two terms in the analogy are undefined, and thus we could substitute any of the following pairs for "macrocosm" and "microcosm": universe/human, heaven/earth, spirit/matter, divine/human, world/person, inner world/outer world. In this essay, I propose to focus on the analogies between planet Earth, or Gaia (as macrocosm), and the individual organism of the species Homo sapiens (as microcosm). My purpose in examining this particular correspondence is to explore whether what we have learned about the transformation of the individual can be applied to the problems of the transformation of global or planetary consciousness.

This approach exemplifies analogical thinking, focusing on qualitative similarities of pattern and function, in contrast to the logical, analytical thinking of mathematics and science, which focuses more on quantitative differences and their precise measurement. Certainly, the worldviews of shamanistic cultures, of Western philosophy up to the time of Newton and Descartes, and of many Asian traditions were permeated by this kind of thinking. In the Tao Te Ching, for example, we read:

> *Mankind follows the Way of Earth. Earth follows the way of Heaven.*
> *Heaven follows the ways of Tao, and Tao follows the Way of Nature.*

The human being, the planet Earth, and the cosmos are modeled on each other: they *co-respond.*

Not that analogical thinking is absent from science, quite the contrary. Most would admit that analogy and metaphor play a role in the discovery of scientific principles, or generalizations.[2] Such intuitions are then tested and validated or falsified (never proved) by empirical observation. Niels Bohr's analogy between the structure of the atom and the structure of the solar system, with the electrons as whirling planets around the solar nucleus, is a case in point. Another is Ernst Haeckel's formulation that ontogeny (individual development) recapitulates phylogeny (species evolution). These are not established laws, from which predictions can be made. Instead, they are intuitive gestalt perceptions, pattern analogies, that may lead to further discoveries and insights.

James Lovelock's Gaia theory is a formulation, in modern biological language, of the correspondences between planet Earth, or Gaia, and a living organism upon Earth. According to the Gaian view, the entire planet, including fiery core, rocky mantle, oceans, biosphere, and atmosphere, is a single, immense superorganism with myriad systemic interactions, rather than an inanimate rock with a thin film of life and an envelope of air. The atmosphere of Earth, according to Lovelock, is like the shell of a snail or the web of a spider; it is a part of the organism, generated from within itself.[3]

Recognizing and developing an analogy is a useful heuristic device that can result in insights and discoveries. *Metaphor* is the term more widely used in linguistics and the humanities for this analogue mode; one pattern is compared to, or stands for, another. We are "carried" *(pherein)* conceptually "beyond" *(meta)*, from one domain to another. We can then see and understand one phenomenon through its likeness to another. The word *symbol* likewise implies a "throwing" *(ballein)* "together" *(sym)*, an apposition of two things so that one can stand for the other or one can be understood in terms of the other. The pervasiveness of metaphors (and symbols, analogies, etc.) in human thought and language has been cogently argued by George Lakoff and Mark Johnson. In their book *Metaphors We Live By,* they show how our ordinary language—which governs how we think, how we talk, and how we act, both consciously and unconsciously—is fundamentally metaphorical in nature and often reflects implicit metaphors. Far from being a mere literary device, metaphors are actually inherent in the very structure of our thought.[4] In my book *The Unfolding Self,* I discuss twelve major metaphors of the process of human self-transformation, as they are found in the mystical and mythic literatures of East and West and in contemporary descriptions of transformative experiences. From examining the accounts of individuals undergoing such transformation, it became clear that these metaphors not only are descriptions of otherwise inexpressible experiences but also stimulate and catalyze psychic transformation. Here we find the practical relevance of these analogies and metaphors for the much-desired and much-needed transformation of global consciousness.

ELEMENTAL ANALOGIES BETWEEN PERSON AND PLANET

When I first became acquainted with the general idea of a pattern correspondence between Earth and the individual human being, I found myself looking for specific examples of this supposed macro-micro analogy. The huge disparity in size and scale between a person and the planet, however, made it difficult for me to see parallels or similarities. I thought perhaps the metaphor was just too vague. I have come to think that this problem of scale, and the perceptual focus of the average specialized scientist on the phenomena at the scale level of that specialization, has prevented science until recently from recognizing any similarities or analogies between an individual organism, animal or plant, and the superorganism we call Earth.

A simpler form of the correspondence doctrine—that world and humans are composed of the same basic elements—poses no difficulty for scientific understanding. It is obvious that we are composed of particles, atoms, molecules, and cells, just like the world of living nature of which we are a part. As Theodore Roszak has written, "We were mothered out of the substance of this planet. Her elements, her periodicities, her gravitational embrace, her subtle vibrations still mingle in our nature, worked a billion years down into the textures of life and mind."[5] Although any unbiased observer would concede that, logically, the individual human being is a living organic system that exists on or in—as part of—the larger living organic system that we call the biosphere, or Earth, conventional science and ordinary awareness scarcely acknowledge this plain truth. Deep ecology, ecofeminism, and other schools of radical ecophilosophy have critiqued the anthropocentric claim that humans are somehow essentially different and therefore have privileged status in relation to Earth. Likewise, the traditions of indigenous peoples, including Native Americans, have always acknowledged and respected the organic coherence and interrelatedness of humans with all of nature.

What, then, are some of the specific structural and functional analogies between the human being and the planet Earth? At first sight, shape would seem to be an unpromising comparison. We are two-legged mammals, with a central axis perpendicular to the planet surface, while the Earth is a spinning sphere. The esoteric traditions of East and West teach us, however, that the human being has an energy field (sometimes called *aura*) that is appoximately spherical. The planetary energy field is also spherical, like the body of the planet itself.

The human body and energy field have a central vertical axis, an invisible central energy channel that is recognized in yoga as the axis (called *sushumna*) on which the energy centers, or *chakras*, are aligned. This is the axis of our bilateral symmetry, of the left/right polarity that extends throughout the body and the structures of human consciousness. The planet Earth also has a central vertical axis, the axis of its rotation, that brings about the circadian rhythm of alternating day and night, affecting the life of all animals and plants. For the Chinese Taoists, this light–dark, day–night rhythm is the starting point for the *yin/yang* polarity that extends throughout all of nature.

Although the mere fact of being constituted of the same elements does not make an analogy between Earth and human being, the relative *configuration of the elements*, as states of matter or conditions of material existence, does show interesting parallels. Medieval hermetic philosophers often drew up elaborate tables of correspondences of the four elements, which they inherited from Greek philosophy. The element "earth" comprised all solid matter, all substance; the element "water" constituted all liquids and fluids; "air" was matter in its gaseous, vaporous state; and "fire" was heat-generating radiation and electromagnetic energy. Below is a small sample of what such tables of correspondences looked like.

ELEMENTAL CORRESPONDENCES

	INDIVIDUAL	PLANET
Earth	Bones, muscles, flesh, tissues	Soil, minerals, rock, vegetation
Air	Breath, respiration, sound, voice	Winds, atmosphere, clouds
Water	Blood, lymph, humors, hormones	Oceans, tides, lakes, rain, rivers
Fire	Brain, nerves, subtle energies	Lightning, bioelectricity, radiation

Much traditional symbolism expresses similar elemental analogies. Such philosophy reflects a worldview in which human nature is perceived as embedded or nested within the larger world of nature. This worldview is again gaining favor in living systems theory, which describes a world of complex, patterned interrelationships at many levels of reality. In modern science, only that part of the element earth that corresponds to what we call the biosphere would be considered living; the rest of earth (rocks, minerals, crystals) as well as water, air, and solar fire energy are considered inanimate nature. According to the Gaia theory, however, the whole planet is a living organism within which there are living and nonliving components, just as there are within a tree or a human body.

Air

The winds were often referred to as the breath of Earth. The word *atmosphere* means sphere of *atmos,* which is Greek for "vapor" or "breath," and is related to the German *atem,* "breath," and Sanskrit *atman,* "spirit" or "self." In Indian, Tibetan, and Chinese medical and yogic systems, the energy currents in the body that are activated by special breathing practices are referred to as "winds." These winds course through the body, can become polluted or blocked, and are purified and energized through yogic practices and such methods as acupuncture. Air is the medium for sound and breath and underlies our capacity for vocalizing, hence also song, speech, words, and thoughts. Air is traditionally associated with the mental realm of thoughts, ideas, and communication.

Water

We know that about three-fourths of the mass of human (and other animal) bodies is fluid, or water, and that the salty chemistry of blood resembles that of seawater. Likewise, about three-fourths of Earth's surface is covered in water. Life on Earth is a water-based system. Biological tides ebb and flow through the bodies of animals and plants, in synchrony with the ocean tides, pulled by lunar and solar gravity. Expanding the analogy, we can think of rivers and lakes as arteries and blood vessels and rain as the fertilizing downpour of hormones and sexual fluids. Psychically, the water element traditionally symbolizes the realm of feelings and emotions, referred to esoterically as the astral world.

Fire

The elemental symbolism of fire includes not only such planetary phenomena as the sun, lightning, volcanoes, and forest fires but also all forms of energy and radiation, including the entire electromagnetic spectrum, cosmic radiation, and various forms of life energy or bioelectricity. In the human organism, fire is seen in the phenomenon of bodily heat, in the electromagnetic activity of the nervous system, and in bioelectrical

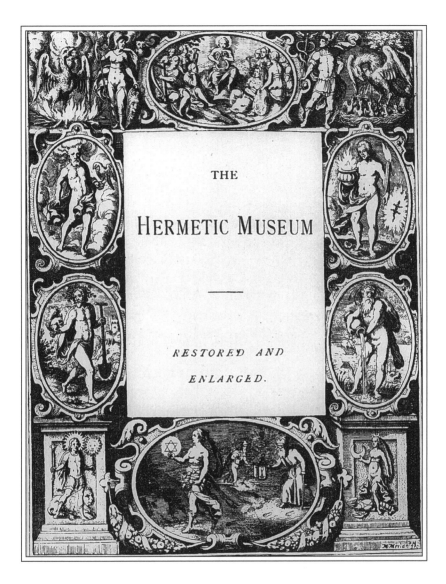

Spirits of the four elements, air and earth on the left, fire and water on the right. At the bottom, short-sighted alchemist-scientists follow the female Spirit of Nature, carrying light (lumen naturae). *(Title page of the* Hermetic Museum, *a collection of alchemical texts, published in Germany, 17th century.)*

phenomena of healing and regenerating electrical fields.[6] There also exist various formulations of subtle life-energy processes, referred to in such concepts as *chi, prana, kundalini,* orgone, bioenergy, and the like. At the psychological level, fire and flames are symbolically associated with ardor, sexual passion, anger, excitement, vitality, inspiration, vision, perception, imagination, and intuition. All of these states and experiences are linked to the functions of the nervous and neuroendocrine systems as well as to conditions of the subtle life-energy field and the energy chakras.[7]

THE SPIRITS OF NATURE

According to alchemical philosophers such as Paracelsus, as well as the primal worldview of tribal cultures, the elements are not only the major structural divisions of the organism, both the planetary and the personal, they are also living, intelligent, autonomous, spiritual forces, with modes of expression on many levels. To the ancient seers and philosophers of nature, each element was the field of expression of an intelligent, conscious being, with which the shaman, alchemist, sorcerer, healer, or magician could communicate. The spirits of the elements, like the spirits associated with plants and animals, were sometimes regarded as a collective entity, as in the Paracelsian notion of *elementals:* air elves and faeries, water sylphs and undines, fire salamanders, earth gnomes, and dwarves.

In many traditional cultures, including the American Indians, the planetary elemental realms were personified as a great goddess or god: Mother Earth, Father Sky or Brother Wind, Grandmother Ocean, Grandfather Fire. Saint Francis, whom Lynn White Jr. proposed as the patron saint of ecology, wrote a canticle in which he addressed Brother Sun and Sister Moon as well as Brother Wind, Sister Water, Brother Fire, and Mother Earth. There is considerable cross-cultural and cross-religious consistency in the attribution of male god characteristics to fire and air, with their dynamic and upward rising energies and female goddess characteristics to water and earth, with their magnetic and downward-sinking energies.

Here we come to what is, to my mind, the most significant of the person/planet analogies. The individual human organism-person is viewed as the created vehicle or form of an immortal spirit or divine being—and so is Earth. The physical planet Earth is the body of a deity living within it, as the human organism is the physical or earth body of a divine being. This was, in fact, the view of the ancient, animistic cultures, including the Greeks, Egyptians, and Mesopotamians, from whom Western culture is generally held to have arisen. In our time, the planets still have the names of the Graeco-Roman deities with whom they were associated. The modern Gaia theory restricts itself to the notion that Earth is one unitary organism and regards Gaia as only a mythic, symbolic allusion. The ancients believed that Earth is not only alive, it is also a conscious being with whom one can communicate in altered states of consciousness, such as divination. And it is a sacred being, the body of a goddess, to whom reverence is due. Spirit is the immanent essence within natural, biological form at every level.

To accommodate this perception of the spiritual essence of Earth and all living organisms within our worldview, we must go beyond the mechanistic models of conventional scientific thinking. In biology, this points to a recovery of vitalism, which held that all natural processes are imbued with a vital force, an élan vital in Henri Bergson's terms, that is absent from synthetic, man-made materials. Additionally, we must concern ourselves with the exploration and restoration of animistic and panentheistic views, which regard all life-forms of plants and animals, as well as the mineral kingdom, the natural landscape, the elements, and the whole Earth itself, as animated by living spirits or souls, by divine or angelic intelligences.

EARTH MOTHER, WORLD TREE, AND GAIA

In traditional animistic cultures, there are two main symbolic world images, both of which were incorporated into numerous myths. One is the idea of Earth as Mother. Our paleolithic and neolithic ancestors, observing the miraculous process of birth in humans and other mammals, such as bears, found it natural to see all life-forms emerging from the body of Earth Mother. Among the earliest religious icons are those of the birth-giving female, with swelling abdomen, breasts, and buttocks. This metaphor has a familial warmth to it. All living beings are the children of Earth Mother; animals, trees, and rocks, as well as rivers, winds,

Alchemical image of Earth as nourishing mother. (From Atalanta Fugiens, *alchemical text by Michael Meier, Prague, 17th century.)*

Paleolithic Earth Mother Goddess. (Willendorf figurine; from 28,000 B.C.E.)

and mountains, are "all our relations," as the Sioux put it in their prayer songs. The feeling of all belonging to one family can be the basis of an ecological ethic, based on respect and the perception of relatedness.[8]

A variant of this world image as Mother, also found in many shamanistic societies, is the image of the World Tree. We find this symbolism in Asiatic shamanistic beliefs, in Nordic-Germanic mythology, as well as in Hinduism, in the Hebrew Kabala with its Sephiroth Tree, and in the visions of the renowned Sioux holy man Black Elk. This image is also unitary, since every branch and every leaf and flower is connected to the one great tree that constitutes the world. Shamans can travel along the branches of this tree, to journey to other worlds. Humans and other living beings are like the leaves on this great tree, drawing sustenance and strength from their connection to the branches, trunk, and roots. This image, too, can provide the basis for an ecological ethic, because of the unitary interconnectedness and interdependence of all parts of the tree.[9]

A third organic analogy for the relationship between humans and Earth derives from the Gaia theory. According to this metaphoric image, Earth is an organism, and individual organisms (human, plant, or animal) are cells in the vast planetary organism. This perspective allows us to understand that such expressions as "saving the Earth" or "healing the Earth" overlook the difference in scale involved. It is impossible for a cell, or a group of cells, to undertake the healing of the whole organism. What individuals and groups *can* do, however, is to change their relationship to Earth and the ecosystem in which they live—and this would contribute to the healing of Earth as a whole.

From a systems point of view, there are actually one or two levels of order between the cell and the organism and therefore also between the individual organism and the planet Earth. Developing this analogy systemically, we could formulate the relationships as in the table below.

Table 2. Organismic Correspondences

INDIVIDUAL	PLANET
Organism	Gaia, or biosphere
Organ systems	Ecosystems
Specialized tissues	Species
Cells	Organisms (plants, animals)

The organ systems of the human (or other animal or plant) body function as energy-transforming, metabolic systems, much like the great ecosystems of Earth, such as rain forests, oceans, prairies, tundras, and so forth. Lovelock develops this analogy between ecosystems and organ systems at length in his book *Healing Gaia*, in which he also introduces the term *geophysiology* for the science of the self-regulating planetary energy systems and their structures and functions.[10] If we realize that such analogies are not mere fanciful metaphors, but instead encapsulate important insights, then we would want to take this analogy seriously. Doing so, we might arrive at a deeper understanding of the human-to-Earth relationship and a better environmental ethic based on such understanding.

Humans as Gaian Nervous System?

There is another question that arises from consideration of this set of analogies: If different species correspond to the specialized tissues of the different organs of the planetary body, then what are human beings? Are we the heart, the brain, the genitals of Earth? If we ascertain the answer correctly or appropriately, we might have the means to understand the nature of humanity's natural role or organic function within the greater whole that is Gaia. Most people, when asked this question, independently arrive at the conclusion that humans must be the brain and nerve cells of the human body. And while popularity of a belief is, per se, no criterion for its validity, this popularity does suggest that there is truth to the analogy. Lovelock himself, in his first book on the Gaia theory, raised the question whether "we as a species constitute a Gain nervous system and a brain which can consciously anticipate environmental changes?"[11] Peter Russell, in his book *The Global Brain*, developed the notion that soon there will be as many humans on Earth as there are neurons in a typical human brain, and the collectivity of nerve cells that is humanity is in the process of becoming integrated as a brain, making connections with other neurons in conscious networks—in the process sometimes referred to as the globalization of information networks.[12]

The functions of the nervous system in animals (including humans) include perception of the internal and external environment, coordination among different parts of the organism (such as, hand and eye), and the creation of interpretations or representations of reality. In the case of the human, the brain and nervous system are, in addition, involved in the communication of perceptions and interpretations using words, images, and the various symbolic codes of science, art, and religion. While other animals with nervous systems also communicate, and even plants may have forms of communication, humans clearly specialize in it and have developed symbolic languages to a high degree of complexity and articulation. Many philosophers have also pointed out that reflective consciousness, also associated with brain function, seems to be a peculiarly human specialization.

Some people take exception to this metaphor of humanity as the Earth's brain and nervous system, feeling that it represents human arrogance and hubris once again. This objection to the analogy is valid, however, only if one holds to a belief that the brain is a superior organ in the body. It should be noted that in physiology, there is no assumption that the brain is somehow superior to, better than, or more advanced than other parts of the organism. We could say that the brain generates and communicates interpretations of reality just as the lungs breathe air, the heart circulates the blood, and the muscles provide for locomotion. Each organ has a specialized role, but none has a privileged or controlling function.

In pursuing the analogy that we are Earth's nervous system and brain, one could develop a more balanced and integrative understanding of the human being's natural role or organic function. Is it not true that we do function on Earth somewhat like a nervous system and brain? In the Bible, there are two sets of instructions from God to Adam and Eve. In one they were told to "subdue the earth and have dominion over the animals." This has often been cited as the original theological justification for the human domination and exploitation of nature. In a second set of instructions, Adam was instructed to *name* the animals and plants, that is to recognize and to speak. Clearly, "naming" here encompasses all the functions of the human brain and mind (interpreting, categorizing, etc.) that also follow from the analogy of humans as the nerves and brain of the biosphere. The domination and exploitation that have characterized so much of human behavior toward the biosphere could not be accepted or sanctioned within the framework of this metaphor.[13]

Although some critics, particularly feminist scholars, have argued that even naming can be seen as the exercise of patriarchal domination and control patterns, it seems to me that the human role of interpreter, categorizer, and communicator of nature is much more compatible with an egalitarian, respectful, and nonprejudicial attitude toward the natural world. We can distinguish between the kind of science that is motivated by, and applied to, the acquisition of greater technological power over nature ("dominion") and, on the other hand, the kind of science that is noninvasive, naturalistic, noncontrolling, and yet empirical and faithful to the discipline of verification that has made science so spectacularly successful ("naming").

Seeing ourselves as communicating nerve cells in the body of Gaia, Earth, necessitates a shift in perspective. It does not make ecological sense for a cell, or a group of cells such as the nervous system, to regard the rest of the body as existing for its use and convenience, to cannibalize and destroy other parts of the integrated ecosystem that is the body. It is also ecologically unhealthy, unwholesome we might say, for cells of one kind to proliferate wildly and spread all over the body with reckless disregard for the delicately balanced interrelationships of the whole system. In the individual organism, we call such cellular behavior "tumors." And the analogy of humankind as a cancer or infestation upon Earth has occurred to quite a few observers.[14]

In a healthy body, the brain or nervous system does not dominate or exploit or try to control the functions of the other parts of the whole. Using the analogy of humans as Gaia's nervous system, one can recognize the parallels between the human domination and exploitation of nonhuman nature on the planetary level and, on the individual human level, the (attempted) dominating relationship of the brain-mind to the rest of the body that we see in neurotic (literally, "nerve-related") and psychosomatic conditions. When the brain-mind, out of misguided assumptions of its own superior knowledge, tries to exert too much control over the bodily functions of breathing, circulation, digestion, or others, the unhealthy and ultimately destructive consequences are only too apparent.[15]

TRANSFORMATIONS OF THE ELEMENTS
IN THE PSYCHE AND ON EARTH

For several years I was using the alchemical symbolism of the elements as a framework for guided imagery work in individual psychotherapy and in group workshops and rituals. I have experimented with the use of slides, sounds, music, movement, and guided inner journeys as means to enhance one's ability to tune in to the different realms of consciousness. I found that visual and auditory imagery of the elements in nature consistently induced in people's experience the qualities of consciousness associated with the elements in the alchemical and other earth-based traditions.

- Images and sounds of air and winds, of clouds and winged creatures, triggered associations of the mental realm, the expansive and swiftly changing world of thoughts and ideas, of words and poems and songs.
- Images and sounds of the water element, of oceans, tides, sea creatures, waves, rivers, springs, lakes, and rain, often released

powerful emotions and feeling memories, both positive and negative.

- Images and sounds of fire energy, such as the sun, lightning, volcanoes, and electrical fields, were associated in people's experience with creativity, imagination, enthusiasm, vision, and intuition.
- Images and sounds of the earth element, of rocks and mountains, land and forest, plants and minerals, induced associations of kinesthetic and somatic awareness, of sensory contact and pleasure, of solid and substantive form.

Such multimodal meditative rituals using alchemical symbolism foster the practice of discriminative awareness and objective observation of one's own psychic processes for the purpose of bringing them into a consciously greater harmony and integration.[16] I found that this multisensory method of facilitating intrapsychic awareness worked quite well, in that participants often reported a deepened sense of their own interconnectedness, through the elements, with their environment and with all life. I learned a great deal from presenting and guiding these image journeys, constantly discovering new ramifying levels of meaning and unexpected associations.

During this time, I also participated in a number of sweat-lodge rituals and healing-circle ceremonies conducted by Native Americans or white people who had studied the Native American traditions. In these rituals there are often invocations and prayers to the spirit of each element as well as the spirits of the four directions—not in the pleading or beseeching mode I had always associated with prayer but in a mode of dignified and respectful mutuality. It seemed to me that these ceremonialists were cultivating and encouraging an attitude of searching for a right relationship to the elements as well as to the animal and plant realms. I began to understand that in an animistic worldview, the elements of the individual psyche and organism and the planetary elements were regarded as necessarily implicated with one another. As Gregory Bateson put it in the title of his book, "mind and nature—a necessary unity."

A quantum step in consciousness expansion for my workshop participants (and for myself) occurred when I began to suggest, through the presented words, sounds, and images, that the participants also allow themselves to become aware of the shadow side of each element. Each of

The four elements in a state of chaos and confusion.
(Allegorical alchemical illustration, 17th century,
France.)

the elements has characteristic fear images and sensations associated with
it. With air, it is the fear of flying and of falling; with water, the fear of
drowning or flooding; with fire, the fears of burning, exploding, or being shot; and, in the case of earth, the fear of being trapped underground
or buried in a landslide or earthquake. These are the most commonly
noted personal fear images and traumatic memories associated with the
elements. We can assume that they are based either on biographical traumatic experiences or possibly on memories carried over from other life-
times. This is work of the kind that C. G. Jung, who stands solidly in the
tradition of philosophical alchemy, called integrating the (unconscious)

"shadow" with the (conscious) ego image. Evoking and confronting such primordial fear complexes, when done in a safe, ritualistic, or therapeutic format, often lead to a significant expansion of one's sphere of awareness, as aspects of one's total experience previously denied or suppressed are accepted and integrated.

It was a natural next step to also consider the shadow side of the elements on the planetary level. Here, there are two kinds of negatively charged elemental phenomena that have great numinous power in the depths of the psyche. One encompasses the images of the elements of nature in their violent and destructive manifestations: tornadoes and hurricanes; swollen, flooding rivers and ocean storms; wild forest fires; volcanic eruptions and searing desert heat; landslides and earthquakes. No one who has been in or near such cataclysmic manifestations can fail to be touched with awe at nature's immense and unpredictable power. Such manifestations of nature's violence may have their counterpart or correspondence, in ways yet poorly understood, in the violent and cataclysmic disturbances of the collective psyche (such as, wars, revolutions, mass movements) that from time to time sweep through large human populations. Certainly, such a correspondence is implied and expressed in many eschatological visions and myths, in which the "end of the world" is perceived and prophesied as taking place simultaneously in the collective human psyche and on the planetary earth level (for instance, as seismic, volcanic or meteorological events).[17]

The second set of collective or planetary shadow expressions comprises those that are a function of man's technological interventions in the biospheric web of life and disruptions of the elemental cycles. Here we have the pollution of the atmosphere through industrial waste products; the poisoning of rivers, wetlands, and oceans; planetary warming and shredding of the protective ozone layer; soil degradation through industrialized farming practices; deforestation; desertification; and the whole well-known litany of ecological destruction. In addition to the disruption and pollution of the planetary energy cycles by the industrial machine, there are also, in the case of the element fire, two further shadow manifestations uniquely due to human invention: the burning of energy from nonrenewable fossil fuels and the violently destructive misdirection of "firepower" as weapons of killing and war—culminating in the specter of nuclear annihilation (and the actual, continuing accumulation of radioactive wastes that are lethal for hundreds of thousands of years).

The reckless application of technology, harnessed to greed, degrades and destroys the ecosystems in which the energies of the elements are maintained in exquisite balance and interrelationship (albeit with occasional catastrophic natural interruptions). We each participate in that degradation of our ecosystems, our own habitats, insofar as we participate, however unconsciously, in the pollution and misuse of the elements. Since the elements constitute *us*, we are also being degraded in the process. We are engaged in an ongoing assault on the planetary elements as well as the decimation of plant and animal species and the relentless suicidal degradation of our own habitats. In short, the situation can be called *ecocide*. Humankind is at war with nature.[18]

Many scientists, philosophers, naturalists, deep ecologists, visionary poets, and elders of indigenous cultures have long recognized and warned of this condition of ecocidal destruction. Indigenous cultures, such as the Native Americans, have for millennia practiced rituals of reconciliation and rebalancing with the spirits and powers of nature. In such rituals and prayer ceremonies, conscious intention is focused on peacemaking with the elemental energies of the ecosystem in which the particular society is at home, as well as with the plant and animal communities of the local bioregion. Such rituals, as I've observed and participated in them, involve a kind of realignment, the establishment of a "right relationship" we might say in Buddhist terms, at the spiritual and psychic levels, between humans and the rest of the nonhuman natural world. A shift then occurs in the way we perceive the natural world, a kind of gestalt figure-ground reversal. Once we recognize our inescapable embeddedness in the living, organic ecosystem and our mutual interdependence with all other coexisting species, our sense of separate identity, so strenuously acquired and desperately maintained, recedes more into the background. Instead, the *relationships*, whether balanced or imbalanced, take the foreground and become the focus of concern. This is the perceptual basis for the new and ancient point of view of the Gaian scientists, philosophers, and artists: it is holistic and inclusive and inevitably accompanied by a sense of wonder and reverence.[19]

From my experience with individual and group consciousness transformation processes as well as with the writings mentioned, I have reluctantly come to the conclusion that the metaphor of war for our antagonistic relationship with nature is most apt. It implies the need both for understanding the causes and origins of this war and for finding a way to end it, which has somehow become our central challenge as a species. It seems to me, furthermore, that the wars between people cannot be reduced or eliminated as long as the war with nature proceeds quite unconsciously. At the very least, one would have to work on both areas simultaneously.

Speaking as a psychologist, I am inclined to the view that both situations of war may ultimately be seen as externalizations of the conflicts and wars within human consciousness. If this is so, then our task becomes one of recognizing and confronting the "inner enemy," the inner antagonist. We need to recognize and withdraw the projections of this inner enemy onto external agents or forces—whether this be other human beings or the world of wild nature.[20]

In conclusion, the metaphor of the human relationship to Earth as a war against nature and the elements is one that many philosophers, visionaries, and indigenous elders have given us. Humankind's age-old dominating and conquering approach to the world of nature has, through the development of powerful industrial technologies, been taken to the extreme of threatening the entire biosphere. On the individual level, it represents the shadow side of our preoccupation with individual separateness and power. On the planetary level, human activities are disrupting all the major elemental energy cycles. At the same time, there are concepts and practices of shamanistic traditions, and of indigenous animistic cultures and also contemporary holistic and ecophilosophical worldviews that promise a way out of these self-created dilemmas of humankind.

Gaia. (Painting by Alex Grey)

A Vision Quest Experience

From my work with the psychic symbolism of the elements and the realization of the critically disturbed relationship between humankind and the elements in nature, I came to the conclusion that a change in our attitude toward the elements, as toward nature in general, is necessary and desirable. From my participation in several Native American sweat-lodge and other ceremonies, I saw that such prayer rituals are one way to bring about such changes in consciousness. Similar ritual forms are found in the Celtic-Druidic traditions of pre-Christian Europe; in shamanistic cultures of South America, Africa, Asia, and Australia; and in the ceremonies formulated by modern practitioners of witchcraft and paganism. These rituals are, in fact, the means by which the elders, healers, and teachers of the ancient Earth Wisdom traditions align themselves with natural forces and with the "spirit of the place" (genius loci), to cultivate a balanced attitude and relationship with the environment.

In such ceremonies, one addresses and invokes the spirits of earth, air, water, and fire as well as the powers of the four directions (or six, including above and below). Such ceremonies are therefore based on the premise that each of the elements as well as each species of animal and plant, constitute the domain of immense, suprahuman, living, intelligent, conscious, spiritual beings—beings with whom it is possible to communicate and attune oneself. These are the beings ancient cultures have called gods and goddesses, nature spirits, devas (in the Indian tradition), or angels and archangels (in the Judaeo-Christian esoteric tradition). Native Americans most often address these spirits as parents or grandparents—for example, "Mother Earth" or "Grandfather Fire"—thus emphasizing a familial feeling, a sense of kinship with all of nature.

When I began to practice these ancient ways, in my own ritual workshops and in those conducted by others, I noticed in myself an increasing sense of balance and interrelatedness. I began to understand what the Native Americans mean when they speak of "walking in balance on Earth." A sense of well-being and feeling at home in the world resulted from periodic reattunement and harmonizing with the elemental energies. I felt that the spirits of the elements were powerful and quite neutral toward any personal goals or concerns I might have—but that communication with them was possible. I experienced them as neither beneficent nor antagonistic toward humans. In that sense, I began to think of the metaphor of "Mother Earth" as misleading. Wilderness questors who think Earth will take care of them as a mother takes care of her children can be in for a rude awakening. In the wilderness, inadequate preparation, a moment's inattention, being overly preoccupied with subjective or personal issues can easily lead to accidental injury or even death. Such painful consequences would not be evidence that nature is "harsh" or "cruel" or "dangerous" to humans—only that nature operates on a different scale than humans do, just as the bodily organism operates on a different scale than the individual cells that make it up.

For me, the most difficult element to relate to, in any kind of psychic or spiritual communion, was the element fire. Nuclear energy clearly belongs in this domain, along with solar energy, lightning, and electromagnetic and bioelectric energies, yet the thought of trying to communicate with or attune to the spirit of nuclear energy frightened me. I was able to proceed, however, when I realized that this intelligent spirit and its energy manifestation, like the others, was not "evil" or opposed to human life and strivings in any way. That communication was both possible and desirable was the first message I received. I was reminded that thermonuclear fire, in essence, is the fire of the stars and, hence, the same solar fire that sustains life on this planet. I saw that it was only through human misuse and perverted applications of this energy that a chronically dangerous crisis situation, risking mass annihilation and irreversible damage to the biosphere, had developed. Again, there was a shift in my attitudes and feelings about nuclear energy and the environment. I felt increased confidence that significant changes in consciousness, and therefore in actions and policies, are possible.

With these kinds of understandings developing out of my increasing involvement in shamanic ritual processes of various kinds, I was finally able, on my fiftieth birthday, to participate in a structured vision quest experience that culminated with four days and nights of fasting alone in the Mojave Desert of southern California. Steven Foster and Meredith Little, of the School of Lost Borders, in Big Pine, were the expert and sensitive guides for our group of four, preparing and protecting us while each went into solitude to empty ourselves and pray for vision. We went into the barren, blistering canyons of the Inyo Mountains, where our companions were a few gorgeously hued lizards; birds; insects; desert flowers and shrubs; hot rust-colored rocks and stones; roaring winds; the sun's ferocious heat; Earth herself; and the night sky with stars.

My intention in going on a vision quest was not so much to attain a vision of what to do but to discover how I could more effectively express what I was learning and seeing. I received a great deal on those four days on the mountain and in the following days of assimilation and "reincorporation," which our guides assisted with perspicacity and caring. I was shown that we want not only to "walk in balance" but also to "speak in balance" and "act in balance." I learned the value of confronting and accepting bodily weakness, and I learned how I normally close off my senses and how they can open, both inwardly and outwardly. I learned a significant lesson with regard to my son, who had died twelve years earlier at the age of eight and with whom I was able to reconnect in a new way. And I was shown that the answer to my request lay in my use of ritual prayer meditations, some of which emerged in the course of those four days.

These prayers integrated for me the symbolism of the four directions of objective space (north, south, east, and west) and the powers of the four elements, the inner and outer, the physical, and the psychic and spiritual. Recognizing that the symbolism of such prayers may very well be appropriately different in different geographical locations on Earth

Vision quest landscape with giant sand dune, Eureka Valley, Mojave Desert, California. (Photo by Ralph Metzner)

Ralph Metzner being "smudged" with sage smoke by Meredith Little, prior to departure on vision quest. (Photo by Cathy Coleman)

and in different cultural traditions, I nevertheless experienced these verses
I was given as a contribution toward the project of making peace with
Gaia and her elemental powers. I was told to turn toward each of the
four directions as the prayer is said, going around clockwise starting
with the east; alternately, one could turn one's back receptively toward
the direction.

Four Elements Medicine Wheel Prayer:
Turtle Island West Coast[1]

O Great Spirit of the East,
radiance of the rising Sun,
spirit of new beginnings
O Grandfather Fire,
great nuclear fire of the Sun.
From you comes life-energy,
vital spark, power to see far,
and to envision with boldness;
with you we can purify the senses,
our hearts and our minds.
We pray that we may be aligned with you,
so that your energies may flow through us,
and be expressed by us,
for the good of this planet Earth,
and all living beings upon it.

O Great Spirit of the South,
protector of the fruitful land,
and of all green and growing things,
the noble trees and grasses.
Grandmother Earth, Soul of Nature,
great power of the receptive,
of nurturance and endurance,
of bringing forth and growing,
flowers of the field,
fruits of the garden.
We pray that we may be aligned with you,
so that your powers may flow through us,

and be expressed by us,
for the good of this planet Earth,
and all living beings upon it.

O Great Spirit of the West,
spirit of the great waters,
of rain and rivers, lakes and springs;
O Grandmother Ocean,
deepest matrix, womb of all life.
With you comes the dissolving
of boundaries and holdings,
the power to taste and to feel,
to cleanse and to heal.
Great blissful darkness of peace.
We pray that we may be aligned with you,
so that your powers may flow through us,
and be expressed by us,
for the good of this planet Earth,
and all living beings upon it.

O Great Spirit of the North,
invisible spirits of the air,
and of the fresh, cool winds;
O vast and boundless Grandfather Sky,
your living breath animates all life.
From you comes clarity and strength,
and the power to hear inner sounds,
to sweep out old patterns,
and bring challenge and change.
The ecstasy of movement and the dance.
We pray that we may be aligned with you,
so that your powers may flow through us,
and be expressed by us,
for the good of this planet Earth,
and all living beings upon it.

Mystical Greenness:
The Visions of
Hildegard von Bingen

The visions and teachings of the 12th-century Abbess Hildegard von Bingen are of stunning relevance to our time. Her concept of viriditas (greenness) as spirit manifest in the creation and her emphasis on the Mother principle are forerunners of an ecofeminist, creation spirituality that yet remains within Christianity. Her visions of elemental degradation are eerily prophetic of the ecological dilemmas of our time.[1]

Born in 1098 as the tenth child of German aristocrats in the country known as Rheinhessen, Hildegard was placed into a convent at the age of eight a tithe, as an offering of "one-tenth," to the Church and to God. In this convent, which was attached to the Benedictine monastery of Disibodenberg, Hildegard came under the tutelage of a renowned hermit teacher named Jutta von Spanheim. At the age of sixteen, Hildegard chose to enter the Benedictine order and continue to live in the convent, where she was educated in the Benedictine devotional practices and arts. In 1136, when Jutta died, Hildegard was elected to be the head of the small community of nuns. Four years later in 1141, at the age of forty-three, she had a momentous spiritual awakening, in which she was given visions together with a command from God to express and reveal these visions.

Later she was to state that she had had mystical visions even as a very young child, but this was the first time that she had felt the confidence to share them with others; this confidence was clearly based on the instructions she received. In the introduction to her first book *Scivias* ("Know the Ways"), she relates her first experience of visionary instruction:

In the forty-third year of my life journey, when I grasped at a heavenly vision with great fear and trembling attention, I saw the greatest brilliance. In it a voice from heaven was saying to me, "O fragile one, you who are ash of ashes, decay of decay, speak and write what you see and what you hear. . . . But speak and write these things, not according to human speech and invention, but according to the way you yourself see and hear these things in the heavens, the wonders of God. Be like one who hears and understands the words of the teacher and tells them just as the master indicates. So write what you see and hear! Speak and tell what I will reveal to you!" . . . A fiery light came down like lightning from the open sky. The light streamed through my brain and glowed in my heart and breast like a flame that warmed but did not burn me. Suddenly I could understand the meaning of Biblical scriptures and the Gospels, though not the literal verbal and grammatical forms.[2]

She took ten years to record her first book of visions. In the manuscript of her work are several exquisite illuminations, apparently painted under her direction, one of which shows the black-robed nun sitting on a stool with tongues of reddish flame streaming down from above into her head; in her lap she holds a writing instrument and tablet. Nearby stands the monk who was her secretary and assistant.

In 1147, at a bishops' synod in Trier, after an examination of her writings, Pope Eugene III publicly declared that Hildegard's visions were authentic and encouraged her to continue recording them. It is a relatively rare occurrence that a mystic's visions have received papal approval. It is characteristic of Hildegard that she would seek to maintain her stance of obedience toward the Catholic hierarchy. It was also characteristic, however, that in her letter responding to and acknowledging the papal endorsement, she took the opportunity to admonish the pope to make needed reforms in the Church. Throughout her life she was outspoken

Hildegard the seeress receiving and recording divinely inspired visions. (From Scivias, *"Know the Ways")*

in her counsel and fiery in her criticism where she encountered abuse or injustice. She acted as adviser and counselor to popes, bishops, and heads of monasteries as well as various feudal lords, princes, kings, and Frederick I, the Emperor Barbarossa.

While continuing her social and political activism, teaching, preaching, scolding, and cajoling, she also built and administered the convent of Rupertsberg, where a growing community of nuns gathered around her. In addition to her symbolic visions, she wrote poems and set a number of them to music—in a style musicologists describe as a variant of Gregorian chant, unique in its melodic inventiveness and passionate feeling. She entitled her collection of devotional songs *Sinfornia of the Harmony of the Heavenly Revelations*. She even wrote what may be the first opera, a kind of morality play set to music called *Ordo Virtutum,* "The Rite of the Virtues."[3] This work, which has been performed and recorded in modern times, regularly astounds people with its dramatic power.

Hildegard also apparently directly supervised the execution of the painted illuminations that accompanied her written work and that depict in visual images of striking vividness the visions that she received. She wrote two other books of her visions: the *Liber Vitae Meritorum,* the "Book of the Merits of Life," which appeared when she was in her fifties, and *Liber Divinorum Operum,* "On the Works of God," which was completed when she was seventy-five. She also wrote a book on physics and two books on medicine and herbal remedies, which remain among the best sources on medieval herbalism. She wrote biographies of two Irish Christian monks from the early medieval period, to whom she evidently felt connected. In 1178 she became involved in a dispute with the prelates of Mainz, and her monastery was placed under a Church interdict. She died at the age of eighty-one, after her position in the dispute had been vindicated.

We have here a woman with a remarkable range of talents—an organizer, administrator, social activist, champion of justice, writer, poet, composer, artist, natural scientist, physician, healer. With inordinate and tireless energy she devoted herself to teaching, serving, healing, advising, and succoring and comforting her fellow human beings. She supported and encouraged reforms in the Church and vigorously opposed corruption. Throughout her life she maintained an unbroken connection with her source of divine inspiration—putting forth visions and teachings of extraordinary depth and power.

Hildegard's Visionary Gift

In the introduction to *Scivias,* Hildegard gives us her own description of her clairvoyant process:

> The visions that I see are not received in a dreamlike state, not during sleep nor any kind of mental disturbance, not with the eyes of

the body or the ears of the outer person, and not in remote areas, but rather when I am awake, fully conscious and with a clear mind, and with the eyes and ears of the inner person, and in easily accessible open locations, as God wills.[4]

These are not what contemporary psychology would call trance or mediumistic states, in which the seer or medium is more or less dissociated from awareness of external reality. Hildegard's visions are the clear, articulate, symbolic sequences of an Apollonian temperament, not the products of a Dionysian, devotional, god-intoxicated condition.

Hildegard goes on to relate that though she had visions in childhood, she did not tell anyone about them; later, as an adult, she heard a "voice from heaven" saying, "I am the living light that illuminates all darkness." The voice from heaven continued to accompany all her visions, giving her instructions when she was to "speak and write what you see and hear" and offering interpretations of the meaning of the symbolic pictures she was shown—analogous to what recording engineers call a "voice-over." The next point, then, about Hildegard's visions is that they are both heard and seen and they are experienced as coming from a divine source. This is the classic mystical vision, in which religious teaching accompanies the symbolic visions and which combines clairaudience and clairvoyance. The symbolic expressions of the mystic differ in this way from the equally rich and varied symbol sequences of myth, ritual, art, and folklore, which leave the meaning to be discovered by whoever perceives them. The mystic is more explicit, whereas the artists and storytellers often disguise the inner meaning.

Hildegard's visions are not only clairvoyant and clairaudient but often have olfactory, gustatory, and tactile aspects as well; thus they exemplify clairsentience, a "clear sensing." A few vivid examples are cited later in this essay. The multisensory nature of her images is unique, as far as I know, in the classic literature of mysticism and prophecy, although it is surely not unknown among the shaman-seers of preliterate tribal cultures. The multidimensional nature of the visions that Hildegard was given is reflected in the multidimensionality of the media through which she expressed and articulated them. To Hildegard, it took written words, poems, songs, illuminated paintings, vivid dramas, as well as the practices and rites of a monastic community, her healing and counseling work, her preaching and organizing, to fully communicate her multifaceted visions.

Besides the introduction to *Scivias*, the only other description we have of the process of her "seeing" is from a letter Hildegard wrote in her seventies to the monk Wibert. In the letter she emphasizes her frailty, her fearfulness, and her insecurity about her ability. "I reach my hands up to God, so that I am held by Him like a feather that is carried weightless on the wind." She describes celestial journeys, which are the Christian mystic's version of the shamanic upper-world journeys:

> And my soul climbs in this vision as God wills, to the highest firmament and the various spheres, and visits various beings and people, though these dwell in places that are far removed from me. And as I see these things in my soul, I observe also the changes of the clouds and of the creatures. I do not see all this with my outer eyes, and I do not hear it with my outer ears, and I do not perceive it with the thoughts of my heart, nor by the mediation of my five senses. Only in my soul does all this take place, with my eyes open, so I do not fall into unconscious ecstasy, but rather see while awake, both by day and by night.[5]

Hildegard's writings make it clear that responding to the call of the visions was for her a healing experience. She emphasizes her weakness and frailty, and she was in fact quite ill for long periods of time. When she received her first vision, with instructions to publish them, she was sick in bed.

> I refused to write. Not out of stubbornness, but out of my sense of unworthiness, and my doubts, and my fear of the shrugging shoulders and the frivolous talking of people—until God's scourge threw me onto the sickbed. Then at last, compelled through my suffering, I brought my hand to write and I received help. . . . As I began to write, and began to feel, as I said, the gift of scriptural understanding growing in me, I recovered my strength and raised myself from the illness.[6]

In other words, the expression and manifestation of the gift of the visions brought about the healing of the illness caused by denial and doubt.

This is a theme familiar to us, for example, from the autobiography of the Sioux medicine man and seer Black Elk, who was close to becoming psychotic until he was guided to express and portray the visions and prophecies that he had received but had been too afraid and insecure to communicate.[7] The vision or dream that we are given must, it seems, be shared, for it can turn poisonous if it is held within. With Black Elk and with Hildegard, as with other prophets and visionaries, the visions are given not just for the individual but for the whole tribe, for all the people.

Hildegard identified with the disciples at the Pentecost, inspired by their visions and voices to go forth and teach and preach. She was called the Sibyl of the Rhine. She also identified with Old Testament prophets, such as Ezekiel, Daniel, and Joel. Hildegard felt that her time was a time of propecy, a time for visions, as did the old prophets. Perhaps Hildegard's visions speak to us so strongly now because our time also is a time when new visions and illumined perspectives are desperately needed.

HILDEGARD'S GREEN COSMOLOGY

One of Hildegard's most striking, original, and pervasive concepts is *viriditas*— "the greening" or "green power." She speaks of "the exquisite greening of trees and grasses," and all of creation, all of humanity, is "showered with greening refreshment, the vitality to bear fruit." Viriditas is God's creative power manifest in the created world of nature; it is fruitfulness, growth, and creativity. "In the beginning all creatures were green and vital; they flourished amidst flowers. Later the green figure itself came down."[8] Jesus is called Greenness Incarnate, and Mary is the *Viridissima Virga*, the greenest of all green branches in God's orchard, "full of the greening power of springtime."

In one extraordinary poem-song, entitled "Hymn to the Virgins," Hildegard unites the imagery of greenness with the life-giving fire of the sun:

> *O most noble greenness* (nobilissima viriditas),
> *rooted in the sun,*
> *shining forth in splendor*
> *upon the wheel,*

no earthly sense can comprehend you.
You are encircled
by the arms of divine mystery.
You glow as the dawn
and burn with the intensity of the sun.[9]

The worldview expressed in Hildegard's visions and writings is vast and inclusive, ranging from the deepest mysteries of the Holy Trinity and the structure of the cosmos to the animals, plants, and elements of nature; they include the teachings and destiny of the Church, the fall and redemption of humanity, the role of the Savior, and the hazardous adventure of the human soul. As one modern commentator expresses it, "The life and activities of the little world were for her not only the welcome object of sincere observation, . . . but the individual being is always organically situated in the integrated macrocosm of the whole."[10] Thus, although there is no "psychology" as such in her writings (the concept of psychology was not invented for another four hundred years), yet within the totality of her visionary work there are teachings concerning the human constitution and penetrating insights about the transformative potentials of the human being—all of which are of great interest and relevance to our current attempts to understand the human situation.

Hildegard's psychological teachings are totally integrated with her theology, her cosmology, her physics, her ecology, and her interest in healing. As a twelfth-century scientist, she believed passionately in the theory of a harmonic correspondence of macrocosm and microcosm. "God has built the human form according to the structure of the world, of the cosmos, just as an artist creates his vessels according to certain patterns."[11] This idea, which was central to medieval thought and to the worldview of the ancients, became lost to the Western world with the rise of scientific rationalism and materialism in the sixteenth and seventeenth centuries; it continued only in the teachings of Hermeticism, certain esoteric schools and traditions of magic, and the visions of such mystics as Jakob Boehme and Emanuel Swedenborg.

A most profound difference in fundamental paradigm between Hildegard and modern psychology, even the so-called transpersonal school, lies in Hildegard's use of symbolism and metaphor and their depiction in art and poetry as well as in descriptive narration. As Matthew Fox observes, "Hildegard awakens us to symbolic consciousness, . . . to deeper connection-making, to deeper ecumenism, to deeper healing, to deeper art, to deeper mysticism, to deeper social justice."[12] Symbolism speaks to the emotional and sensual aspects of mind, not just to the abstract conceptual mind. The language of symbols and images connects our ordinary awareness with the experience of the deep, living, organic, archetypal patterns of nature and cosmos.

To illustrate Hildegard's symbolic psychology, I will draw further on the remarkable images and interpretations of the fourth vision of the first part of *Scivias*. In one passage she describes her vision of the human soul as a spherical energy ("fiery sphere"), animating and nourishing the body as it flows through it like the nourishing sap flowing through the tree. Hildegard's oracular commentary elaborates this analogy: the tree becomes fruitful through the measured changes of weather, the warmth of the sun, and the moisture of rain.

> Like the sun, the compassion of God's grace provides illumination for humankind; like rain or like dew comes the breath of the Holy Spirit; and in appropriately measured cycles, like those of the weather, comes the ripening of the fruits [activities and products]. The soul is for the body as the sap is for the tree, and the soul energies unfold as the tree unfolds its *gestalt*. Understanding corresponds to the greenness *[viriditas]* of the branches and leaves, will [or desire] corresponds to the flowers and blossoms, feeling is like the first fruit sprouting forth, and intellect like the fully ripened fruit. Sense perception is like the height and breadth of the tree. Thus, the soul provides the inner solidity and strength of the body.[13]

The metaphor of the soul as the sap of the tree that is the body is one of the nature-based organic analogies that characterize Hildegard's theology and psychology. It is in marked contrast to prevailing images of "soul" as something that is ethereal and nonmaterial and could even leave the body or become "lost."

Another one of Hildegard's images, remarkable for its integrative organicism, is her threefold view of the human constitution. And she says, "The human being has three pathways, on which life's activities take place: the soul, the body, and the senses. The soul animates the body and brings the breath of life into the senses. The body attracts the soul to itself and opens the senses to the exterior world. The senses touch the soul and mediate the stimuli [of the sensory world] to the body."[14] This particular psychological threefold division is characteristic of Hildegard's thought in the emphasis given to the sensual and the carnal and their balanced interrelationship with the spiritual.

VISIONS AND PROPHECIES ON THE ELEMENTS

Hildegard's worldview is that of a visionary scientist of the European Middle Ages. It included the ancient idea that all of creation is composed

Hildegard's vision of the circle of life: the fourfold mandala of Earth, with its nourishing plants and trees, is surrounded by circles of water, air, and fire; animals are breathing toward the plants. (From De Operatione Dei, *"The Works of God")*

of four elements, four states of matter: air, the gaseous; water, the liquid; earth, the solid; and fire, as energy or radiation. Several of her illuminations symbolically portray the elements as constituting a fourfold mandala of creation. In her books of visions she repeatedly presents the image of the four elements forming not only the structure of the macrocosm but also, correspondingly, the structure of the human being, the microcosm. She demonstrates a thorough familiarity with the principles formulated in the Hermetic maxim "As above, so below." Humanity is part of the God's beloved creation, existing in intimate interdependence with the elements and all living creatures.

Hildegard not only employs the elemental imagery to describe the physical world of nature and the human role in it, but she also used this symbolism in its psychological meaning. Her metaphors are grounded in the folk wisdom of common speech, harkening back to the natural knowledge of shamanic cultures and anticipating the insights of modern depth psychology and the new discipline of ecopsychology. In her book *Liber Vitae Meritorum,* Hildegard gives an astonishing vision of the disruption of the elements through human intervention—which reads eerily like a prophecy of twentieth-century environmental degradation:

> The elements are complaining with strident voices to their Creator. Confused through the misdeeds of humans, they are exceeding their normal channels, set for them by the Creator, through strange and unnatural movements and energy currents. Thereby they are expressing that they can no longer fulfill their natural functions, as ordained by God, because through mankind's destructive works they have become inverted, turned upside down. Therefore they are emanating disgusting odors and pestilential vapors, caused by the misdeeds of humans, and reflecting hunger for absent justice. For humans no longer cultivate the elements in the appropriate manner; instead, they are attracted to the smoke of stinking punishments and participate in the world stench. Humans are interrelated with the elements, just as the elements are connected to humans.[15]

We are dealing here with a vision from a time five hundred years before the Industrial Revolution, and yet its relevance to our time seems painfully obvious. Can we not observe how the pollution and poisoning of our air and our water, the gouging, stripping, and eroding of our earth, our soil, are causing "pestilential vapors" and "world stench"? Do we not feel the injustice in the reckless exploitation of natural resources that leaves millions of people in Third World countries exposed to malnourishment or drought and famine? Do we not wonder at the blunting of our sensitivity that leads us to be "attracted to the stinking punishments," that is, to continue to poison, pollute, and degrade the environment even as we react in disgust at the consequences?

The passage quoted above ends with a statement that could be regarded as a formulation of the law of karma. "To the same degree that the elements of the world have been ruined by the misdeeds of human beings, so will they be purified and cleansed through the suffering and hardship of humans—for God wills that all be cleansed and purified before His face." Here we have a prophecy of purification and balancing vis-à-vis the elements and creatures of the natural world—a type of prophecy that has been made numerous times in the centuries since Hildegard and particularly frequently in relation to the present time, at the end of the second millennium after Christ.

The imagery of apocalyptic upheaval, turbulence, and chaotic disturbances of the natural order of the elements occurs also in the penultimate of the twenty-six visions of *Scivias*. The passage has the title "The Day of Great Revelation." ("Revelation" is the meaning of the Greek word *apocalypse*.) These visions point the way to the inevitable transformation and regeneration that has to take place in planetary consciousness and in the physical world of human activities. "I continued to see. Behold, the elements and all creatures were shaking with an all-pervasive vibration. Fire, air, and water broke out, so that the Earth trembled. There were explosions of lightning and thunder, mountains and forests collapsed, and all mortal creatures exhaled the breath of their life. The elements were being cleansed so that all impurities in them were removed."[16]

As the theologian Matthew Fox has pointed out, it is important not to take these apocalyptic, millennial prophecies too literally in terms of historical time. The last judgment is at hand for everyone who undertakes the spiritual mystical journey of transformative death and rebirth. The "prophecies" may describe the sights and terrors encountered by all at the moment of death.

In the manuscript illumination depicting this vision in *Scivias*, we

see disembodied heads of spirits being overpowered by streams of water, billows of air, and flames. This is the lower panel; in the panel above
Christ is seated on a throne within a circle of red fire, accompanied by
choirs of angels. The chaos of the elements is being transmuted into the
harmonies of celestial music. Thus it is shown in this apocalyptic vision,
and thus it is experienced in the heart of every mystic seeker when the
time of revelation has come. Between the lower picture of degeneration
and collapse and the upper picture of order and harmony, there are the
bones of the dead, whom Christ is awakening and who are being reconstituted, re-collected. Dying and the seeming suffering associated with it
are shown as a prelude to a new life, a new consciousness.

After the stormy disruption of the elements, there comes a great peace
in Hildegard's vision. "The elements then shone with a wonderful clarity,
as if a dark covering or skin had been removed from them. Fire had no
searing heat, air was free of dense clouds, water did not rage and flood,
and the earth was not fragile and crumbling. Sun, moon, and stars
sparkled in brilliant illumination and beauty, as radiant celestial gems.
They stood still, . . . so that there was no night, but only day."[17] All the
destructive manifestations of the elements cease, and there reign peace
and harmony, both inner and outer. This is the time of "last judgment,"
when we no longer judge and are no longer tempted by the paths leading to darkness and stench.

Since the body, as well as the psyche, is composed of the elements,
there is great healing as the scattered and bruised fragments of our being are brought together again, in wholeness. By using the phrases and
words from Hildegard's own vision (in quotation marks) and connect-
ing them to the human psyche, the inner meaning of these extrordinary
revelations becomes evident. The fiery aspect of our nature "glows golden
like the dawn, without heat"; the airy part, the air of our mind, "is clear
and shining, without any condensation or thickening"; the water currents of our body and the emotional currents of our psyche become
"transparent and still, without excessive flooding and turbulence"; the
earthy part of our nature, our flesh and bones, becomes "strong and
well-proportioned, without fragility or deformation."[18] Here is revealed
a vision of the total transformation possible for the human being, a
psycho-alchemical transmutation of the elements from a state of disorder and conflict to a state of harmony and balance.

There are many more fascinating details to this and other visions of the Rhineland seeress. These extracts provide merely a partial glimpse of Hildegard's vision of human destiny. According to her visions, the wholeness, or integrity, of Creator and creation was established in God's plan and promised in Christ's mission of deliverance. This is the vision of the mystics of ancient and modern times, as it was the vision of Hildegard—speaking to us in her prophetic voice across the centuries. This self-described "simple-minded woman" who was "companion to angels" inspires us with her love and delight in the natural wonders of creation, her respect for the feminine principle, her awe at the marvels of the Creator, and her insight, admiration, and compassion for the complex mysteries of the human heart. "All of creation," says Hildegard, "is a symphony of joy and jubilation."

The Role of Psychoactive
Plant Medicines

Originally, my interest was in the potentials of psychedelic drugs for the transformation of consciousness. Subsequently, I became interested in the role of altered states of consciousness (induced by plants and other methods) in the three great traditional systems of transformation—shamanism, alchemy and yoga. I now regard shamanic ritual use of such plants, along with herbal medicine and organic farming, as part of a worldwide movement toward a more balanced and conscious relationship with the plant realm. In this essay, I review the role of psychoactive plant medicines in the three transformative traditions and speculate on how they might be integrated into society in a healthy way. [1]

There is a question that has troubled me, and no doubt others, since the heyday of psychedelic research in the 1960s, when many groups and individuals were preoccupied with the problem of assimilating new and powerful mind-altering substances into Western society. The question, simply stated, was this: Why did the American Indians succeed in integrating the use of peyote into their culture, including its legal use as a sacrament to this day, when those interested in pursuing consciousness research with drugs in the dominant white culture succeeded only in having the entire field made taboo to research and any use of the substances deemed a criminal offense punishable by imprisonment? The use of peyote spread from Mexico to the North American Indian tribes in the latter half of the nineteenth century and has found acceptance as a sacrament in the ceremonies of the Native American Church. It is recognized as one kind of religious ritual that some of the tribes practice; and it is acknowledged by sociologists for its role as an antidote for alcohol abuse.

This intriguing puzzle in ethnopsychology and social history was relevant to me, since I was one of the psychedelic researchers who saw the enormous transformative potentials of "consciousness expanding" drugs, as we called them, and were eager to continue the research into their psychological significance. It would be fair to state that none of the early explorers in this field, in the fifties and early sixties, had any inkling of the social turmoil that was to come or of the vehemence of the legal-political reaction. Certainly Albert Hofmann, the Swiss chemist who discovered LSD—the epitome of the cautious, conservative scientist—has testified to his dismay and concern over the proliferation of patterns of abuse of what he so poignantly called his "problem child" *(Sorgenkind)*.[2]

Thus resulted the strange paradox that substances regarded as a social evil and a law enforcement problem in the mainstream dominant culture are the sacrament of one particular subculture within that larger society. Since the Native American subcultures are older and ecologically more sophisticated cultures than the European white culture that attempted to absorb or eliminate it, and since many sensitive individuals have long argued that we should be learning from the Indians, not exterminating them, the examination of the question I have posed could lead to highly interesting conclusions. The answer to the ethnopsychological puzzle became clear to me only after I started observing and participating in a number of other American Indian ceremonies that did not involve the use of peyote, such as a healing-singing circle, a sweat lodge, and a spirit dance. I noted what many ethnologists have reported—that these ceremonies were simultaneously religious, medicinal, and psychotherapeutic. The sweat lodge, like the peyote ritual, is regarded as a sacred ceremony, as a form of worship of the Creator; they are also both seen and practiced as a form of physical healing, and they are performed for solving personal and collective psychological problems. Thus it was natural for those tribes that took up peyote to add this medium to the others with which they were already familiar, as a ceremony that expressed and reinforced the integration of body, mind, and spirit.

In the dominant white society, by contrast, medicine, psychology, and religious spirituality are separated by seemingly insurmountable paradigm differences. The medical, psychological, and religious professions and established groups each separately considered the phenomenon of psychedelic drugs and were much too frightened by the unpredictable transformations of perception and worldview that they seemed to trigger. The dominant society's reaction was fear, followed by total prohibition, even of further research. None of the three established professions wanted these consciousness-expanding instruments, and neither did they want anyone else to be able to use them of their own free choice. The implicit assumption was (and is) that people are too ignorant and gullible to be able to make reasoned, informed choices as to how to treat their illnesses, solve their psychological problems, or practice their religion. The fragmented condition of our whole society is mirrored back to us through these reactions.

For the Native Americans, on the other hand, healing, worship, and problem solving are all subsumed in the one way, which is the way of the Great Spirit, the way of Mother Earth, the traditional way. The integrative understanding given in the peyote visions is not feared, but accepted and respected. Here the implicit assumption is that everyone has the capability, indeed the responsibility, to attune themselves to higher spiritual sources of knowledge and healing—and the purpose of ceremony, with or without medicinal substances, is regarded as a facilitator of such attunement.

Psychedelics as Sacrament or Recreation

Several observers, for example, Andrew Weil, have pointed out the historical pattern that as Western colonial society adopted psychoactive plant or food substances from native cultures, the use of such psychoactive materials devolved from sacramental to recreational.[3] Tobacco was historically regarded as a sacred or power plant by Indians of North, Central, and South America and is still so regarded by Native Americans.[4] In white Western culture, and in countries influenced by this dominant culture, however, cigarette smoking is obviously recreational and has become a major public health problem. The coca plant, as grown and used by the Andean Indian tribes, was treated as a divinity, Mama Coca, and valued for its health-maintaining properties. The concentrated extract cocaine, on the other hand, is purely a recreational drug, and its indiscriminate use as such causes numerous health problems. In this, and other instances, desecration of the plant drug has been accompanied by criminalization. Coffee is another example. Apparently first discovered and used by Islamic Sufis, who valued its stimulant properties for long nights of prayer and meditation, it became a fashionable recreational drink in European society in the seventeenth century and was even banned for a while as being too dangerous. And cannabis, used by some sects of Hindu Tantrism as an amplifier of visualization and meditation, has become the epitome of the recreational "high."[5]

Since sacramental healing plants were so rapidly and completely profaned upon being adopted by the West's increasingly materialistic culture, it is not surprising that newly discovered synthetic psychoactive drugs have generally been very quickly categorized as either recreational or narcotic—even those, like the psychedelics, whose effects are the opposite of narcotic ("sleep inducing"). Concomitantly, as the indiscriminate, excessive, nonsacramental use of psychoactive plants and newly synthesized analogues spread, so did patterns of abuse and dependence. Predictably, established society reacted with prohibitions, which in turn spawned organized crime activities. This took place in spite of the fact that many of the original discoverers of the new synthetic psychedelics, such as Albert Hofmann and Alexander Shulgin, are individuals of deep spiritual integrity. Neither their efforts nor those of such philosophers as Aldous Huxley, Alan Watts, and Huston Smith or psychologists such as Timothy Leary and Richard Alpert, to advocate a sacred and respectful attitude toward these substances, were able to prevent the same profanation.

The newly discovered phenethylamine psychedelic (also called empathogenic—"empathy generating") MDMA provides an instructive example of this phenomenon. Two patterns of use seem to have become established during the seventies. Some psychotherapists and spiritually inclined individuals began to explore its possible applications as a therapeutic adjuvant and as an amplifier of spiritual practice. Another, much larger group of people began using it for recreational purposes, as a social "high" comparable in some respects to cocaine. Its irresponsible and widespread use in this second category by increasing numbers of people understandably made the medical and law enforcement authorities nervous. The predictable reaction occurred. MDMA was classified as a Schedule I drug in the United States, which puts it in the same group as heroin, cannabis, and LSD—making it a criminal offense to make, use, or sell the substance and sending a clearly understood off-limits signal to pharmaceutical and medical researchers.[6]

After Albert Hofmann had identified psilocybin as the psychoactive ingredient in the Mexican magic mushroom that the Aztecs called *teonanácatl,* he took some of the synthesized psilocybin to the Mazatec shamaness Maria Sabina, to obtain her assessment of how closely the synthesized ingredient resembled the natural product. In doing so, he was following the appropriate path of acknowledging the primacy of the botanical over the synthetic. It has been suggested that for every one of the important synthetic psychedelics there is a natural plant that has the same ingredients and that perhaps it should be our research strategy to find the botanical "host" for the psychedelics emerging from the laboratory. Research on the shamanic use of the hallucinogenic morning glory seeds called *ololiuhqui* in ancient Mexico, which contain LSD analogues, has allowed us a deeper understanding of the possible uses of this substance.

If Gordon Wasson, Albert Hofmann, and Carl Ruck are correct in their proposal that an LSD-like ergot-derived beverage was used as the initiatory sacrament in Eleusis, the implications are profound.[7] According to Rupert Sheldrake's theory of morphogenetic fields, rituals, like any patterned activity, gain their power through precise repetition of all the elements.[8] One could suppose that by regrowing or rehybridizing this particular plant, as it was used in ancient times, we could "tune in" to and reactivate the morphogenetic field of the Eleusinian Mysteries, the ancient world's most awe-inspiring mystical ritual.

There is no inherent reason why sacramental use and recreational use of a substance in moderation cannot coexist. In fact, among Native Americans, tobacco often plays this dual role; after a sacred pipe ritual with tobacco and other herbs, participants may smoke cigarettes to relax. We know the sacramental use of wine in the Catholic Communion rite, and we certainly know the recreational use of wine. We are able to keep the two contexts separate, and we are also able to recognize when recreational use becomes dependence and abuse. One could envision a similar sophistication developing with regard to psychoactive plant products. There could be recognized sacramental and therapeutic applications, and certain patterns of use might develop that are more playful, exploratory, and hedonistic—and yet contained within a reasonable and acceptable social framework that minimizes harm. The abuse of a drug in such a rational and sensible system would not be a function of who uses it, or where it originated, or its chemical classification—but rather the behavioral consequences of the drug user. Someone becomes recognized as an alcoholic, that is, an abuser of alcohol, when his or her interpersonal and social relationships are noticeably impaired. There should be no difficulty in establishing similar abuse criteria for other psychoactive drugs.

PSYCHEDELICS AS GNOSTIC CATALYSTS

In 1968, in an article called "On the Evolutionary Significance of Psychedelics," I suggested that the findings of LSD research in the areas of psychology, religion, and the arts could be considered in the context of the evolution of consciousness. "If LSD expands consciousness and if, as is widely believed, further evolution will take the form of an increase in consciousness, then can we not regard LSD as a possible *evolutionary instrument?* . . . Here is a device which, by altering the chemical composition of the cerebro-sensory information processing medium, temporarily inactivates the screening-programs, the genetic and cultural filters, which dominate in a completely unnoticed way our usual perceptions of the world."[9] From the perspective of almost thirty years' experience and reflection, I would now extend and amplify this statement in two ways:

1. The evolution of consciousness is a transformational process that consists primarily in gaining insight and understanding, or gnosis.
2. The acceleration of this process by molecular catalysts not only is a consequence of new chemical discoveries but also is an integral component of traditional systems of transformation, including shamanism, alchemy, and yoga.

In the field of consciousness research, the "set-and-setting hypothesis," which was first formulated by Timothy Leary in the early sixties, helps us understand psychoactive drugs and plants as one class of triggers within a whole range of possible catalysts of altered states.[10] The theory states that the content of a psychedelic experience is a function of the set (intention, attitude, personality, mood) and the setting (interpersonal, social, and environmental) and that the drug functions as a kind of trigger, or catalyst, or nonspecific amplifier or sensitizer. The hypothesis can be applied to the understanding of any altered state of consciousness, when we recognize that other kinds of stimuli can be triggers—for example, hypnotic induction, meditation techniques, mantra, sound or music, breathing, sensory isolation, movement, sex, natural landscapes, a near-death experience, and the like.

An important clarification results from keeping in mind the distinction between a state (of consciousness) and a psychological trait, between state changes and trait changes. For example, psychologists distinguish between state anxiety and trait anxiety. William James, in his classic *Varieties of Religious Experience,* discussed this question in terms of whether a religious or conversion experience would necessarily lead to more "saintliness," more enlightened traits. This distinction is crucial to the assessment of the value or significance of drug-induced altered states. Only by attending to both the state changes (visions, insights, feelings) and the long-term consequences, or behavioral or trait changes, can a comprehensive understanding of these phenomena be attained.

Having an insight is not the same as being able to apply that insight. There is no inherent connection between a mystical experience of oneness and the expression or manifestation of that oneness in the affairs of everyday life. This point is perhaps obvious, and yet it is frequently overlooked by those who argue, on principle, that a drug cannot induce a genuine mystical experience or play any role in spiritual life. The internal factors of *set,* including preparation, expectation, and intention, are the determinants of whether a given experience is authentically religious. Equally, intention is crucial to the question of whether an altered state results in any lasting personality changes. Intention is the bridge from the ordinary or "consensus reality" state to the state of heightened consciousness; and it also provides a bridge from that heightened state back to ordinary reality.

This model allows us to understand how the same drug(s) could be claimed by some to lead to nirvana or religious vision and in others (for example, Charles Manson) could lead to perverse and sadistic violence.

The drug is only a tool, a catalyst, to attain certain altered states; which altered states depend on the intention. Furthermore, even where the drug-induced state is benign and expansive, whether it leads to long-lasting positive changes is also a matter of intention or mind-set.

The drug indeed seems to reveal or release something that is *in* the person. This is the factor implied in the term *psychedelic,* which means "mind manifesting." An alternate term that has been proposed is *entheogenic,* "releasing (or generating) the deity within." My reservation about this term is that it might convey the misleading idea that the divinity within is "generated" in these states. To the contrary, most people realize in these states that the divine within *is* the generator, the source of life energy, the awakening and healing power. For someone whose conscious intention is a psychospiritual transformation, the psychedelic *can* be a catalyst that reveals and releases insight or knowledge from higher aspects of our being. This is, I believe, what is meant by *gnosis*— sacred knowledge, insight concerning the fundamental spiritual realities of the universe in general, and one's individual destiny in particular.

The potential of psychedelic drugs to act as catalysts to a transformation into gnosis, or direct, ongoing awareness of divine reality, even if only in a small number of people, would seem to be of the utmost significance. Traditionally, the number of individuals who have had mystical experiences has been very small; the number of those who have been able to make practical applications of such experiences has probably been even smaller. Thus, the discovery of psychedelics, in facilitating such experiences and processes, could be regarded as one very important factor in a general spiritual awakening of collective human consciousness. Other factors that could be mentioned in this connection are the revolutionary paradigm shifts in the physical and biological sciences, the burgeoning interest in Eastern philosophies and spiritual disciplines, and the growing awareness of the multicultural oneness of the human family brought about by the global communications networks.

PSYCHEDELICS IN TRADITIONAL SYSTEMS OF TRANSFORMATION

In earlier writings I emphasized the newness of psychedelic drugs and the unimaginable potentials to be realized by their constructive application.

I viewed them as first products of a new technology, oriented toward the human spirit. I still appreciate the potential role of the new synthetic psychedelics in consciousness research and perhaps in consciousness evolution. My views have changed somewhat, however, under the influence of the discoveries and writings of cultural anthropologists and ethnobotanists, who have pointed to the role of mind-altering and visionary botanicals in traditional cultures across the world.[11]

Shamanism

One cannot read the works of R. Gordon Wasson on the Mesoamerican mushroom cults; or the work of Richard E. Schultes on the profusion of hallucinogens in the Amazon region; or the cross-cultural studies of such authors as Michael Harner, Joan Halifax, Peter Furst, and Luis Eduardo Luna; or the cross-culturally oriented medical and psychiatric works of such researchers as Andrew Weil, Claudio Naranjo, and Stanislav Grof; or more personal accounts, such as the writings of Carlos Castaneda, Florinda Donner, the McKenna brothers, or Bruce Lamb's biography of Manuel Cordova, without gaining a strong sense of the pervasiveness of the quest for visions, insights, and nonordinary states of consciousness in the worldwide shamanic traditions. These studies demonstrate incontrovertibly that psychoactive plants are used in many, but by no means all of the shamanic cultures that pursue such states.[12] For this reason I have been led to a view closer to that of aboriginal cultures, a view of humanity in a relationship of co-consciousness, communication, and cooperation with the animal kingdom, the plant kingdom, and the mineral world. In such a worldview, the ingestion of hallucinogenic plant preparations to obtain knowledge—for healing, for prophecy, for communication with spirits, for anticipation of danger, or for understanding the universe—appears as one of the oldest and most highly treasured traditions.

The various shamanic cultures all over the world know a wide variety of means for entering nonordinary realities. Michael Harner has pointed out that "auditory driving" with prolonged drumming is perhaps equally as widespread a technology for entering shamanic states as hallucinogens. In some cultures, the rhythmic hyperventilation produced through certain kinds of chanting may be another form of altered-state trigger. Animal spirits become guides and allies in shamanic initiation. Plant spirits can become "helpers," too, even when the plant is not taken internally by either doctor or patient. Tobacco smoke is used as a puri-fier as well as a support to prayer. Crystals are used to focus energy for seeing and healing. There is attunement, through prayer and medita-tion, with deities and spirits of the land, the four directions, the ele-ments, the Creator Spirit. The knowledge obtained from other states and other worlds is used to improve the way we live in this world. The use of hallucinogenic plants is part of an integrated complex of interre-lationships among nature, spirit, and human consciousness.

Thus it seems to me that the lessons we are to learn from these consciousness-expanding plants in shamanism have to do not only with the recognition of other dimensions of the human psyche but also with a radically different worldview—a worldview that has been maintained in the beliefs, practices, and rituals of shamanic cultures and almost totally forgotten or suppressed by the materialist culture of the mod-ern age. There is, of course, a certain delightful irony in the fact that it has taken a material substance to awaken the sleeping consciousness of so many of our contemporaries to the reality of nonmaterial energies, forms, and beings.

Alchemy

In discussing alchemy as the second of the three traditional systems of consciousness transformation mentioned earlier, I would emphasize first that we have only the minutest shreds of evidence that ingestion of hal-lucinogens played any part in the European alchemical tradition. The use of solanaceous (nightshades) hallucinogens in European witchcraft, which is related to both shamanism and alchemy, has been documented by Harner.[13] Likewise, in Chinese Taoist alchemy, the use of botanical and mineral preparations to induce spirit flight and other kinds of al-tered states, has been discussed by Michel Strickmann.[14] A complete account of the role of hallucinogens in alchemy has not as yet been written. Possibly, our ignorance in this field is still a consequence of intentional secrecy on the part of the alchemical writers.

Mircea Eliade, in his book *The Forge and the Crucible,* made a strong case for the historical derivation of alchemy from early Bronze Age and Iron Age metallurgy, mining, and smithing rites and practices.[15] One could argue that alchemy is one form of shamanism—the shamanism of those who worked with minerals and metals, the makers of tools and weapons. Many of the concerns and interests of the alchemists parallel shamanic themes. There is the strong interest in purification and healing, in discovering or making a "tincture" or "elixir" that will impart health and longevity. There are visions and encounters with animal spirits, some clearly from the imaginal realms. There are stories and visions of divine and semidivine figures, often personified as the deities of classical mythology. There is the recognition of the sacredness, the animating spirit, of all matter. And there is the integrated worldview, which sees spirituality, religion, health and illness, human beings, and the natural world and its elements all interrelated in a totality.

It is true that there does not seem to be the equivalent of a shamanic journey in alchemy, no clear indication of an altered state of consciousness in which visions or power or healing abilities are attained. It appears to me, however, that the alchemical equivalent of the shamanic journey is the opus, the "work," the experiment with its various operations, such as *solutio, sublimatio, mortificatio,* and the like. The focus would seem to be more on the long-term personality and physical changes that the alchemical initiate has to undergo, just like the shaman in training. The operations in alchemy were meditative rituals, during which visions might be seen in the retort or furnace, and interior psychophysiological state changes triggered by the empathic observation of chemical processes.

Furthermore, R. J. Stewart has argued that in the Western tradition of magic and alchemy, which has roots in pre-Christian Celtic mythology and beliefs and of which traces can still be found in folklore, ballads, popular songs, and nursery rhymes, the central transformative experience was the Underworld journey.[16] This Underworld or "otherworld" initiation involved taking a "journey" into other realms, encounters with animal and spirit beings, attunement with the land and the ancestors, meditative rituals centering around the tree of life symbolism, and other features that place this tradition clearly in the ancient stream of shamanic lore found in all parts of the globe.

Yoga

Turning now to yoga as the third of the traditional systems of evolutionary transformation of consciousness, we need not try to resolve the questions of whether the use of psychoactive plant preparations is a decadent form of yoga, as Eliade seems to believe, or whether the use of hallucinogens was primary, in the Vedic Indian tradition of the soma cult, as Wasson has proposed.[17, 18] Some have suggested that methods of yoga were developed when the psychoactive plant or fungus was no longer available, as an alternative means for attaining visionary states. Suffice it to say that in the Indian yogic traditions, in particular the teachings of Tantra, we have a system of practices for bringing about a transformation of consciousness, with many parallels to shamanic and alchemical ideas.

The use of hallucinogens as an adjunct to yogic practices is known to this day in India, among certain Shaivite sects in particular.[19] Those schools and sects that do not use drugs tend to regard those that do as decadent, as belonging to the so-called left-hand path of Tantra, which also incorporates ritual food and sexuality *(maithuna)* as valid aspects of the yogic practice. Under the influence of nineteenth-century Western occult and theosophical ideas, this left-hand path was equated to "black magic" or "sorcery." In actuality, the designation "left-hand path" derives from the yogic principle that the left side of the body is the feminine, receptive side; thus, the left-hand path is the path of those who worship the Goddess *(Shakti),* as the Tantrics do, and incorporate the experience of body, the delight of the senses, food, and sexuality into their yoga. Thus, as in shamanism and alchemy, we find here a strand of the tradition that involves respect and devotion to the feminine principle, the Mother Goddess, the earth and its fruit, the flesh-and-blood body, and the seeking of ecstatic visionary states.

It is true that the Indian yogic traditions seem not to have the same concern for the natural world of animals, crystals, and plants as is found in shamanism and alchemy. The emphasis is more on various inner and subtle states of consciousness. Nevertheless, there are interesting parallels among the three traditions. The focusing of inner light-fire energy in different centers and organs of the body, as practiced in Agni Yoga and Kundalini Yoga, is similar to the alchemical practice of purification by fire and to shamanic notions of filling the body with light.[20] The Indian alchemical Tantric tradition embraced the concept of *rasa*, which is akin to the European alchemical concept of "tincture" or "elixir." Rasa has internal meanings—feeling, mood, "soul"—and external referents— essence, juice, liquid. *Rasayana* was the path or way of rasa, the way of fluid energy flow, which involves both external and internal essences.[21]

As a third parallel, I will only mention the Tibetan Buddhist Vajrayana system, which is a remarkable fusion of Tantric Buddhist ideas with the original Bon shamanism of Tibet—a system in which the various animal spirits and demons of the shamans and sorcerers have become transformed into personifications of Buddhist principles and guardians of the dharma.[22]

Conclusions

It appears incontrovertible that plant (and fungal) hallucinogens played some role, of unknown extent, in the transformative traditions of shamanism, alchemy, and yoga. If we regard psychotherapy as the modern descendant of these traditional systems, then a similar, if limited, application of hallucinogens could be made in various aspects of psychotherapy. And this has, in fact, already occurred, as the various studies of psychedelics in alcoholism, terminal cancer, obsessional neurosis, depression, and other conditions testify.[23] It seems likely that these kinds of applications of psychedelics, as adjuncts to psychotherapy, will continue—if not with LSD and other Schedule I drugs, then with other, newer and perhaps safer psychedelics.

What appears unlikely to me is that this kind of controlled psychiatric application will ever be enough to satisfy the inclinations and needs of those individuals who wish to explore psychedelics in their most ancient role, as tools for seeking visionary states and hidden forms of knowledge. The fact that the serious use of hallucinogens, outside a psychiatric framework, continues despite severe social and legal sanctions suggests that this is a kind of individual freedom that is not easy to abolish. It also suggests that there is a strong need in certain people to reestablish their connections with ancient traditions of knowledge, in which visionary states of consciousness and exploration of other realities, with or without hallucinogens, were the central concern.

It may be that such a path will always be pursued by only a limited number of individuals—much as the shamanic, alchemical, and yogic initiations and practices were pursued by only a few individuals in each society. I find it a hopeful sign that some people, however few, are willing to explore how to reconnect with these lost sources of knowledge, because, like many others, I feel that our materialist-technological society, with its fragmented worldview, has largely lost its way and can ill afford to ignore any potential aids to greater knowledge of the human mind. The ecologically balanced and integrative framework of understanding that the ancient traditions preserved surely has much to offer us.

Furthermore, it is clear that the visions and insights of the individuals who pursue these paths are visions and insights for the present and the future and not just of historical or anthropological interest. This has always been the pattern: the individual seeks a vision to understand his or her place, or destiny, as a member of the community. The knowledge derived from expanded states of consciousness has been, can be, and needs to be applied to the solution of the staggering problems that confront our species. This is why the discoveries of the mystical chemists and ethnobotanists have immense importance—for the understanding of our past, the awareness of our presence, and the safeguarding of our future.

Psychopathology of the Human-Nature Relationship

It is widely agreed that the global ecological crisis which confronts the world today is one of the most critical turning points that human civilization has ever faced. Furthermore, the realization is spreading that the root causes of environmental destruction lie in human psychology—in certain distorted perceptions, attitudes, and values that modern humans have come to hold. In this essay I discuss some of the diagnostic analogies that have been proposed to account for the destructive imbalance in the human-nature relationship.[1]

Several different diagnostic metaphors have been proposed to explain the ecologically disastrous split, the pathological alienation, between human beings and the rest of the biosphere. None of these psychological diagnoses, incidentally, have been made by psychologists, who seem to have taken absolutely no interest in this question thus far. We can view these concepts as metaphors or analogies, transferred from the realm of individual psychopathology to the level of society and to the level of the human species in its relation to the nonhuman natural world. There are historical precedents for applying diagnostic concepts from individual psychology to the realm of collective or mass psychology. Wilhelm Reich's work on the mass psychology of fascism and, more recently, Lloyd deMause's psychoanalytic interpretations of historical and political trends are examples of this approach.[2] To those who would question the relevance of such diagnostic speculation, the answer is simply that we are trying to discern the nature of the psychological disturbance that appears to have Homo sapiens in its grip, to be able to apply the appropriate treatments to the amelioration of the present ecocatastrophe.

THE AILING BIOSPHERE: METAPHORS OF ORGANIC PATHOLOGY

A number of people have proposed that in view of the excessive population growth of human beings in many parts of the biosphere, the best analogy to describe the situation is in terms of a malignant tumor. Tumors are made up of cells multiplying uncontrollably and destroying the surrounding tissue. The anthropologist Warren Hern has said, "A schematic view of the growth of London from 1800 to 1955 looks like nothing so much as an expanding, invasive, metastatic, malignant tumor."[3] He proposes the term *Homo ecophagus* ("ecosystem-devourer") as the appropriate name for this pathological species. In pointing to the obvious malignancy of large megacities, Theodore Roszak has written about "Gaia's city pox," the spread of large urban conglomerations associated with the Industrial Revolution.[4] The disease metaphor for our planetary condition depends on the following underlying analogy: Earth (Gaia) is a living organism, and humans and other individual organisms are the cells in this superorganism. The phenomenal expansions of human populations that we are now seeing, particularly the sprawling urban aggregates, can then be seen as clusters of cancer cells, spreading to more and more areas of Earth's land surface.

Al Gore has taken the disease metaphor to task, writing that "the internal logic of the metaphor points toward only one possible cure: eliminate people from the face of the earth."[5] This is an incorrect reading of the disease analogy, however. On the level of the individual organism, eliminating the pathogens is by no means the only possible cure for cancer. There are several different approaches to the treatment of cancer, including changes in diet, lifestyle, attitude, self-concept, and imagery, all of which have been shown to have some success. The implications for the collective human situation are obvious and quite hopeful. There is also the well-documented existence of so-called spontaneous remission, in which cancerous cells stop multiplying and tissues revert to a healthy condition, or in which the organism's immune system reduces the numbers of pathogenic microbes to a tolerable level. The normal inhibitory mechanisms that prevent excessive growth can become reactivated. Perhaps this could be analogized to conscious individuals restraining their reproductive rate and conscious communities setting boundaries on urban sprawl.

The most completely articulated formulation of the disease analogy is by James Lovelock, in his last book, *Healing Gaia*. Trained in medicine, Lovelock has long been suggesting that *geophysiology* should be the name of the science of the structures and functions of Earth's ecosystems and energy cycles (hydrogen, oxygen, nitrogen, etc.). Planetary medicine then concerns the disturbed functioning of this great organism. Lovelock's preferred diagnosis is that Gaia is suffering from a parasitical infestation by the species Homo sapiens, a disease he calls *disseminated primatemia*. He points out that parasite-host relationships can have four possible outcomes: first, the invading microorganisms are destroyed by the host's immune system; second, host and parasite settle down to a long war of attrition—the condition known as chronic infection; third, the parasite destroys the host and thereby eliminates its own life support; and, fourth, the parasitical relationship is transformed into one of mutualism or symbiosis. "The last [scenario], symbiosis, is obviously desirable. As intelligent microbes, we have the advantage of knowing the risks of failure and the lasting benefits of symbiosis. But will we achieve it?"[6] Lovelock states that there are several strong precedents in nature for this kind of symbiosis between life-forms of very different scale, but he adds that there are inherent properties of humans that make it difficult for us to act sensibly and achieve symbiosis within Gaia. With this statement we enter the realm of human behavior and attitudes as the crucial levers of global change.

ANTHROPOCENTRISM AND THE HUMAN SUPERIORITY COMPLEX

Environmental thinkers, or ecophilosophers, were the first to point to the crucial role of distorted human attitudes, beliefs, and values in the generation of the ecological crisis. The concept of anthropocentrism, or homocentrism, was offered as a philosophical diagnosis of the human species' ecological maladjustment and biocentrism or ecocentrism as the healthier corrective. This idea has been put forward by a number of twentieth-century philosophers, ecologists, and writers, including Aldo Leopold, Paul Sears, Aldous Huxley, Loren Eiseley, Rachel Carson, Lynn White Jr., Robinson Jeffers, Paul Shepard, Gary Snyder, Edward Abbey, and others; forebear of this kind of thinking can be traced to such nineteenth-century thinkers as John Muir, Henry Thoreau, and Ralph Waldo Emerson as well as to the ethical cosmology of Baruch Spinoza.[7] The anthropocentric critique has been articulated most cogently by the Norwegian philosopher Arne Naess (himself strongly influenced by Spinoza) and by those identified with the philosophical orientation known as deep ecology, founded by Naess. To use the term anthropocentrism as a critique of the human attitude to nature in the modernist worldview parallels the use of "ethnocentrism" to critique racial discrimination and the use of "Eurocentrism" to critique the colonialist exploitation ideology of Western culture.

Although the role of anthropocentric attitudes in creating or aggravating the ecological imbalance of industrial civilization is unquestionable, there are reasons to question the use of that term, since it actually covers two distinct meanings. *Anthropocentric* literally just means "human-centered," and some critics have pointed out that the human, like every other species, necessarily looks at the world from its own point of view, seeking to maximize its own survival advantages. A nonanthropocentric viewpoint, in this criticism, is both impossible and unnatural. But whether our human-centered perspective can be transcended is surely an empirical question—a question about the possibility of psychological change. Even if we assume that a homocentric attitude is a basic fact of human nature, this still leaves open the possibility that humans can learn to transcend their inborn homocentrism. This is, in fact, what Arne Naess, Warwick Fox, and others propose with their notion of extending identification to the natural world. Perhaps this is something humans can do and animals cannot. Or perhaps animals, or some animals, can also empathically escape their species-centered points of view and look at the world through human eyes. Certainly this seems to be the view of shamanistic cultures, which have much lore and mythology about how in ancient times humans could understand the language of animals, and animals could understand humans, even to the point of marrying them sometimes. Interspecies empathic identification may have been the norm in the paleolithic world, a capacity that has become atrophied through disuse in humans.[8]

The deep ecologists' critique of anthropocentrism, however, is really saying more than just that the fixation in a human-centered perspective is deplorable—just as ethnocentrism implies more than holding a perspective (naturally) centered on one's own ethnic group. There is an implicit meaning of assumed superiority and right to dominate others. This has been referred to as human chauvinism or human imperialism (two metaphors from the political arena) as well as *speciesism*—on a parallel with such prejudicial ideologies as racism, sexism, classism, and nationalism. In each of these forms of prejudice, one group of human beings assumes its superiority to other beings (human or nonhuman) and therefore arrogates the right to dominate and exploit those judged inferior.[9] It is really human "speciesism" that we are talking about here, the human assumption of superiority to other species—what the ecologist David Ehrenfeld called "the arrogance of humanism" in his book of that title.[10] This leads to the surprising and depressing conclusion that humanism, that much prized core idea of Western culture, has become a kind of pathological mind-set involving discrimination, prejudice, and domination, precisely analogous to racism, sexism, classism, and nationalism.

Because this is an idea quite distinct from the fixation on the human-centered perspective, I suggest we call this diagnostic metaphor the *human (or humanist) superiority complex*. In a subsequent chapter, we will delve more deeply into the interesting cultural-historical question of how this superiority complex came to be such a pervasive feature of the Western worldview. The "dominion" imagery of the creation myth in Genesis has been identified by several historians as one obvious source. Some Christian theologians have argued that "dominion" really meant "stewardship," but for many, even the notion of stewardship is still based on assumed human superiority. Do we really know enough to be stewards? Hunter-gatherers are clearly not stewards, which is a term derived from animal husbandry ("sty-warden"). Oversimplified interpretations of Darwinian evolutionary theory have lent seeming support to the notion of the human as the superior animal, more evolved and more complex than other life-forms and therefore, it was assumed, having both the knowledge and the right to tinker with nature and use it as we saw fit. "Superiority striving," a Nietzschian "will to power," is a central element in the developmental theory of Freud's contemporary Alfred Adler. Adler believed that conscious feelings of superiority are always a compensation for an unconscious inferiority complex and that such inferiority feelings tend to arise normally in childhood, as a result of prolonged dependency and immaturity. Jung and other psychodynamic psychologists accept the notion of conscious attitudes compensating for unconscious ones, even if they do not accept the centrality of the superiority-inferiority complex. If we want to apply this analysis to the collective ideology of humanist arrogance, we would look for unconscious fears and feelings of inadequacy toward the natural world underlying the attitude of conquest and domination. With this speculation, we come close to Paul Shepard's ideas on the loss of paleolithic relatedness and developmental initiation rites.

DEVELOPMENTAL FIXATION:
THE VIEWS OF PAUL SHEPARD

The first person to clearly formulate a psychopathological metaphor for the destructive and exploitative behavior of the human species toward the natural world was the ecologist Paul Shepard, in his book *Nature and Madness*. Drawing on the work of such psychoanalytic developmental psychologists as Erik Erikson and Harold Searles, Shepard brilliantly dissected the cultural pathology of Western Judaeo-Christian civilization as a case of arrested development, or what he calls "ontogenetic crippling." He traced the progressive distortion of normal developmental pathways, which could still be seen in surviving hunter-gatherer societies, through four historical stages: the agricultural domestication, the Desert Fathers, the Puritans, and the founders of mechanistic science. In his 1993 essay "A Post-Historic Primitivism," Shepard summarizes his earlier work by saying that "incomplete, ontogeny runs into the dead end of immaturity and a miasma of pathological limbos."[11]

A particularly interesting feature of Shepard's analysis is his discussion of the interplay between neoteny, the extended period of immaturity and dependency of the human child, and the developmental support provided by culture. In the case of a species with such marked neoteny as the human, the failure or disappearance of culturally provided developmental supports would have particularly devastating consequences. In his use of paleolithic hunter-gatherer societies as models of ecologically balanced lifestyles, including child-rearing, Shepard seems to be saying that with the advent of domestication, circa twelve thousand years ago, civilized humanity began to lose or pervert the developmental practices that had functioned healthily for hundreds of thousands of years.

He sees two stages where ancient patterns of development may have become chronically incomplete: infant-caregiver relationships and adolescent transition rites. Shepard argues that agriculture increased the distance between the growing child and the nonhuman, or "wild," world of nature: "By aggravating the tensions of separation from the mother and at the same time spatially isolating the individual from the nonhumanized world, agriculture made it difficult for the developing person to approach the issues around which the crucial passages into fully mature adult life had been structured in the course of human existence."[12]

In Erikson's developmental model, adolescence is the time when the child is enmeshed in a conflict between "identity and identity diffusion." The notion of a collective fixation at the stage of early adolescence fits with the kind of boisterous, arrogant pursuit of individual self-assertion that characterizes the consumerist, exploitative model of economic growth, where the short-term profits of entrepreneurs and corporate shareholders seem to be not only the dominant value but the *only* value under consideration. It also fits with the aggressive and predatory militarism and the emphasis on the values and ideals of male warrior cults that have characterized Western civilization since the Bronze Age. Adolescents who have difficulty negotiating the turmoil of this stage often become, as Erikson writes, "remarkably clannish, intolerant and cruel in their exclusion of others who are 'different,' in skin color or cultural background." [13]

To provide guiding structures for negotiating the transition from the family matrix to the larger society was the function of rites of passage in traditional societies. The progressive deterioration and loss of adolescent rites of passage in the modern age are well known. As Robert Bly has pointed out, even the minimal father-to-son apprenticeship bonding that existed before the Industrial Revolution has since been lost. The only transition rites of manhood we still have involving elders, such as they are, are the boot-camp and combat initiations afforded by the military. Beyond that, there is only the stunted futility of attempted peer group initiation, whether in the pathetic form of college fraternity hazing or in the casual violence of juvenile street gangs, where twelve-year-olds may carry handguns to school to avenge imagined insults to their "home" band.

Besides the loss of adolescent initiation rites, Shepard points to the "unity pathology" that develops if the earliest stage of infant-caregiver bonding is disrupted or disturbed. This is the stage Erikson identifies as the stage where the child's developing sense of self is dealing with issues of "basic trust vs. mistrust." If this stage is not negotiated successfully, we may have at best an attitude of chronic insecurity and at worst the suspiciousness and proneness to violence of the paranoid psychotic. Jean Liedloff's studies of mother-infant bonding among Amazonian Indians and her "continuum concept" support Shepard's assertion that in hunter-gatherer societies, the intense early attachment leads not to prolonged dependency but to a better functioning nervous system.[14]

Shepard summarizes his theory of ontogenetic crippling by stating that "men [presumably he means "Western industrialized humans"] may now be the possessors of the world's flimsiest identity structure—by Paleolithic standards, childish adults."[15] One of the worst consequences of this collective madness is "a readiness to strike back at a natural world that we dimly perceive as having failed us." On the other hand, adults who in infancy developed a basic trust that the world of nature and society can provide for their needs are not likely to be attracted to a worldview that demands a relentless struggle for competitive advantage. Government leaders and opinion makers in the United States are now in the habit of promoting "competitiveness" as the value or goal that the educational system should develop in the nation's children. We are suffering, Shepard says, from "an epidemic of the psychopathic mutilation of ontogeny."

Shepard does not say much about the possible treatment for such a case of collective arrested development. Presumably the reinstitution of initiation rituals for adolescents, carried out by respected elders, and a much greater sensitivity to the fragility of early infant bonding should be two key ingredients in any attempt to reverse this pathology. Similar proposals have been made by many people. "An ecologically harmonious sense of self and world is . . . the inherent possession of everyone; it is latent in the organism, in the interaction of the genome and early experience. The phases of such early experiences, or epigenesis, are the legacy of an evolutionary past in which human and nonhuman achieved a healthy rapport."[16]

AUTISM

A related psychopathological metaphor put forward by theologian-turned-*geologian* Thomas Berry is that the human species has become autistic in relationship to the natural world.[17] He traces the origin of this autism to Descartes's invention of the mechanistic worldview: "Descartes . . . killed the Earth and all its living beings. For him the natural world was mechanism. There was no possibility of entering into a communion relationship. Western humans became autistic in relation to the surrounding world." Autistic children do not seem to hear or see or feel their mother's presence; they do not respond to touch or voice or gesture. Like them, we have become blind to the psychic presence of the living planet and deaf to its voices and stories that nourished our ancestors in preindustrial societies. This situation can be remedied, according to Berry, only by "a new mode of mutual presence between the human and the natural world."

Psychiatrists still debate whether infantile autism is the same as or different from childhood schizophrenia. The official diagnostic manual of the American Psychiatric Association, the DSM-IV, calls it a "pervasive developmental disorder" characterized by "qualitative impairment in reciprocal social interaction, . . . lack of social or emotional reciprocity, . . . qualitative impairments in communication, . . . stereotyped and repetitive use of language and markedly restricted repertoire of activities and interests."[18] A preoccupation with parts of objects, absence of imaginative play, and lack of awareness of the feelings of others are also typical of autistic children. These characteristics can readily be observed in many adults of industrial cultures, when compared with those brought up in traditional tribal societies.

The cause of infantile autism is not known. Earlier views that it was caused by deficient mothering have given way to the general belief that it is a biochemical brain disorder. Some autistic children respond to vitamin B_6 therapy, others to heroic and prolonged efforts by caregivers to dissolve the perceptual-affective barriers. Most children are untreatable. It is clearly an extreme form of developmental deficit—and if this diagnosis of our cultural malaise is indeed correct, the prospects for humanity are not good.

ADDICTION

A third analogy from the field of psychopathology that offers considerable insight, in my view, is the model of addiction (or compulsion, more generally). We are a society whose scientists and experts have been describing for forty years, in horrifying and mind-numbing detail, the dimensions of global ecocatastrophe. Just think of some of the book titles: *Silent Spring, The Population Bomb, The Limits to Growth, The Death of Nature, The End of Nature.* Our inability to stop our suicidal and ecocidal behavior fits the clinical definition of addiction or compulsion: behavior that continues in spite of the fact that the individual knows that it is destructive to family, work, and social relationships. This metaphor of addiction or compulsion, on a vast scale, also parallels in many ways the teachings of the Asian spiritual traditions, especially Buddhism. These traditions teach that suffering or dissatisfaction is an inevitable feature of all human existence and that craving or desire is at the root of suffering.

One of the first to develop the addiction diagnosis was the deep ecologist and mountaineer Dolores LaChapelle, in her book *Sacred Land, Sacred Sex.* In a chapter entitled "Addiction, Capitalism and the New World Ripoff," she analyzes the interrelationships between the pursuit of addictive substances, including gold, silver, sugar, and narcotics, and the phenomenal growth of the capital-accumulating industrial society from the sixteenth century to the present. "The entire development of capitalism consists in making a group of people addicted to some 'substance' and selling it to them. Capitalism 'worked' as long as we had an enormous source of cheap natural resources (primarily in the New World)... Continuing its history of 'addiction,' capitalism is now relying more and more on addictive drugs to fuel its growth."[19]

Several other authors have also pointed to the addictive nature of our relationship to fossil fuels, another major engine of unrestrained industrial growth and ecological destruction. More generally, one can see the spread of consumerism and the obsession with industrial-economic growth as signs of an addictive society. Chellis Glendinning, drawing on ideas from Lewis Mumford and Jacques Ellul, has analyzed the "techno-addiction" that characterizes industrial civilization—with its compulsive craving for faster and more powerful machines, its pervasive denial, and its blatant attraction to retraumatization.[20] The addiction model is quite useful. In the past forty years, we have learned something about addiction, how to treat it and how to prevent it. The twelve-step recovery movement does attract individuals who want to break the cycle of addiction, and it also appeals to people with spiritual values and interests.

NARCISSISM

Environmentalists have long argued that one of the key dynamics of the global runaway system of ecological destruction is overconsumption, particularly in the heavily industrialized, modernized societies. Consumerism—more and more people wanting and buying more and more goods—represents a fairly precise collective analogy to compulsion-addiction on the individual level. Although consumption is massively and artificially pumped to extreme levels by advertising, there is much evidence to suggest that an underlying narcissism may play a major role. Narcissism is a personality disorder characterized by an inflated and grandiose self-image as well as feelings of entitlement that mask deep-seated feelings of unworthiness and emptiness.

The psychologist Philip Cushman has drawn explicit parallels between narcissism and the consumer culture. The relentless pursuit of ever more expensive and technologically advanced consumer goods feeds the entitled "false self," while the insecure and empty inner self remains anxious and wounded—driven then to buy even more goods to cover up the inner emptiness. As Cushman writes, "the empty self seeks the experience of being continually filled up by consuming goods, calories, experiences, politicians, romantic partners and empathic therapists in an attempt to combat the growing alientation."[21]

Ecopsychologists Allen Kanner and Mary Gomes have expanded on this line of work to argue that if the diagnosis of mass narcissism in

American culture is correct, it represents a difficult challenge for environmentalists. Since the average consumer feels inwardly inadequate and is constantly bombarded with a torrent of advertising designed to induce him or her to spend more and more to cure this unworthiness, the environmentalist's plea for less material consumption may fall on ears made deaf by entitlement and fear. "When they [consumers] are criticized for excessive materialism, there is a danger that these admonishments will primarily increase their overall sense of failure rather than significantly alter their environmental habits."[22]

Amnesia

Yet another useful diagnostic analogy is the notion that we as a species are suffering from a kind of collective amnesia. We have forgotten something our ancestors once knew and practiced—certain attitudes and kinds of perception, an ability to empathize and identify with nonhuman life, respect for the mysterious, and humility in relationship to the infinite complexities of the natural world. It may be that at several crucial turning points in the history of human consciousness, we chose a particular line of development and thereby forgot and neglected something else—with fateful consequences. I take this to be one aspect of Paul Shepard's view: we forgot the adolescent initiations, we forgot the humility and relatedness of the paleolithic hunter-gatherer, and we forgot the perceptual sensitivity to the ceaseless cycles of energy transformations occurring in the natural world. Paul Devereux and his collaborators, in their book *Earthmind*, write, "For a long time now, we have been unable to remember our former closeness with the Earth. Due to this amnesia, the ecological problems now thrust upon us have come as a shock . . . we notice the emergence of an amnesia that is really a double forgetting, wherein a culture forgets, and then forgets that it has forgotten how to live in harmony with the planet."[23]

An elaboration of the amnesia metaphor would be to consider the possibility of *traumatic amnesia*. We know from studies of the effects of child abuse and rape, of reactions to combat in wartime, and of accidents and natural disasters that when the person experiencing the trauma is in a completely helpless position, out of control, the memory of the experience can be lost—even though physical effects on the body and such symptoms as nightmares and panic attacks may remain. Such buried memories can sometimes be recovered with hypnotic or psychedelic psychotherapy. If this paradigm applies to humanity's amnesia for knowledge of an interdependent relatedness that seems to have been normal and natural for paleolithic culture, the question that present itself is this: Was there some event that in a terrifying way threatened this sense of relatedness and harmony?

One person who proposed and defended this view with verve and brilliance was the psychoanalyst Immanuel Velikovsky, who, in his book *Mankind in Amnesia,* argued that planetary near-collisions in historic times caused massive and violent earth changes, leading to almost total amnesia and permanent fear and insecurity among human beings. Even if we do not accept his theory of cosmic catastrophe, there are plenty of candidates for extremely violent natural cataclysms, such as volcanic and seismic events, with widespread loss of life and forced migrations, during the past four to five thousand years as well as earlier. For example, in the fifteenth century B.C.E., a volcanic eruption on the island of Thera in the eastern Mediterranean, accompanied by earthquakes and tidal waves of awesome destructiveness, obliterated the highly advanced ancient Minoan culture—and may have provided the historical prototype for the legend of the sinking of Atlantis.[24] Other possible events causing traumatic amnesia may have been periods of prolonged rain and freezing, prolonged drought and aridity, sudden weather changes, or invasions by marauding warrior bands. In medieval Europe it is not difficult to imagine the traumatic effect of Christianity's prolonged onslaught on the pagan nature religion as well as of the Black Death, which wiped out at least one-third of the population in the fourteenth century.

The amnesia analogy, in general, is more hopeful than some of the others, since it is clearly much easier to remember something that we once knew than it is to develop an entirely new adaptation. We can also see that the indigenous peoples of the Fourth World, whether in North and South America, Southeast Asia, or Australia, have been trying for some time to help us remember certain vital attitudes and values that they have preserved and maintained in their own ways of life but that "civilized" humans appear to have forgotten.

REPRESSION OF THE ECOLOGICAL UNCONSCIOUS

Theodore Roszak, in his book *The Voice of the Earth,* has argued that ecology and psychology need each other and that since "repression of the ecological unconscious is the deepest root of the collusive madness in industrial society, open access to the ecological unconscious is the path to sanity."[25] Roszak points out that Jung's idea of the "collective unconscious" originally included prehuman animal and biological archetypes but later came to concentrate primarily on pan-human religious symbols. He proposes that we take the original meaning and call it the "ecological unconscious" as "the living record of cosmic evolution." This may turn out to be a terminology that has wide appeal, although I have reservations about it. Calling an image or understanding "unconscious" or, even more, reifying it as "the unconscious" may function to keep that understanding unconscious. After all, we are trying to foster ecological consciousness, not unconsciousness. An even better term, in my view, is Aldo Leopold's "ecological conscience," since it implies a moral value, an ethical consideration.

Roszak wants to rehabilitate or revise the Freudian id; instead of the predatory, lecherous beast the founder of psychoanalysis imagined, it should be seen as the repository of ancient ecological wisdom in Roszak's view. "The id is the Earth's ally in the preservation of the biosphere . . . [and] Gaia gains access to us through the door of the id."[26] I believe that this idea will not do what Roszak wants it to do, however. While it is true that our Western modern child-rearing practices mostly stifle any innate ecological sensibility the child may have, it is also true that in traditional societies ecological knowledge and respect for nature are passed on from parents and elders to children and do not just emerge without such training. That is one of the reasons why the disruption of traditional cultures has been so environmentally devastating. "Open access to the ecological unconscious," whatever that may mean, is not going to be sufficient for a path to sanity, unless it is supplemented by a recovery of ancient traditions of initiation and ritual celebration and a strong dose of ecological literacy.

DISSOCIATION

In contrast to the Freudian and post-Freudian view of the centrality of repression in the creation of the "unconscious," there has been in recent years a revival of interest in the concept of dissociation. Dissociative disorders, such as "post-traumatic stress disorder" (PTSD) and "multiple personality disorder" (MPD), are being diagnosed much more frequently, though it is not known whether this rate of diagnosis is due to an increase in the actual occurrence of such disorders or to improved recognition of conditions previously misunderstood. Dissociation is actually a normal and natural cognitive function, the opposite of association. Dissociation plays a role in hypnotic and other forms of trance, when we progressively disconnect perception of the external world, to attend to interior images, memories, and impressions. Even the simple act of focusing or concentrating attention clearly involves some degree of dissociation, a screening out of awareness of anything that is not in focus.

In the Freudian view, psychic material (thoughts, images, feelings, etc.) that is in the repressed unconscious (also called id) is disorganized, primitive, and childish, functioning according to the "pleasure principle"; the conscious mind (ego), on the other hand, functions according to the "reality principle" and is capable of adjusting or adapting to the demands of reality in a rational, organized manner. The dissociationist view, as originally put forward by Freud's contemporary Pierre Janet and in the neo-dissociationism of Ernest Hilgard and others, is that dissociation involves a "vertical" separation of strands of consciousness that may be equally well organized, rational, and in touch with reality. For example, the mental and emotional components of a painful experience may be dissociated, so that we remember what we saw and thought but not what we (appropriately) felt; vice versa, a certain stimulus may trigger a feeling of panic, but the cognitive memory of what happened remains dissociated. In MPD, the most extreme form of dissociative disorder, which has been shown in 99 percent of cases to have developed in response to repeated abuse in early childhood, two or more fragments of identity, sometimes called "ego states" or "alters," are created. They maintain a continuity of their own, often with different names and different personality characteristics. As Hilgard says, "the concealed [or dissociated] personality is sometimes more normal or mentally healthy than the openly displayed one. This accords better with the idea of a split in the normal consciousness rather than with the idea of a primitive unconscious regulated largely by primary process thinking."[27]

The notion of the "splitting" of two or more equally rational and organized psychic fragments or identities was also used by Robert J. Lifton in his analysis of the Nazi doctors, who were able to enjoy listening to Beethoven in the garden and playing with their children after a day of torturing and killing people.[28] I believe that this concept of dissociation, or splitting, provides a more accurate and more useful understanding of the collective human pathology vis-à-vis the environment than the notion of a repressed and primitive "ecological unconscious." The entire culture of Western industrial society is dissociated from its ecological substratum. It's not that our knowledge and understanding of Earth's complex and delicate web of interdependence is vaguely and inchoately lodged in some forgotten basement of our psyche. We *have* the knowledge of our impact on the environment; we *can* perceive the pollution and degradation of the land, the waters, the air—but we do not attend to it, and we do not connect that knowledge with other aspects of our total experience. Perhaps it would be more accurate, and fair, to say that individuals feel unable to respond to the natural world appropriately, because the political, economic, and educational institutions in which we are involved all have this dissociation built into them. This dissociative alienation has been a feature of Western culture for centuries or, in some respects, even for millennia, if Paul Shepard is right.

In the Western psyche, the dissociative split between humans and nature is entangled with a split between the spiritual and the natural. In a subsequent chapter, we shall consider the complex historical roots of this dissociation. Basically, it's as if we had two selves. One is spiritual, which we think of as rising upward into higher realms. The second, the natural self, which includes bodily sensations and feelings, sinks or draws us downward. As a result of this dualistic, value-laden conception, the spiritual (and human) is then always regarded as superior to the natural (and animal). With this notion, we find ourselves back with the humanist superiority complex described earlier.

In some versions of this core image, the contrast between the two realms, or tendencies, is even sharper; not only is there a separation of the two tendencies, but there is also opposition between them. Then we are taught that to be spiritual, to attain salvation or enlightenment, we have to overcome our "lower" animal instincts and passions and conquer the bodily ego. In the alchemical tradition, which mostly was based on following and imitating nature, this special kind of spiritual work was called the *opus contra naturam*, "the work against nature."

This dissociative split between human spiritual values and the realities of nature, the flesh, and the senses, survived the demise of the religious worldview and appears again as a purely psychological pattern in Freudian psychoanalysis. In this version of the ancient split, the conflict is between the ego, which is basically human consciousness, and the id, which is the body-based animal instincts and impulses. The ego has to struggle against the id to attain consciousness and become truly human. At the collective level of culture, Freud held that this conflicted relationship with the natural brought about the discontents of civilization *(Das Unbehagen in der Kultur)*—this was the inevitable price we had to pay for the possibility of civilization.

The ecologically disastrous consequences of this dissociative split in Western human beings' self-concept becomes clear when we reflect upon the fact that if we feel ourselves mentally and spiritually separate from our own nature—our body, instincts, sensations, and so on—this separation will also be projected outward. We see and experience ourselves as separate then from the great realm of nature and Earth all around us. If we believe that to advance spiritually, or to be true human beings, we have to go against, to inhibit, and control the natural feelings and impulses of our own body, this same kind of antagonism and agenda of control will also be projected outward, supporting the well-known Western "conquest of nature" ideology. For most people in the West, their highest values, their noblest ideals, their image of themselves as spiritual beings striving to be good and come closer to God have been deeply associated with a sense of having to overcome and separate from nature.

It does not take much imagination to see how the consequences of this distorted perception have been played out in the spread of European civilization around the globe. And it *is* a distorted, counterfactual image: we human beings are not, in fact, separate from or superior to nature, nor do we have the right to dominate and exploit nature beyond what is necessary for our immediate needs. We are part of nature—we are in Earth, not on it. We are the cells in the body of the vast living organism that is planet Earth. An organism cannot continue to function healthily if one group of cells decides to dominate and cannibalize the other energy systems of the body.

Furthermore, the idea that the spiritual and the natural are opposed or that spirituality must always transcend nature is a culturally relative concept not shared by polytheistic religions or traditional animistic societies. In indigenous cultures around the world, the natural world is regarded as the realm of spirit and the sacred; the natural *is* the spiritual. From this belief follows an attitude of respect, a desire to maintain a balanced relationship, and an instinctive understanding of the need for considering future generations and the future health of the ecosystem—in short, sustainability. Recognizing and respecting worldviews and spiritual practices different from our own is probably the best antidote to the West's fixation in the life-destroying dissociation between spirit and nature.

Historical Roots of the Split between Humans and Nature

Once we recognize that the human exploitation and destruction of the biosphere is related to a dissociative split within human consciousness between the spiritual and the natural, then the question becomes—how did this separation come about? In this essay, I trace its origins in the mind-set of the founders of modern science, as well as further back in the ascendancy of transcendental monotheism.[1]

It is widely agreed that the global ecological crisis that confronts the world today represents one of the most critical turning points that human civilization has ever faced. While earlier cultures, including the classical civilizations of Mesopotamia, Greece, Rome, Mesoamerica, and China, have left in their wake a legacy of environmental destruction, it has always been possible, in the past, to migrate elsewhere. In fact, escape from ecological destruction and overcrowding was probably one of the chief unacknowledged motives behind the mass migrations from Europe to the Americas during the sixteenth, seventeenth, and eighteenth centuries. Today, however, that great icon of the twentieth century, the view of the blue-green Earth from space, reminds us of two inescapable and challenging facts: first, that national boundaries do not exist on Earth, except in the maps and minds of humans, and, second, that Earth is finite and its carrying capacity is limited.

Because of these two fundamental facts, the oneness and the finitude of Earth, the present situation represents a profound historical discontinuity. First, the globe-encircling power of the multinational, techno-industrial, profit-driven economic growth system is now destroying the entire biosphere, including major life-support systems for humans. Second, the relentless operation of the exponential population-growth curve, acting as a multiplier on all the other factors of pollution, toxic waste accumulation, loss of soil fertility, loss of biodiversity, impoverishment, famine, urban decay, and so on, is exceeding the carrying capacity of the biosphere, the inevitable result of which is (and will be) massive ecological and societal collapse. Some environmentalists estimate that we have less than a decade to turn things around before the entire global system goes into irreversible catastrophic collapse.

There is reason to believe that the present situation may even represent not just a historical crisis, but a discontinuity on the evolutionary time scale of planet Earth. While species have become extinct in previous periods of Earth's evolutionary history, some scientists calculate that the present rate of extinction, which is estimated to reach 50 percent of all remaining species within the next one hundred years, is unprecedented since the climatic catastrophe that brought about the extinction of the dinosaurs sixty-five million years ago. In the series of five major periods of mass extinction, the present one is the only phase being brought about by the actions of one species, namely, the human.[2] Not only humanity but also Earth itself is at a turning point. I would like to address the question of how it is possible that our species, Homo sapiens, the "knowing human," has contrived to get itself into this predicament of truly terrifying proportions.

There is a growing chorus of agreement that the roots of the ecological crisis must lie in the attitudes, values, perceptions, and basic worldview that we humans of the global industrial society have come to hold. The worldview of the Industrial Age is a product of European and Euro-American culture that has spread throughout the Western world and is now being extended with unparalleled vigor and speed throughout the entire globe. The underlying and explicit ideology of this globalization is that economic growth (which is the prime value) will come about through the operation of the so-called free market, which affords the maximum accumulation of capital and return on investment. The capital accumulation model of economic growth is still being presented, as the desirable (indeed, the only) model to imitate and apply to Third World, underdeveloped countries, who cannot even feed their impoverished populations and keep their children from dying.

The apparent short-term successes of this capitalist model (at least for a small percentage of the ruling elites) and the complete collapse of the only alternative, communism, have blinded us to the insidious factors of social degeneration inherent in this system. They have also made us seemingly oblivious and helpless in the face of the catastrophic ecological destruction taking place in almost all the planet's major ecosystems. Meanwhile, the indigenous people of Earth are not at all inclined to follow this model and are watching in disbelief while the techno-industrial and consumerist growth complex self-destructs before their very eyes—threatening to destroy the last surviving remnants of rain forests, wetlands, and wilderness.

THE RISE OF MECHANISTIC SCIENCE

The conquering and controlling attitude of humans toward nature, with its implicit assumption of human superiority, began in the Middle Ages and, to an extent (as we shall see in subsequent chapters) even earlier. It was an attitude that condoned or even encouraged the exploitation of nature for human use, in the absence of any ecological sensibility or ethical consideration of the rights of nonhuman life-forms. This mind-set increased dramatically in its influence during the scientific revolution of the sixteenth century and then again with the Industrial Revolution of the eighteenth and nineteenth centuries. The astounding breakthroughs in knowledge and technology that originated with the work of Galileo, Copernicus, Isaac Newton, Johannes Kepler, Francis Bacon, and René Descartes, brought about the shift away from the medieval worldview toward the mechanistic-materialistic worldview of the modern era.

No longer was Earth the center of God's creation and humans the "crown of creation," halfway between beasts and angels in the Great Chain of Beings. According to the new "mechanical philosophy," as it was called, the sun-centered cosmos was like a gigantic clockwork, with Earth and the other planets orbiting with measured regularity, designed and set into motion by the Creator God but otherwise not interfered with. The human role, enhanced by the already considerable successes of science in mastering natural processes, was to function to improve on nature— to discover her secrets by experimental and quantitative means and to put them to use for better living conditions for humans. In short, humans were to be God's appointed mechanics, formulating and applying the new mechanical science.

The psychological motivations and the social-historical situation of the founding fathers of modern science were complex and challenging. Their political struggles with the spiritual and magical conceptions of medieval Hermeticism, and their evident masculine gender bias, have been documented and analyzed by feminist scholars.[3] They were men of religious conviction and some, like both Newton and Kepler, were deeply involved in studies of the Hermetic spiritual traditions of alchemy and astrology.[4] I also do not by any means wish to minimize their achievement, particularly in helping free European culture from the dogmatic excesses of the hierarchical, theocentric ideology of the medieval world, which gave us such systemic collective perversions as the Crusades and the Inquisition and was helpless in dealing with the ravages wrought by plagues, famines, and incessant feudal warfare. I only wish to point out two crucial aspects of this worldview transition that have generally not been appreciated.

One is that a kind of deal was struck between religion and the new science, resulting in a split worldview, a culture of two worlds. The world of the Creator, of spirit, of divinity, of transcendent realities, and of moral concern was the realm of religion, and science agreed to stay out of it. On the other hand, the world of matter and of forces that could be perceived through the senses and measured and manipulated was the realm of science, and the Church gave the scientists free rein to develop it. As a result of this deal, the new mechanistic science was to be free of any considerations of value, purpose, signficance, or ethics—a totally deterministic, mechanistic conception of the universe. Thus the stage was set for a further and complete separation of the sacred from the natural world, as the realm of the sacred was made off-limits to science.[5]

In the course of the next four centuries, the transcendent creator, the divine clockmaker so to speak, was progressively marginalized as the realms of spirituality and religion were ignored by science. Thus we come to the desecrated, nonsentient, purposeless world of the modern age, in which knowledge is pursued solely for its own sake or for the ends of warfare and profit. The destruction of the environment by technological-industrial means in this world is ignored or rationalized as an inherent consequence of "progress." Many individual scientists and ordinary people have, of course, resisted these developments and formulated alternative approaches, but their views have failed to change the overall momentum of the scientific-technological enterprise.

There is another feature of the modern scientific worldview that has tended to support the human assumption of superiority toward animal and natural life, namely, certain unexamined value judgments inherent in the popular understanding of the Darwinian theory of evolution. Darwin dealt a severe blow to our human self-esteem and humanist self-importance by showing that humans are not the "crown of creation" but "descended from the apes." We were able to salvage our battered self-image somewhat by arguing that at least we are the most advanced and complex of mammals. Evolution had clearly progressed from the simple to the complex—as in the nineteenth-century "tree of life" diagrams, where one-celled organisms were at the root and Homo sapiens at the top, the crown of the tree. This view permitted a comfortable continuation of the old belief that we humans are superior to all other animals, because we are the most highly evolved species and therefore have both the knowledge and the right to tinker with nature and use it as we see fit, for our own purposes.

Current evolutionary biology has shattered all of those assumptions, depriving us of this last rationalization for the human superiority complex toward nature.[6] Evolution is not equivalent to progress. Evolving later in time does not mean being more advanced, and more complex organisms are not more "highly evolved" than the simple. Evolution is defined simply as *changing adaptations to changing environments.* Since the discoveries of the Burgess Shale, it can no longer even be said that later organisms are more complex than earlier ones. The evolutionary tree of life is not so much a single-trunk progression from simple to complex, as an exuberantly branching bush with many past experimental forms that nature has long discarded because they failed to adapt to changing conditions.[7] Nor is it true that more complex organisms are better adapted or more successful than simple ones. If anything, there is some reason to believe that complex, specialized organisms are more delicate and hence vulnerable to slight variations in environmental conditions. Indeed, by the criterion of adaptive longevity, the evolutionary champions on this Earth are the single-celled prokaryotic bacteria, which originated three and a half billion years ago. They were the only life-forms for two-thirds of the total duration of life before complex, multi-celled organisms arrived on the scene, and they will almost certainly survive us, if Homo sapiens contrives to make the planet uninhabitable for the so-called higher forms of life.[8]

HUMANISM, PROTESTANTISM, AND COLONIALISM

With the rise of the new mechanistic-materialistic worldview during the Renaissance, there occurred synchronistically (that is, not coincidentally) the birth of Renaissance humanism, the Protestant Reformation, and the first explorations of the Americas. Each of these movements, unintentionally and unconsciously, further deepened the split between human consciousness and the natural world.

Renaissance humanism, with the rediscovery of the culture of antiquity, celebrated the intrinsic worth of human beings and gave a much-needed boost to human self-esteem, burdened as it was with a thousand years of indoctrination about original sin. The early Italian humanists, like Marcilio Ficino and Pico della Mirandola, who wanted to affirm the nobility, spirituality, and wisdom of the human, surely could not foresee that this doctrine was to undergo a gradual shift over the next four hundred years to a position of human superiority, the "arrogance of humanism" in the twentieth century.[9]

The Protestant Reformation, with its emphasis on the individual's direct access to spiritual and moral guidance from scripture, free of the corrupted and controlling hierarchical priesthood, attacked the exaggerated idolatry of medieval Catholicism, with its Mary cult and numerous images of saints and pilgrimage shrines. Early Christianity had incorporated, to some extent, the old European pagan nature religion by placing chapels and churches on natural sacred sites, by turning ancient seasonal festivals into Church holy days, and by transforming some of the ancient gods and goddesses into Christian saints. The Protestant reformers and Puritans, in their iconoclastic zeal, contributed to the elimination of the last vestiges of pre-Christian European paganism, thereby further deepening the alienation of the urban populations from the psychic renewal found in a spiritual perception of the natural world.[10]

The third of these movements that changed the world in the fifteenth and sixteenth centuries was the beginning exploration and colonization of the Americas. This initiated a period in which first the Spanish and Portugese and later the English, French, and Dutch colonial imperialists were able to extract and ship to Europe unbelievable quantities of gold, silver, foodstuffs, spices, drugs, and other raw materials, providing the fuel for the explosive growth of capital accumulation.[11] This laid the foundation for the growth to worldwide dominance of the Euro-American capitalist-industrial economies, continuing to this day to ravage the biosphere with ever increasing efficiency and intensity.

The shadow side of this European colonialist enterprise—the genocidal holocaust perpetrated upon uncounted millions of the indigenous people of South and North America, via the introduction of virulent new diseases, outright massacre, dislocation and theft of land, slavery, and socioeconomic oppression, is to this day not fully known or acknowledged by the dominant Euro-American society.[12] Indians of North and South America, in the year 1992, did not celebrate the "discovery of the New World" by Columbus, but instead their history of "500 years of resistance." They remember and mourn the loss and destruction of ancient cultures (more than six hundred separate nations with different languages existed in the Americas before Columbus), the devastation brought to unimaginably beautiful lands, and the irreversible loss of numerous species of wildlife. Nor should it be thought that this injustice and the oppression of Native Americans is a thing of the past, even in the United States.[13]

THE ASCENDANCY OF TRANSCENDENTAL MONOTHEISM

The historian Lynn White Jr. has shown that in Europe, the controlling and conquering relationship to nature began in earnest during the Middle Ages, at the high point of ascendancy of the Christian worldview.[14] A combination of factors played a part, among them, the invention of the iron plow, which allowed greater food production compared with wooden ones but also increased soil depletion, and the rapid deforestation of Europe's vast forests to feed the growing number of iron foundries and metal shops, needed to make plows and tools, armors, and weapons and to build houses for the growing populations as well as ships for the navies of the warring monarchies.

The domination and exploitation of nature was not an explicit teaching of the Christian Church, of course, but it was condoned and not prevented by transcendental theology. As Thomas Berry has written, "Our identification of the divine as transcendent to the natural world makes a direct human-covenant relationship possible, but also we negate the natural world as the locus for the meeting of the divine and the human."[15] In the medieval Christian worldview, the divine realm, the *civitas dei*, was high above and inaccessible to human beings. By contrast, the natural world of earth and water, animals and plants, flesh and blood, feelings and pleasures of the senses was the corrupted world of the Fall, of sin, and of the Devil, one of whose names was "Lord of This World."

The idea of a covenantal relationship between a transcendent Creator and the human implies that humans are superior to other beings in the world of nature. Humans were the "chosen people," chosen over the animals. This story provides a religious justification for the human assumption of superiority that has been with us ever since. In the first book of the Bible, God gives instructions to Adam and Eve: "Be fruitful and multiply, and replenish the earth, and subdue it: and have dominion over . . . every living thing that moveth upon the earth" (Gen. 1:28). Ecologically minded theologians have justly argued that "dominion" does not necessarily mean "domination/exploitation" but can mean "wise stewardship or management," like a gardener tending his garden. It cannot be denied however, that in historical fact, domination, control, and exploitation have been Western humanity's guiding values in relationship to nature.

Clearly, stewardship, which is much less destructive of the environment than conquest has also been practiced through the ages in different countries and regions. At the present juncture, however, the prevailing ideology of the global industrial system is much more geared toward control, use, and profitability. Stewardship and preservation are definitely secondary concerns in the mainstream policies of most industrialized countries.

The oppositional dualism between spirit and nature grew out of Judeo-Christian transcendental monotheism. Even after the decline of the medieval Christian worldview and well into the modern age, we still find this same separation appearing in influential writings. Perhaps its most vivid formulation is by the eighteenth-century German poet-philosopher J. W. Goethe, who formulated this core dualistic image in a famous passage in his drama *Faust*. The story of Faust, with his restless and ruthless quest for knowledge as personal power, strikes us as somehow a mythic key to the European psyche.

Zwei Seelen wohnen, ach, in meiner Brust,
Die eine will sich von der anderen trennen:
Die eine hält, in derber Liebeslust,
Sich an die Welt mit klammernden Organen;
Die andre hebt gewaltsam sich vom Dunst
Zu den Gefilden hoher Ahnen.

Two souls, alas, are dwelling in my breast,
One strives to separate from the other.
One holds, with sensual, passionate desire,
Fast to the world, with clinging senses;
The other rises strong from earthly mist
To the ethereal realms of high ancestral spirits.[16]

Even in the twentieth-century Freudian view of the psyche, we still find this same separation beween the spiritual and natural, although the reality of any spiritual realms is denied. Now the split has been transferred to the psychological realm. To attain truly human consciousness, according to psychoanalysis, the rational mind, or ego, has to free itself from the constraints and distractions of the natural realm (the id) of bodily impulses and feelings. The similarity of these formulations lies in this dualism. We could say that throughout the history of Western consciousness there has been a conception of two selves—a natural self, which is earthy-organismic and tends downward, and a spiritual or mental self, which is airy-ethereal and tends upward.

The deep-rooted pervasiveness of this spirit-nature dualism in European consciousness is such that it is difficult for us to imagine how it could be otherwise. Indeed, in speaking here as a psychologist and historian of ideas, I am not concerned with assessing the metaphysical truth or validity of this conception. I personally believe there is an essential valid core to this image, although it has become distorted and oversimplified. Its disastrous consequences become clear when we reflect upon the fact that if we feel ourselves mentally and spiritually separate from our own nature (body, instincts, sensations, and so on), this separation will also be projected outward, so that we think of ourselves as separate from the great realm of nature—Earth—all around us.

Western culture—this great civilization of which we are so proud, in both its religious and its humanist scientific worldview—has this dualism built into it. The material world is inert, insentient, and nonspiritual, and no kind of psychic or spiritual communication or communion between humans and Earth or nature is possible, according to this worldview. In an ironic linguistic twist, the Magna Mater, the Great Mother Goddess of ancient times, has become the dead *matter* of modern materialism.

Toward a Reconsideration of Polytheistic Animism

The conceptual difficulty we might have in extracting ourselves from the oppositional dualism between the spiritual and the natural can be alleviated when we compare this conception with the worldview of the indigenous inhabitants of North and South America or, indeed, of primal, shamanistic cultures all over the world. Not just indigenous cultures the world over but also the pre-Christian ancestors of Europeans had radically different worldviews. The Celtic, Nordic-Germanic, Baltic, and Slavic peoples who inhabited Europe before the Christian era worshiped gods and goddesses and spirits of nature in forest groves and sacred springs, on mountaintops and in great stone circles.[17]

For these people, spirituality is not separate or above nature—the spiritual *is* the natural. Spiritual practice consists in communing with the living intelligences perceived to be indwelling in nature, with conscious respect and reverence. Methods of heightening consciousness to bring about such communion include altered-state "journeys" with hallucinogenic plants or drumming, wilderness vision quests, sweat-lodge and other healing ceremonies involving singing, and trance states induced through maintaining certain postures, dancing, fasting, and other practices. This is the worldview known to anthropologists as animism, which sees all life-forms, including animals, plants, rocks, forests, rivers, mountains, fields, seas, winds, as well as sun, moon, stars, and the total cosmos, as pervaded by and interconnected with spiritual energy and intelligence. In theological language such a view is known as immanentism, or panentheism, which holds that divinity, the creative spiritual forces, exist within and pervade all the realms of nature.

Even though the dualistic split between spirit and nature has dominated collective consciousness in European history, there have been exceptional individual mystics and artists who have articulated a view closer to the animistic beliefs of antiquity. Here are three examples. As we have seen, there are the visionary teachings of the Hildegard von Bingen, who spoke of *viriditas* (greenness) as the creative power of God manifest throughout creation. Hildegard said that "the soul is in the body the way the sap is in the tree"—in other words, the soul nourishes and sustains the body instead of having to rise above it or struggle against it.[18]

A second example of the animistic undercurrent in the European psyche is found in the works of the visionary English poet and painter William Blake. In *The Marriage of Heaven and Hell,* Blake wrote that "the ancient poets animated all sensible objects with Gods or Geniuses, calling them by the names and adorning them with the properties of woods, rivers, mountains, lakes, cities, nations, and whatever their enlarged and numerous senses could perceive."[19] Blake is saying that the polytheistic animism of antiquity was accompanied by much greater clairvoyant spiritual perception. The change came, according to Blake, when a system was formed to "enslave the vulgar by attempting to realize or abstract the mental deities from their objects: thus began priesthood." In other words, the loss of direct perceptual communion with the spirits of nature was brought about by a political move—the institution of priesthoods as intermediaries between the human and the divine.

My third example of a philosopher who succeeded in transforming the fateful spirit-nature dualism is J. W. Goethe. In the second part of the *Faust* drama, the sorcerer who has made a pact with the Devil has a series of visionary experiences while traveling through multiple worlds with multiple deities. The dualism of God and Devil, heavenly and earthly impulses, is dissolved into a pluralistic, polytheistic vision. In the lines immediately following the passage I quoted earlier, about the two souls moving upward and downward, Faust says:

> *O gibt es Geister in der Luft,*
> *Die zwischen Erd und Himmel herrschend weben,*
> *So steiget nieder aus dem goldenen Duft,*
> *Und führt mich weg zu neuem bunten Leben!*

> *If there be spirits of the air,*
> *that float and rule 'twixt earth and sky,*
> *descend, I beg you, from the golden ethers,*
> *and sweep me forth to rainbow-colored life!*

It is interesting to note that the "intermediate spirits" that the poet-sorcerer is here invoking, the spirits of the air, are precisely the spirits that the early Christian fathers, including Saint Augustine, said were demonic spirits and should be avoided (concerned as they were with counteracting pagan animism).

To return to indigenous societies, we would expect that societies with an animistic, shamanistic, panentheistic worldview would have a very different—more respectful and less destructive—relationship with their natural environment. And, indeed, although pre-conquest Native Americans intervened in sometimes drastic ways with their environment, there is no evidence that in the tens of thousands of years of habitation of the American continent, they ever achieved anything even close to the kinds of massive destruction that have occurred in the past five hundred years. Ecologists in all parts of the world have increasingly come to the realization that the indigenous peoples, with their so-called primitive animistic and shamanistic beliefs, have, in fact, been practicing the sustainable lifestyles that we are now trying to develop.[20] Indeed, how could it be otherwise? An ecological adaptation has to be sustainable to have survived. The primal cultures of today far exceed our Western civilization in longevity.

The Assault on Paganism

The nature religion of the indigenous European peoples was eliminated by Christian monotheism during the first few centuries of our era. The monotheistic religions have always devoted considerable energy to eliminating the competition, to establish the reality of their one and only god. In doing so, they denied and denigrated the creative spiritual energies inherent in nature that the ancients had worshiped from the earliest times. The Hebrew priests and prophets railed against those of their people who followed the Canaanite Great Goddess called Asherah, whose devotional shrines, known as *asherim*, were set up in trees, or rocks, or other wild places. Saint Augustine and other church fathers wrote that the many deities and spirits, known as *daimones*, with whom the Greeks and Romans were apt to consult and commune were really demonic evil spirits.[21] Since God is a transcendent creator, far removed from the affairs of humans, one could not communicate with him directly.

Pagan deities were either disparaged or demonized. The image of Pan, the goat-bodied nature god of the Greeks, became the Christian image of the horned and hooved Devil. Likewise, Odin-Wotan, the Nordic-Germanic god of ecstatic trance, of warriors, shamans, and poets, became demonized. Many of the goddess figures, including the Germanic Freya, goddess of love, sexuality, and fertility, were equated to maleficent witches. Those who followed the old nature religion were branded as "pagan" or "heathen," which originally simply meant "country dwellers" or "heath dwellers." These country folk were more likely to have preserved beliefs in spirits and knowledge of healing and magical herbs than those who lived in towns with walls, who worshiped in churches of stone under the direction of priests.

Starting in the eleventh century, the Church began a movement to consolidate its worldly power and wealth by attacking what it considered external or internal "enemies of the faith." Crusades were launched against the Islamic "infidels"—ethnically, the African Moors—who were occupying the Palestinian Holy Land. Simultaneously, internal crusades and inquisitions were launched against so-called heretics, Christians who had allegedly turned away from the Church, such as the reform-minded Cathars in Provence and the Knights Templar, who were envied because of their wealth. The next group to be targeted, to become scapegoats, were the Jews, who were made to choose between converting or leaving. The Spanish monarchy forced the remaining unconverted Jews out of Spain in 1492, the same year that Columbus sailed for America. Finally, in the fourteenth century, the Church turned its full inquisatorial fury against the pagan witches, who were branded as being in league with the Devil and therefore heretical and punishable by burning to death. A simple accusation of witchcraft, which was defined as "harm doing" *(maleficium),* was enough to set into motion the process of extracting confessions by torture, followed by burning. The hapless victims of torture provided the names of more suspected witches, who would then also be tortured and burned and their property confiscated by the Church and civic authorities.

No one knows to this day how many witches were killed—estimates range from two to nine million. It seems clear that the vast majority were women, many of them simple country women, although town dwellers and even aristocrats were not exempt. Some of the country women were herbalist healers, practicing especially herbalism and healing related to midwifery, contraception, and abortion. Some were shamans who used hallucinogenic plants (particularly of the solanaceous, or nightshade, variety) to induce visionary experiences of shamanic flight, referred to as flying through the air to the witches' Sabbat. The brutal persecution and extermination of witches, originally simply the "wise women of the woods," that continued for three centuries in all the countries of Europe rank as a biophobic, misogynistic holocaust, a karmic stain on the history of the Church that has not to this day been fully acknowledged, much less atoned for.

It also cut Christianity off even more from the natural world, by denying and demonizing its pagan heritage. It is my belief that the Christian churches will not regain their diminishing spiritual authority until they can reconcile with their historical suppression of paganism and witchcraft. There is nothing in the nature of a religious movement that requires these kinds of forced and brutal conversion methods. For example, Buddhism spread from its native India to Tibet, Southeast Asia, China, and Japan, in each country integrating in a peaceful and respectful manner with the preexisting animistic, shamanistic religions in those countries.

CONCLUSIONS

I have suggested that at the core of the psychic alienation of Western humanity from the natural world, with its disastrous consequences of global ecological destruction, is a humanist superiority complex that is a deeply rooted feature of the Western psyche. For a complex variety of historical reasons, Europeans have come to experience spirituality and nature as separate or opposed. "Two souls, alas, dwell in my breast." It was not always so, but for the past two thousand years, under the influence of Judaeo-Christian transcendental monotheism, we have grown futher and further removed from the kind of direct awareness of the spiritual presences in nature that our pagan ancestors enjoyed.

As the worldview of medieval Christianity gave way to the mechanistic-materialistic worldview of modern science, the alienation from Earth has become even more profound. Humanity in the modern era confronts nature as an alien and terrifying realm, without even any of the otherworldly solace that religion has provided. In the modern atheistic, materialistic worldview, there is no spiritual being anywhere, either in this life or after death, either in nature or above it. Nature, consisting of inert, random, machinelike processes, had to be conquered, subdued, controlled, and dominated—and a phenomenal technology was developed to do just that.

In pointing to the role of mechanistic science and industrial technology in aggravating our alienation from Earth, I do not suggest an impossible neo-Luddite return to a preindustrial era. I do suggest that it is possible to recall certain values that we have lost and that it is desirable to examine the value systems with which we develop and apply technology. Economist-philosophers such as E. F. Schumacher, Ivan Illich, and others have suggested "small-scale" and "appropriate technologies." Instead of being used to feed runaway cycles of exploitation and addictive consumerism ("producing more and more goods for more and more people"), technology needs to be redirected toward the preservation and restoration of damaged ecosystems, which can sustainably support all forms of life, including but not limited to the human being. Models and designs for this kind of ecologically sensitive technology exist—we only have to muster the political will to choose them.

Similarly, in pointing to the role of transcendental monotheism and the Christian antipagan bias in the severing of our spiritual connection to the natural world, I do not imply that we must all become pagans and deny two thousand years of Christianity, plus Judaism and Islam. These traditions have become an indelible part of our psychic constitution. I do believe it is possible for Christians, Jews, and Muslims to reconnect with the nature religion of their ancestors and that when they do so, a tremendous spiritual revitalization can take place, in which the natural world and the divine world are recognized as one and the same. I see this as a kind of remembering, like Odin the shaman-god drinking from the well of remembrance situated at the root of the great world tree— from which he gained ancestral and evolutionary knowledge of the origins of things and the value of such remembering for the present and the future.

Sky Gods and
Earth Deities

One very significant and very ancient source of the split between humans and nature in the Western world came with the transition from earth goddess to sky god religions and the concomitant institution of patriarchy. Very different and conflicting stories began to be told, reflecting a more distanced, fearful, and aggressive relationship between humans and nature, and between humans and gods. In this essay, I discuss the conflict-laden mythic legacy resulting from these profound cultural upheavals.[1]

About six thousand years ago, the first wave of Indo-European Kurgan tribes began to migrate out of their presumed homeland in southcentral Asia. Backed by the power and mobility of horses and wheeled chariots, these people (previously known also as Aryans) invaded and conquered the relatively peaceful agrarian Earth Goddess cultures of Old Europe as well as Anatolia, Iran, and India. Over the course of the next two to three millennia, these nomadic pastoralists imposed an entirely new set of ideologies and values that have formed the foundation of the Western worldview ever since. For the matrilineal, matricentric order of the Neolithic village, they substituted a patrilineal and patriarchal system that became the norm in the Bronze Age, Iron Age, and all subsequent ages up to the present. A pantheon of sky and warrior gods was super-imposed on the Earth and nature divinities of the original inhabitants of Old Europe. A similar transition from goddess-centered religions to the cults of male lawgiver gods, also reflected in radically transformed mythologies, took place in the Semitic cultures of Mesopotamia, Egypt, and the eastern Mediterranean.

The pervasiveness of the Indo-European language family and the associated parallels in religion, worldview, and mythology have been known since the nineteenth century, when scholars first thought of San-skrit as the mother tongue of Indo-European languages. Numerous par-allels were found to exist between words and names, such as that for the ruling deity, the "Lord of the Shining Sky": Sanskrit Dyaus and Deva, Baltic Dievas, Old Germanic Tiwaz or Ziu, Greek Zeus, and Latin Deus. Although earlier scholars, such as Bachofen, had described an archaic period of *Mutterrecht,* there was only fragmentary knowledge about the pre–Indo-European cultures, and much was misunderstood. What we now understand as undercurrents of Old European religion, persisting beneath the Indo-European overlay, went unrecognized and were typi-cally characterized as "mysterious," "obscure," "very old," "minor dei-ties," or even "an older generation of gods."

However, persistent residues of the Old European religion and cul-ture do indeed exist and are identifiable in myths, symbols, folklore, and ritual practices. Thanks in large measure to the work of the archaeolo-gist-mythologist Marija Gimbutas, the symbolic language and mythic imagery of these most ancient cultures have been rediscovered and ex-tensively described in the second half of the twentieth century. As Gimbutas writes in the concluding section of her monumental work *The Civilization of the Goddess,* "The functions and images of Old European and Indo-European deities, beliefs in an afterlife, and the entirely differ-ent sets of symbols prove the existence of two contrasting religions and mythologies. Their collision in Europe resulted in the hybridization of two symbolic structures in which the Indo-European prevailed while the Old European survived as an undercurrent."[2] During the hundreds, even thousands of years of cultural interaction, there was undoubtedly not only conquest, assimilation, and superimposition of an alien religion but also intermarriage of peoples, a blending and combining of religious and mythic images. Gimbutas's concept of *hybrid mythologies* provides a kind of corrective lens through which many previously obscure and incomprehensible features of European mythology can be understood.

I should point out that whereas, originally, my approach to mythology, heavily influenced by Joseph Campbell and C. G. Jung and his followers, was to see it as an expression of intrapsychic symbolism and psychospiritual growth processes, I am now convinced of the view represented by Marija Gimbutas, Robert Graves, Mircea Eliade, and others, who see mythology in a more inclusive vein as the total knowledge tradition of an oral culture, including cosmology, science, and history as well as psychological insight and instruction.

The poet-mythologist Robert Graves, in his book *Greek Myths,* first published in 1955, wrote that "in the Hellenic invasions of the early second millennium B.C. . . . small armed bands of herdsmen, worshipping the Aryan trinity of gods—Indra, Mitra, and Varuna—attached themselves peacefully enough to the pre-Hellenic settlements in Thessaly and Central Greece. . . . Thus a male military aristocracy became reconciled to female theocracy, not only in Greece, but in Crete, where the Hellenes . . . exported Cretan civilization to Athens and the Peloponnese."[3] The ancient nature-goddess cults were appropriated and their stories twisted for ideological purposes. Hera, one of the forms of the ancient Great Goddess, whose cult was overrun by the Hellenes, almost certainly with much resistance by her worshipers, is ridiculed in Greek myths as the complaining wife of a robust, adulterous father-god. Athena, a form of the ancient life-giving bird goddess, is transformed into a cool warrior-strategist, born fully armed from Zeus's head—thus eliminating any traces of her true origin and status and turning her into a "brainchild" of the father-god.

The invading Hellenes' takeover of the preexisting matricentric goddess cults is vividly portrayed in the well-known stories of the Olympian gods, including Zeus and Apollo, with their seduction (more accurately called rape) of local goddesses, nymphs, and nature spirits as well as human women, priestesses of the Goddess. One example is the substitution of the solar god Apollo for the Earth goddess Gaia as the protector deity of the cave oracle at Delphi. Another is found in the story of the Cretan princess Europa, after whom the continent is named: Zeus changed himself into a gorgeous bull, whom Europa trustingly rode, not suspecting his intent to seduce her. According to Graves, this myth reflects the

Olympian's takeover of the Minoan sacred bull cult, in which the priest-esses rode on the bull in processions and danced with the bull in the games. A third well-known example is the abduction and rape of Persephone, daughter of the Cretan Earth goddess Demeter, by Hades, ruler of the Underworld and brother of Zeus, with the latter's complicity.

Some Greek gods and goddesses, however, were not Olympians. They clearly belong to the older stratum of Earth- and Goddess-centered religion. Pan, the horned, goat-bodied god of wild and domesticated animals, was invoked by lusty country people in orgiastic celebrations. Robert Graves suggests that the satyrs, portrayed as goat-bodied with rampant erections, were goat totem tribesmen whose chosen god was Pan. To the Christians, with their life-negating attitudes, he was the embodiment of the horned and hooved Devil. Around the time of the beginnings of Christianity, a legend arose that sailors on a ship in the eastern Mediterranean had heard a supernatural voice proclaim, "Great Pan is dead!" In the underground pagan traditions of witchcraft and folklore, however, Pan survived; he became the Lord of Animals, the wild man covered with hair, who represented our connection with the nonhuman natural world, particularly animals. His feminine counter-part was the Lady of the Beasts, whom the Greeks knew as Artemis and the Romans as Diana, the protectress of witches. In the Celtic world, Pan resembles Cernunnos, the shaman-god with deer antlers, holding a snake and surrounded by animals.

Another non-Olympian, the androgynous Dionysus, was an ancient vegetation deity, originally from Asia, who spread the wine cult through-out the Mediterranean. The Hellenic Greeks co-opted his cult, among others, by inventing a fantastic story of Zeus carrying and birthing him from his thigh. He was the god of intoxication and ecstatic transcen-dence, and to deny his power was to risk madness. His cult followers were primarily women, who found in his annual rites temporary escape from domination by their men. These *maenads* and accompanying sa-tyrs moved in processions and danced through the night woods in his honor, singing and shrieking in wild abandon, provoked perhaps by the ingestion of wine with hallucinogenic mushrooms. In the later classical period, the Dionysus cult was adopted and adapted into the Orphic mys-teries of death and rebirth, where Dionysus symbolized the immortal soul, transcending death.[4] In the European Middle Ages, Dionysus, the vegetation god, reincarnates as the leaf-masked Green Man of folklore, whose mysterious visage graces many Gothic churches.[5]

In Egyptian mythology, the parallel to Dionysus was Osiris, the green-skinned god of vegetation and regeneration whose repeated deaths, followed by resurrections with the aid of his sister and consort, Isis, symbolize the recurring cycles of death and renewal in vegetative life. The conflict between Osiris and his violent and envious brother, Seth, reflects the ongoing clash and competition between the matricentric farming cultures along the Nile and the marauding bands of herder-warriors who lived in the harsh, arid conditions of the peripheral desert regions. On a more cosmic level, the struggle between Osiris and Seth became a metaphor for the opposition between the generative forces associated with water and plant life and the destructive, life-threatening force of desert heat. The Greek mythographer Plutarch wrote that "they [the Egyptians] give the name of Osiris to the whole source and faculty creative of moisture, believing this to be the cause of generation and the substance of life-producing seed; and the name Seth (or Typhon) they give to all that is dry, fiery, and arid, in general antagonistic to moisture."[6]

In India, one can see marked similarities and mythic parallels between Dionysus and Shiva. Alain Daniélou has argued that Shiva was actually the phallic vegetation god of the pre-Aryan Dravidians of India, who was co-opted by the Brahmins and turned into the ascetic god of the yogis as well as the Lord of the Dance (Nataraja), who dances the universe into being.[7] Thousands of shrines containing the *lingam-yoni* (phallus-vulva) stone carving are found all over India, testifying to his androgynous erotic potency and the disguised persistence of the old fertility cults. During the Tantric revival, in the first few centuries of the common era, there was a resurgence of Shakti (Goddess) worship, and sensual-sexual experience in the context of sacramental ritual was acknowledged as a path to spiritual realization. Shiva and Shakti in ecstatic embrace became the guiding images of Tantric yogis. They embody the reconciliation and mutuality of male and female energies and the healing of the dissociative split common in the patriarchal and ascetic traditions.

Among the Semitic peoples of ancient Mesopotamia, the thousand-year-long transition from a matricentric Goddess-oriented culture to a patriarchal culture is reflected in the transformations between Sumerian and Babylonian religious mythology. In the Sumerian religion, Inanna is Queen of Heaven and Earth Goddess, whose temples contain the granaries and whose priestesses express their devotion to the Goddess through sacred sexual rites. Inanna's son and lover, Dumuzi, the shepherd-king, is sacrificed each year to ensure the continued fertility of the land and reborn each year with the renewal of springtime vegetation. In Babylonian mythology, the solar warrior-god Marduk is the leader of a rebellion against the power of the older Creatrix Mother, personified in the form of a great female dragon, Tiamat, whom Marduk slays. He first splits her in half like an oyster, the two halves becoming the sky and the sea; afterward comes the rest of creation—the planets, the seasons, plants, animals, and humans. Eventually, in a kind of compromise or accommodation with the older religion, the Babylonians established a male-dominated family or council of gods with their consorts and children, much like the Vedic pantheon in India, the Greek Olympian family, and the Nordic-Germanic family of Aesir gods.

In the Babylonian *Gilgamesh* epic, the oldest written literature in the Western world, the two mythic-religious strands are closely interwoven. The epic opens with an ironic paean of praise to the semidivine hero-king Gilgamesh, builder and ruler of Uruk, who is so arrogant and tyrannical that the people of the city complain to their gods, begging them to intervene. The gods then turn to the older Creatrix Mother Goddess—Aruru—asking her to create a counterpart to Gilgamesh, one who can match his strength and contain his overbearing arrogance. The Goddess does so, and Enkidu is born. Enkidu is a wild man, covered with hair and living with the animals. He is seduced by a priestess of the goddess Ishtar, using her erotic arts. He abandons the wild lifestyle of running and hunting with animals and goes to the city to meet Gilgamesh. The two men first fight and then become best friends, performing numerous heroic deeds and embarking on adventures. Enkidu the wild man is more in touch with nature: he inteprets certain dreams of Gilgamesh's as warnings against abusing and disrespecting the divinities of nature.

Various aspects of the conflicting and blending layers of religious ideology are suggested in this complex and beautiful tale. There is the domination and tyranny of the warrior-hero, as experienced no doubt by the adherents to the older religion. There is resistance on the part of the original people and their Goddess religion, as they ask for help from

the creator deities. The original civilizing role of the feminine is acknowledged, as the wild man is domesticated into urban life by the priestess of
the Goddess. The story further reflects the transition from the hunting-
gathering "wild" state to life in the farming villages and towns of the
Neolithic, with their temples, priesthoods, and warrior-kings.[8]

In the religious mythology of the Nordic-Germanic people, there is
fascinating evidence of the interaction between the Indo-European
Kurgan invaders and the Old European cultures. We find this in the myths
of the prolonged warfare and eventual peacemaking between two families of deities, the Aesir and the Vanir. The clashing and hybridizing of
religions and worldviews between Indo-Europeans and Old Europeans
is clearly discernible here, even though the later Indo-European layer is
obviously dominant. In that sense, Nordic-Germanic mythology serves
as an example of a pattern of cultural transformation that occurred all
over Europe and the Near East over the course of many centuries.[9]

The Aesir are primarily sky and warrior gods, including Odin, Tiwaz
(or Tyr), and Thor the Thunderer. On the other hand, the Vanir, including Nerthus, Njörd, and the brother-sister pair Freyr and Freyja, are
primarily Earth and nature deities. Archaeological evidence in the form
of carved inscriptions and images on stelae or ornaments indicates that
both the Aesir and Vanir deities were worshiped at particular sites. They
are portrayed in the myths as two different families or clans of divinities who are often at odds and even at war. Presumably this reflects the
conflict, drawn out over many centuries, between the invading Indo-
Germanic tribes from the East and the aboriginal populations of Old
Europe who resisted the attempted assimilation. After the Indo-Germanic
people had settled in Central Europe, the Vanir continued to be the gods
of the farmers and fishermen, while the Aesir were worshiped by the
military aristocracy, who had appropriated the land and established their
domination.

Several early scholars proposed that the myth of the war between
Aesir and Vanir reflects the actual historical conflict, in the second millennium B.C.E., between the indigenous "Megalith culture" of southern
Scandinavia and western Europe, whose gods were the Vanir, and the
invading Indo-Aryan "Battleax culture," whose gods were the Aesir.[10] The
views of the French mythologist Georges Dumézil, who identified a tri-
partite model of divine and human functions in Indo-European cultures,

are often cited as countering this view. Dumézil says that the Aesir-Vanir war myth refers to conflict between two different social classes within Indo-European society, the warriors and the farmers, but this is not really inconsistent with the Indo-European invasion theory. On the contrary, it affirms that the Germanic story fits the pattern of Indo-European conquest and subsequent assimilation of the Old European cultures. As Mircea Eliade, the eminent historian of religion, has written:

> The invasions of the territories inhabited by the Neolithic agricultural populations, the conquest of the autochthons by militarily superior invaders, followed by a symbiosis between these two different types of societies, or even two different ethnic groups, are facts documented by archaeology; indeed they constitute a characteristic phenomenon of European protohistory, continued, in certain regions, down to the Middle Ages. But the mythological theme of the war between the Aesir and the Vanir precedes the process of Germanization, for it is an integral part of the Indo-European tradition. In all probability, the myth served as the model and the justification for a number of local wars, ended by a reconciliation of the adversaries and their integration into a common society.[11]

I would question here only the metaphor of "symbiosis," since it refers to a mutually supportive relationship between two different species. The more appropriate ecological metaphor for the Indo-European takeover would seem to be predation or colonization; it was an aggressive invasion, in which the interests of the agricultural societies of Old Europe were completely subordinated to the interests of the invading Indo-Germanic pastoral warrior societies, at least at first. In time, of course, accommodation must have taken place, as well as assimilation, so that a coherent social order developed with hierarchically organized castes or classes. Hybrid myths were created, with their associated artistic and ritual forms, expressing the strengths and values of both cultures. I like to imagine the situation as analogous to a palimpsest, with the deeper, older strata of religious imagery detectable in fragments through the dominant, later overlay.

When we look at classical mythology, both of the Mediterranean areas and of northern Europe, there are three mythic complexes that clearly reflect this clashing of cultures and blending of mythologies. There is a group of *myths that justify invasion and domination,* the self-justifying stories of the Indo-European or other pastoralist invaders. There is a second group of *myths of resistance and retaliation,* in which the popular resistance to the Aryan takeover is expressed, what one might also call "the revenge of the goddess." And, third, there is a group of *myths of compromise and reconciliation,* which express the harmonizing and accommodation that presumably was reached by the people, who had found a way to reconcile their differences.

MYTHS JUSTIFYING INVASION AND DOMINATION

There is a central myth found in many Indo-European societies, including the Indians, Iranians, Greeks, Romans, Celts, Germans, and Hittites, of a divinely justified cattle raid. Besides the horse, the most revered animal for the Indo-Europeans was the cow. There is, for example, a Nordic-Germanic creation myth in which the first proto-human giants were licked out of salty ice blocks by the primal cow Audhumla, whose milk then also nourished them. The cow also features prominently in Vedic mythology and is revered in India to this day. Among Indo-Europeans and other pastoralists, cattle have always been the measure of a man's wealth. In the cattle-raiding mythic complex, a hero figure (such as the Greek Heracles and the Celtic Cuchulainn) loses his cattle to a monster, who is generally associated with the local non–Indo-Europeans. The hero then recaptures the cattle, sometimes with the help of a warrior-god. According to the historian J. P. Malory, the evidence "suggests that this cattle-raiding myth served as a charter which both helped to define the role of the warrior in Indo-European society (the proper activity of the warrior was cattle raiding), and sanctioned Aryan cattle raiding against foreigners."[12] It seems clear that the Kurgans and other Indo-Europeans typically indulged in cattle stealing as a way of augmenting their herds and wealth and that this activity became so central to them that religious myths grew up to justify and rationalize it.

In the Semitic world, the biblical story of Cain and Abel can also be read as a reflection and justification of the pastoralist takeover and expulsion of the indigenous farmers. Biblical commentators tend to gloss

over God's unexplained unfairness toward Cain: Yahweh favors the offerings of Abel the sheepherder and rejects the offerings of Cain the
farmer. The high moral drama of fratricide, guilt, and divine punishment obscures the underlying message. The farmer is cast in the role of
villain, and the "keeper of sheep" is the innocent victim—a neat reversal
of the historical facts, since it was the Hebrew herders who invaded and
conquered the Canaanite farmers. God curses Cain and punishes him
by driving him out of his lands: "A fugitive and a wanderer shall you be
on the earth" (Gen. 4:12). The invading herders expropriate the land,
driving off the indigenous farmers, and then tell a story that God or-
dained this fate as punishment for the farmers.

In the Bible, this is actually Yahweh's second curse against humans
and the earth. After Adam and Eve's transgression, which consisted of
eating a forbidden fruit, Yahweh, in a fit of vituperation, curses the serpent, the woman, the man, and the earth. He curses the serpent "above
all cattle, and above every beast of the field," by condemning it to crawl
on the ground. He curses the woman by "greatly multiplying the pain"
of pregnancy and birth and making her dependent on and subordinate
to the man. He punishes Adam for listening to his wife, and he curses
the earth: "Cursed is the ground for thy sake; in sorrow shalt thou eat of
it all the days of thy life; thorns also and thistles shall it bring forth to
thee, and thou shalt eat the herb of the field: in the sweat of your face
shall you eat bread, until you return to the ground; out of it you were
taken; for dust you are, and to dust shall you return" (Gen. 3:17–19).

Perhaps these maledictions express the envious resentment that the
desert nomads must have felt toward the lifestyle of comparative ease
and pleasure they found in the Fertile Crescent. The text condemns and
denigrates farming and a fruit-and-vegetable diet, but the implied message goes further. Natural, biological processes—the serpent's closeness
to the ground, the human woman's labor of childbirth—are categorized
as divine punishment. In a larger sense, the curse of Yahweh sets a fateful
tone for the direction of Western civilization. From the beginnings of
the patriarchal, Judaeo-Christian monotheistic takeover, the human
being's (Adam's) relationship to Earth does seem to have suffered from
a curse of scarcity and antagonism. In the twentieth century, we still
seem to be suffering the consequences of this antagonistic attitude, in
the form of massive pollution and ecological destruction. Are we not

still living with the consequences of Yahweh's curse—a traumatic disconnection from the nourishing and regenerative energies of Earth?

Several scholars, including Merlin Stone, Gerda Lerner, Elinor Gadon, John A. Phillips, and Carol Ochs, have analyzed in depth how the biblical myths justify the subordination of women in Judaism.[13] Uniquely in the world's creation mythologies, Yahweh creates the world and all its creatures out of his own head, by proclamation, without even the hint of any female participation. Eve, or Havah, whose name means "Mother of All Living," clearly a form of the ancient Creator Earth Goddess, is reduced to mortal status. Turning the natural order upside down, the woman is brought out of the body of the man and is blamed for the expulsion from the garden of abundance. The Levite priests and prophets cited in the Bible savagely attack the cult of the Canaanite Earth Goddess known as Astarte, Ashtoreth, or Asherah and encourage their followers to destroy her shrines and groves. The ancient initiation ritual of the Goddess, in which eating the fruit of the tree and communing with the serpent provided divinatory insight, is also turned on its head; rewritten, it becomes a story that prohibits participation in the old Goddess cult, justifies the inferior status of women, and places severe strictures and guilt on the woman's autonomy and expression of her sexuality.

Quite similar attacks on the character of the feminine, both human and divine, and on the old Earth Goddess religion came about in other Near Eastern cultures during the millennia of the patriarchal takeover. In the Sumero-Babylonian Gilgamesh myth, as already mentioned, the interweaving strands expressing conflicting ideologies can be clearly discerned. The goddess Ishtar is portrayed as fickle, petulant, and vengeful. The warrior-hero Gilgamesh rejects the amorous proposition she makes to him and, in a bitter tirade, accuses her of betraying, abandoning, and even killing those who were her lovers before, including the lamented Tammuz. Ishtar, stung by the rejection, brings down the "Bull of Heaven," a flooding tempest of destruction. These passages probably represent the male hero's complaint against the authority of the Goddess and her priestesses in the ancient cults, in which a king first became the chosen bridegroom and was then replaced or sacrificed. Psychologically, it is analogous to the petulant projections of an adolescent boy reacting to the uncertain affections of an autonomous woman. The character of the Goddess is ridiculed and denigrated as promiscuous and faithless, thus providing apparent justification for the warrior-kings' attacks and sub-jugation of the matricentric Goddess religion.

In Greek mythology, the story of the Athenian hero Theseus defeat-ing the monstrous Minotaur, which was kept in a maze in Crete, can be read as a justifying myth for the Athenian (Dorian) invasion of Crete. The Greek historian Plutarch describes a raid on Knossos, followed by a peace treaty, with the Greek king marrying the Cretan princess. Accord-ing to the myth, the Minotaur was a bull-headed monster who demanded periodic sacrifices of Athenian youths and maidens. Theseus entered the maze, slew the Minotaur, and found his way back out by means of a golden thread given to him by the king's daughter, Ariadne, whom he married but did not take back to Athens. Cretans revered the bull as an animal sacred to the Goddess and staged fertility dances in a maze and acrobatic games in which youths and maidens danced and leaped over bulls. The myth thus portrays the Minoan religious ceremonies as per-verted and monstrous, in the eyes of the Athenians, to justify the inva-sion and subjugation.

In Nordic-Germanic mythology, as already mentioned, there is ex-tensive treatment of the conflict between rival factions of deities, the Vanir and Aesir, representing the Old European and Indo-European cultures. The question naturally arises, who was seen as causing or origi-nating this war? The story of the origins of this war is referred to in only a few tantalizingly brief and obscure passages, in an Edda poem called "Völuspa," or the "Visions of the Seeress." The verses refer to a sorceress-goddess called Gullveig, one of the Vanir, whose appearance among the Aesir provokes them into trying to kill her—three times, unsuccessfully. The Vanir then fight back, and, we are told, "this is how war came into the world." Gullveig's provocation of the Aesir is unexplained in this ancient song of the Edda. The story of the assault of the Indo-European warrior aristocracy against the Old European matricentric cultures is told with minimal justification.[14]

MYTHS OF RESISTANCE AND RETALIATION

We can surmise that there must have been a great deal of resistance to the Kurgan incursions into the cultures of Old Europe as well as to the patriar-chal takeover in the Near Eastern city-states. The cultural transformation took centuries, in some areas millennia, and it would be strange indeed if there were no evidence in the mythological traditions of resistance and revenge. Indeed, the story of Gullveig and the war between the Vanir and Aesir referred to earlier is a prime example. The ability of the Vanir gods to hold their own against the invading Aesir is also attested to by the continued presence (particularly in Sweden) of shrines to the Vanir, with figures and runic inscriptions, well into the era in which the Aesir cult was dominant.

There are two myths of peacemaking attempts between the rival clans of deities, one that fails and one that succeeds. At the first peace treaty, there is an exchange of emissaries between the two groups. The Aesir send the unknown god Hoenir and the giant Mimir to the Vanir as ambassadors. Mimir (whose name is related to Latin *memor*) is the guardian of the Well of Remembrance at the foot of the Tree of Worlds, the holder of ancestral and evolutionary memory. But the Vanir do not consider these two individuals a worthy exchange. To indicate their displeasure, they decapitate Mimir and send his head back to Odin. This tale has many intriguing aspects. It clearly shows the Vanir Earth religion holding its own against the Aesir sky religion. The decapitation of Mimir, the memory holder, could be seen as a metaphor for the forgetting of evolutionary wisdom, consequent upon disrespect for the old nature divinities.[15]

In Greek mythology, the most dramatic and powerful story expressing the theme of the revenge of the Goddess is the story of Gaia, the Earth goddess, and Uranus, the sky god. It was Gaia whose voice originally spoke through the oracle at Delphi, before it was expropriated by the Olympian Apollo. Uranus, whose name parallels the Vedic pastoral god Varuna, was first Gaia's son and then her consort, fathering the one-eyed Cyclopes and Titans with her. In the historical reading of this myth, we recognize Uranus as the sky god of the invading Aryans, consolidating their takeover by claiming the Earth Goddess as wife and the nature spirits (Cyclopes and Titans) of the indigenous people as offspring.[16]

According to the myth, Uranus banished the Cyclopes to Tartarus, the lower depths. Presumably this reflects a demolition of the old nature cults by the Achaeans. In outrage, Earth Mother Gaia induced the Titans, led by Cronus, to castrate and kill their father with a flint sickle provided by her. Cronus then becomes the world ruler, until he in turn is deposed by his son Zeus. This myth has echoes in several ancient Near Eastern myths, such as that of Cybele and Attis, in which the son-consort of the Goddess is castrated or killed. Ritual self-sacrifice or self-castration was even practiced by the demented priests of that cult.

The Gaia and Uranus myth tells the historical story of the assault on the Earth Goddess religion by the followers of Indo-European sky god cults and the subsequent retaliation against the oppressor cult. The emasculation of Uranus can be read as a metaphor for the loss of generative power, which follows upon the denial and suppression of the feminine and the spiritual energies of the natural world. In modern psychological terms, we have the imbalanced, uncreative, authoritarian men (and many women) typical of patriarchal societies. The Earth Goddess gives birth and health but also disease and death to the human, natural body. When this power is not respected, the painful consequences are unavoidable. The loss of generative and regenerative power, as seen, for example, in the spread of degenerative diseases, is the price paid by us all for the patriarchal suppression of the Goddess.

In the mythology of Celtic Ireland, which also chronicles and reflects the often tumultuous transition from matricentric to patriarchal society, the story of the curse of the goddess Macha symbolizes the revenge of the Goddess in a most poignant and awesome manner. Macha was a form of the ancient Irish horse and sun goddess, who could outrun any horse. When her human husband boasted of her prowess at the annual horse championship races in Ulster (now known as Northern Ireland), the king angrily demanded that she appear to race against his prized horses. Being pregnant, Macha was reluctant to go and consented only when the king threatened to kill her husband if she did not attend. At the race, she appealed to the assembled warriors and king for a delay, since she was about to deliver—"for a mother bore each one of you." The king refused, she ran the race, won easily, and immediately gave birth to twins. At the moment of her victory, she pronounced a curse upon the men of Ulster that "when a time of oppression falls upon you, each one of you in this province will be overcome with weakness, as the weakness of a woman in childbirth." This curse became known as the "Pangs of the Men of Ulster."[17]

In commenting on this story, Irish theologian Mary Condren has written that the cry of Macha "has resounded in Ireland down through the ages" up until the late-twentieth century. A curse, particularly the curse of a deity, was no trivial matter, as we might think of it today. Is it not strange that Northern Ireland is still wracked by seemingly intractable hatred and violence? "The Goddess Macha cursed the patriarchal age that had dawned. . . . Her cry was possibly the last symbolic attempt to appeal to true motherhood as the basis for public social ethics. That her people ignored her meant that the values of relationship and affiliation were effete; violence, death, and the threat of death became the dominant grammar of political relationships."[18]

MYTHS OF COMPROMISE AND RECONCILIATION

The myth of Demeter and Persephone, which provided the central story of the Eleusinian Mysteries, for two thousand years the core religious ceremony of the Greek world, was an acknowledgment of the clash between the Olympian religion of sky and mountain gods and the earlier Earth Goddess cults. Demeter is the Cretan grain goddess (known to the Romans as Ceres, from which we derive the word *cereal*), who taught humankind the cultivation of grain and was revered for her frutifulness and abundance. Her daughter, Persephone, was abducted by Hades, brother of Zeus and ruler of the Underworld, who had displaced Hecate, the earlier Underworld goddess. In this myth, Demeter searches the world in profound grief and despair. When she discovers that her daughter's abduction took place with the complicity of Zeus, grief turns to rage, and she unleashes drought and desolation upon the earth, threatening the survival of all life. Demeter's rage is against the Aryan sky gods and their aggressive disrespect for the religion of the Earth Goddess. The revenge of the Goddess involves the loss of fertility, barrenness, and death.

When the gods realize the enormity of their transgression against the goddess of all earthly life, Zeus works out a compromise: Persephone stays underground for half the year and above ground the other half. Here, this myth blends with earlier myths of the seasonal death and renewal of vegetative life. Demeter then agrees to release the blight she has sent upon the land and teaches again the secrets of agriculture and regeneration. The Eleusinian Mysteries celebrated this whole story of assault, revenge, reconciliation, and renewal in a ritual involving poetry, song, dramatic presentation, and prayer. Albert Hofmann, R. Gordon

Wasson, and Carl Ruck, in their book *The Road to Eleusis,* have argued that the ceremony could have included ingestion of a hallucinogenic potion derived from the ergot fungus that grows on rye or barley (amply available in the region around Eleusis) and contains LSD-like alkaloids. In this case, the entire ritual would have been amplified to the ecstatic intensity of mystical experience. Whether amplified by hallucinogens or not, the Eleusinian Mysteries brought thousands of ancient Greeks to a reconciliation with their pre-Hellenic, ancestral religion and with a reverential attitude to the nourishing Mother Goddess.[19]

In Irish mythology, too, there are hints of reconciliation rituals between the invading patriarchal Celts and the indigenous matricentric cultures, who worshiped the goddess of the land and built great stone circles and passage graves in her honor. These myths often refer to the ritual marriage of the warrior-king to the local goddess of the land, who offered sacred kingship in exchange for having the land named after her. Éire, the ancient name for Ireland, was derived in this way from the goddess Ériu, and the town of Armagh was named after the goddess Macha. As in many Near Eastern ancient societies, the annual ritual mating of the king with the goddess of the land or her priestess ensured the fertility of the land for its people. As Mary Condren wrote, "In a famous story of one of the Celtic invasions, Ériu makes it clear that anyone wishing to enter Ireland would have to revere the goddesses if they wished to prosper and be fruitful."[20]

Nordic-Germanic mythology also has a story of reconciliation, in the long, drawn-out conflict between Aesir and Vanir gods. After their first failed attempt at peacemaking, when the rival families of gods finally decide to cease fighting, they meet, according to the myth, in a council circle around a gigantic cauldron. Each deity spits saliva into the cauldron, and out of their mingled juices an incredibly wise being named Kvasir is born. This Kvasir is then killed by two dwarves, who mix his blood with honey and thereby create a drink that inspires both humans and gods with poetic creativity, the mead of inspiration. The name Kvasir relates to a Slavic word for fermented beverage, and the ritual of mingling saliva reflects archaic practices of inducing fermentation. We have here, as with Eleusis, a mythic ritual of reconciliation, probably referring to the kind of reconciliation and accommodation that must eventually have taken place between the Kurgan invaders and the Old Europeans.[21]

Metaphorically, this is a story about the wisdom and creativity that arises out of the reconciliation of previously antagonistic opposites, what Jung called the *coincidentia oppositorum*. This is the wisdom that comes from loving instead of fighting, from cooperating instead of competing, from partnership instead of domination, and from honoring and celebrating differences instead of fearing them and using them to create scapegoats for our guilt. When we can dissolve the barriers of separation and conflict among nations, races, religions, and the other traditional but artificial divisions of humankind, we would unleash an unparalleled explosion of the arts and creativity in all areas of life—this would appear to be the message of these myths of compromise and reconciliation.

The hybrid mythologies telling of domination, retaliation, and reconciliation are found throughout Europe, the Mediterranean, the Near East, Iran, and India—wherever a patriarchal ideology with cults of male sky and warrior gods was superimposed on matricentric egalitarian societies that worshiped the Great Goddess, with countless manifestations in all the forms of plant and animal life, including especially the human female. The basic pattern is everywhere the same, whether we are talking about the bands of Kurgan pastoralists who invaded Old Europe, the Celtic warriors who invaded Britain and Ireland, the Hebrew pastoralists who invaded Canaan, the Aryan Hellenes who invaded Crete and Greece, or the Mesopotamian city-states, who may have evolved a patriarchal dominator ideology without foreign invasion. There is much we do not know about prehistory, and we may never know the full story about the origins of the patriarchy.

We do know that with the establishment of the patriarchal dominator pattern, there was a partial loss and submergence of the gynocentric Earth spirituality, which was the human heritage from the most ancient times of paleolithic gatherers and hunters. Certain aspects of this archaic worldview were preserved in the animistic and shamanistic traditions of Northern Europe and the polytheistic religions of classical antiquity. With the expansion of Christianity, the suppression of the old pagan nature religions and the oppression of women took a sharp upswing, culminating in the Inquisition, in which, according to some estimates, as many as six to nine million witches were exterminated, the majority of them pagan women. This sustained misogynistic assault on women and paganism must be seen in the context of thousands of years of antagonism toward the ancient Earth Goddess, the "Mother of All the Living."

It has been about six thousand years since the first waves of Kurgan pastoralists migrated westward and established their sky god religion and patriarchal social order in the peaceful farming communities of Old Europe. Perhaps the worldwide environmental and women's movements, and the questioning of Eurocentric ideology that is now going on are signals that the patriarchal dominator system is beginning to be dismantled. The need for rituals of compromise and reconciliation has never been greater and is being increasingly recognized. The wisdom and creativity expressed in the myths of our ancestors can be drawn on to help us find the connection back to a more respectful, harmonious, and joyous relationship with the natural world and all its creatures.

I like to imagine that we are in the civilizational transition that William Blake referred to when he wrote this in his visionary prophecy *The Marriage of Heaven and Hell:*

> The ancient tradition that the world will be consumed in fire at the end of six thousand years is true, as I have heard from Hell. For the cherub with his flaming sword is hereby commanded to leave his guard at tree of life; and when he does the whole creation will be consumed and appear infinite and holy, whereas now it appears finite and corrupt. This will come to pass by an improvement in sensory enjoyment.[22]

The cherub guarding access to the tree of life is a symbol of the patriarchal, foundational myth that our alienation from nature (Eden) is God's punishment (the so-called Fall). The cherub's departure means we can return to the sacred tree of life, to the regenerative nature-reverencing animism and joyous sensitivity of our pre-patriarchal ancestors.

The Black Goddess,
the Green God,
and the Wild Human

*Prior to the rise of transcendental monotheism, the religious worldview of
the ancient world was polytheistic, animistic, and shamanistic. In this essay I explore some of the key mythic images of our pagan ancestors—the
gods and goddesses that personify our relationship to the earth, to the plant
realm, and to the world of animals.[1]*

The religion and worldview of the Celtic, Germanic, Baltic, and Slavic
people, who inhabited Europe before the Christian era, as well as that of
the Greeks and other Mediterranean peoples, was animistic: gods and
goddesses, the living intelligences of nature, were perceived and worshiped
in forest groves and sacred springs, on mountaintops and in great stone
circles. In addition to gods and goddesses, there were other classes of
beings associated with nature who were not human but who were certainly equal, if not superior, to humans and deserving of respect—giants
and dwarfs, elves and trolls, fairies, leprechauns, gnomes, satyrs, nymphs,
and mermaids. These deities and beings could be communed with by
anyone who was willing to practice the methods taught by the shamans
and their successors, the witches, the wise women of the woods—using
magical plants and stones, chants and incantations, dances and rituals.

This is the nature religion that was eliminated by Christian monotheism during the first few centuries of our era. Pagan deities were either banished into nonexistence or demonized. Those who followed the old nature religion were branded as "pagan" or "heathen," which originally simply meant "country dwellers" or "heath dwellers" as I have said. The country folk were more likely to have preserved beliefs in spirits and knowledge of healing and magical herbs than those who lived in towns with stone walls. Some of the pagan deities were absorbed into Christian lore, just as some traditional sacred places had churches or chapels built on them. Others sank into the cultural underground of folklore and popular customs and beliefs. Mythic stories of divine figures devolved into comic or moralizing legends and fairy tales. Under the influence of Judeo-Christian transcendental monotheism, the kind of direct awareness of the spiritual presences in nature that our pagan ancestors enjoyed and cultivated was gradually lost. As William Blake said, "Thus men forgot that all deities live within the human breast."

While I do not mean to suggest that we must all become pagans and worship the ancient gods again, I do believe that by reconnecting with the nature religion of our ancestors, we can recover something of the imaginal sensitivity and ecological spirituality that is the collective heritage of each of us. A tremendous spiritual revitalization can take place when we recognize the natural world and the divine world as intimately interwoven with each other. I see this as a kind of re-membering, through which the dismemberment of human consciousness from Earth could be healed.

In my book *The Well of Remembrance,* I focused on the Earth wisdom mythology of the Nordic-Germanic people.[2] In this same spirit of of healing remembering I would like to discuss several mythic deities from pre-Christian Europe as well as from non-European cultures—god images that embody a perception of the spiritual in nature. There are three groups of such images. One is the Black Earth Goddess, who was absorbed into Christianity as the Black Madonna or Black Virgin. A second group are the plant deities of the ancient world, a variant of which also made it into Christian iconography as the Green Man. The third group are the animal deities and wild men/wild women, who represent the evolutionary memory of our animal ancestry.

The Black Goddess/Madonna

There about five hundred shrine images of the Black Virgin in various churches in Europe.[3] Among the best known are the Virgin in the cathedral of Chartres in France; the protectress saint of Poland in Czestochowa; the protectress saint of Switzerland at Einsiedeln, near Zürich; the Muttergottes ("Mother of God") in Altötting, near München, in Bavaria; and the Madonna in Loreto, Italy. These shrines of the Black Madonna are among the most-visited places in Christendom. Hundreds of thousands of people annually make the pilgrimage to Altötting or Einsiedeln and have done so since the Middle Ages, when most of the shrines were first established.

The reason for their magnetism as pilgrimage sites lies in their reputation for healing efficacy. In Altötting, for example, the tiny chapel that holds the shrine of the Virgin is surrounded by several thousand *ex voto* tablets, some dating back to the thirteenth century and some from the

Black Madonna from Altötting, Bavaria.
Note also the plant designs on her robe.

Black Madonna, with green robe, from Einsiedeln, Switzerland.

current year, in which thanks is expressed for a miraculous healing or recovery, a safe journey or the return of a loved one, or, in earlier times, an exorcism of evil spirits. In the typical story, a person appealed to Maria for help or guidance and vowed to make an offering if the appeal was successful. Thus, the bequest and the tablet come "from the vow" *(ex voto)*. On the outside of the chapel, one can also see numerous crutches and limb prostheses, left as unnecessary by grateful healed pilgrims.

Although they enjoy great popular appeal, the images of the Black Madonna are a source of some embarrassment to the Catholic Church. Usually, the guidebooks make no reference to the color, or when they do, they try to explain it away by ludicrous references to the blackening effect of centuries of smoke from candles and incense burners. Occasionally, there are references to the mysterious line from the Old Testament Song of Solomon, in which the Shulamite, perhaps the Queen of Sheba, sings: "I am black, but I am beautiful, O ye daughters of Jerusalem." For the good Christian pilgrims who cannot bear to contemplate a dark-skinned Madonna, the souvenir shops carry sanitized wax or wooden replicas, in which Mary and the infant Jesus have appropriately white European faces.

The Black Virgin has been identified with several black goddess figures of the ancient pre-patriarchal cultures of the Mediterranean and Near East, including the Phrygian Cybele, the Sumerian Inanna, the Syrian Anath, the Hebrew Lilith, the Indian Kali, the Ephesian Diana, and the Egyptian goddesses Neith and, of course, Isis. In the goddess-worshiping cultures of Old Europe and the pre-patriarchal Mediterranean, black was the color of fertility and abundance, like the rich black soil of the Nile and other river valleys. White, on the other hand, was the color symbolic of death, and images of the death-bringing goddess were carved in bone or marble. For the nomadic pastoralist Indo-Aryans, however, who invaded Europe from the fourth millennium B.C.E. onward, white, gold, and yellow were the colors of the life-giving, shining Sun God, and black was the color of the somber underground death deities, like Hades, Hecate, or Hel.

With the shift to a patriarchal sky god religion, followed by the Judaeo-Christian monotheistic traditions, the nature-reverencing goddess religions of the archaic world were suppressed, desecrated, and demonized. The sacred sexuality associated with the cult of Inanna and Ishtar was condemned as prostitution. Lilith, who represented female sexual autonomy and protection of childbirth and children, was turned into a seductive demoness who stole children. Male priests and theologians found it easy to play up the terrifying aspects of goddess worship, as in the cult of Cybele, whose priests symbolically, and at times literally, offered their genitals in sacrifice to the goddess. The Indian Kali became increasingly polarized as destructive only, although the original image is balanced between birth-giving and death-dealing. Diana became the goddess of the witches. The Black Goddess entered Christianity from below, as it were, in both her healing and threatening aspects. She was strongly associated with the twelfth-century esoteric Christianity of the Cathars, the Troubadours, and the Templars, all of whom tried to overcome the dissociative split between nature/eros and dogmatic ascetic spirituality, and all of whom were savagely destroyed by the Church.

Only the image of the Black Madonna and Child, itself based on the

Egyptian images of Isis with the child Horus, survived the Christian misogynistic onslaught. The cult of Isis was the dominant religion of the Mediterranean during late Roman times and spread into Roman-occupied lands, including Gaul. The city of Paris was devoted to Isis, as Lyons was to Cybele and Marseilles to Artemis. Like other Black Goddess figures, Isis is the life-giving and healing goddess of Earth. In *The Golden Ass* of Apuleius, Isis speaks: "I am Nature, the universal Mother, mistress of all the elements, primordial child of time, sovereign of all things spiritual, queen of the dead, queen also of the immortals, the single manifestation of all the gods and goddesses there are."[4] The text goes on to claim that she is identical to Cybele, Artemis, Aphrodite, Persephone, Demeter, Juno, and Hecate.

The Black Earth Goddess under whatever name, including the Black Madonna, has traditionally always been supportive and facilitative of the natural processes of life: healing the sick, easing the pain of child-birth, bringing fertility, making the milk flow, comforting and guiding the dying, helping the plants grow. As such, she represented the persis-tence of the Great Goddess during the time of dominance by patriarchal sky god cults and the persistence of the Mother Goddess during the as-cendancy of Christian monotheism.

Some years ago, when I was on the Canary Islands off the coast of Africa, I had a vivid dream about the Black Goddess. In the dream I was with a group of AIDS sufferers who had gone to Africa to get to know the Black Goddess. We had been told that the underlying cause of AIDS was a disconnection from the regenerative power of the Black Goddess, and the cure would involve reestablishing the psychic bond with that Goddess. I told that dream to several friends who had AIDS, who felt it symbolized an important truth. Since AIDS represents a breakdown of the body's inherent immune resilience and self-healing capacity, recon-necting with the healing power of the Black Goddess may well be neces-sary on the road to wholeness.

The shrines and images of the Black Virgin have an undeniable psychic and spiritual power, which explains their attraction for tourists as well as those seeking a cure for their ills. The chapel in Altötting, in the lush, fertile farm country of Lower Bavaria, stands in the middle of the town square, surrounded by other churches and monasteries. The outside of the chapel, as already mentioned, is covered with thousands of votive tablets. The entire interior of the chapel is painted black, and the walls are studded with countless gold and silver images and ornaments, especially around the alcove shrine that holds the statue. The light from numerous candles in gigantic silver candleholders sparkles and scintillates off the polished gold and silver objects. The blackness set with shimmering gold and silver gives the whole chapel a mysterious, alchemical, yet strangely comforting aura.

THE GREEN MAN AND OTHER PLANT DEITIES

Another mythic image from pagan times that has survived, unnoticed, in Christian iconography is the Green Man, or Leafy Man, also called *le feuillou* in French or *Blattgesicht* in German. William Anderson, in his book *The Green Man*, has shown that the numerous images in Gothic European churches of a face covered with leaves, or leaves coming out of its mouth, is in fact identical to the figure of British folklore known as the Green Man. There is a leaf-clad green man in many traditional English country dance festivals, and a woodsman with a green hat and coat, carrying an ax, can be seen on pub signs throughout Britain.

In German, French, and English churches from the Gothic period, the leaf-faced figure is found tucked away secretly in the corners, under lintels and pedestals, apparently holding up figures of saints, popes, and bishops. In Bamberg, the Blattgesicht is mounted under the pedestal on which stands the horse with its famous "Bamberger Reiter" (horseman). Like the Black Madonna, this image is relatively unknown and rarely mentioned in guidebooks, and yet the builders of the cathedrals put this figure there as if to say, "This is the hidden root of spiritual power in nature, without which the church could not stand." The leafy face has neither the benign compassion of the saints nor the grotesque savagery of the demons that abound in Gothic churches. Rather the face is neutral, serious but not somber, challenging rather than kind. Like the Black Virgin, this powerful pagan mythic image is now reemerging into public consciousness at a time when a new recognition and remembrance of the regenerative spirituality in nature is desperately needed.

A striking mythic representation of the Green Man image is found in the Arthurian legend of Sir Gawain and the Green Knight, which dates from the thirteenth century but is probably based on much earlier myths.

Leaf-Face, on corbel under ledge on which stands an unidentified rider on a horse—the "Bamberger Reiter." (Bamberg cathedral, Germany, 13th century)

According to this story, the Green Knight (with green face, green armor, green helmet, green shield, and mounted on a green horse) rides into King Arthur's court and issues a challenge to the assembled knights. He will submit to having his head cut off, and the knight who does so must then himself surrender to decapitation one year later. After considerable hesitation, Sir Gawain accepts the challenge and cuts off the Green Knight's head. The Green Knight then calmly picks up his head, tucks it under his arm, and rides away, promising to meet Gawain in a year's time, to fulfill the vow. The rest of the story deals with the tests of his loyalty and integrity that Gawain has to undergo on his way to meet the Green Knight. Only a plant or tree can be decapitated and then be restored and continue to live. Thus, the Green Knight is symbolically a

Head with sprouting oak branches and leaves, carved on inside wall of wooden choir stall. (Exeter cathedral, England, 14th century)

personification of the regenerative power of the plant realm, to which the proud human being submits or pays the price.

A Christian symbolic embodiment of the sacred green plant spirit can be found in Hildegard von Bingen's mystical theology and "creation spirituality." Her most original and vivid metaphor is the notion of *viriditas*—"greenness"—which is God's creative power manifest in the world of nature. In Hidegard's writings Jesus is called Greenness Incarnate, and Mary is the *Viridissima Virga*, the greenest of all branches in God's orchard.[5]

Dionysus

The Green Knight and the Green Man with a leafy face are clearly Christian transformations of the vegetation god of ancient times, the son-lover of the Great Goddess who died each year in winter and was reborn, or regenerated, in the spring. This is the deity whose name in ancient Greece was Dionysus (or Bacchus in Rome), the god of ecstasy and divine rapture who taught people how to turn grapes into wine and drove those mad who refused to acknowledge his divinity. Dionysus was not originally one of the Olympians and therefore probably represents a relic from the pre-Hellenic cults of the Goddess. The myths tell of his coming from Thrace in Asia, accompanied by his band of revelers and spreading the pleasures of the wine cult throughout Greece. The Aryan Greeks co-opted his cult, as they did that of several goddesses, by inventing the story of Dionysus's birth from Zeus's thigh. In the later classical period, the Dionysus cult was adopted and adapted into the Orphic mysteries of death and rebirth, where Dionysus symbolized the immortal soul.

The images of Dionysus show him with feminine or androgynous features, sometimes bearded, sometimes youthful, and sometimes with long hair like a woman. Vine leaves wound around his head and body, and one of his names was Dendrites—the "tree youth." In processions, he and his followers carried a staff called a thyrsus, wound around with vines and with a pine cone mounted on top. He was also associated with animals, especially the bull and the serpent. According to legend, his "train," or procession, was accompanied by panthers, and his followers wore fawn skins. An Orphic Hymn addresses the god as "loud-roaring and reveling Dionysus, primordial, two-natured, thrice-born, . . . wild, unspeakable, mysterious, . . . ivy-covered, bull-faced, . . . wrapt in foliage, decked with grape clusters."[6] Like other ancient vegetation deities, Dionysus is also associated with the Underworld of the dead. Heraclitus said Dionysus and Hades are one and the same.

As Robert Graves, Terence McKenna, and others have suggested, it is likely that the "wine" consumed in the Dionysian and Bacchic rites in-cluded not only fermented grapes but also various hallucinogenic and aphrodisiac herbs—perhaps psilocybin mushrooms related to the fa-mous "magic mushrooms" of the ancient Mexican shamanic tradition.[7] There are accounts of Dionysian orgies, in which ecstatic *maenads* ran through the woods at night, singing and dancing with erotic abandon, offering bare breasts to their androgynous deity, and causing wine, pure water, milk, and honey to flow miraculously from the earth and rocks. There are also derogatory stories of intoxicated maenads supposedly tear-ing to pieces small animals with their bare hands and teeth. It is possible that such stories represent part of the conservative reaction, exaggerat-ing and demonizing the spreading Dionysian wine and hallucinogen cult. It is also possible that in the course of time the cult degenerated as the proportion of wine consumed increased, and sacred visionary celebra-tion gradually became drunken orgy.

Friedrich Nietzsche, in his early work *The Birth of Tragedy*, pointed out that ancient Greek tragedy grew out of musical and dance performances that were originally part of the Dionysian rituals and processions. He argued that there were two imaginal strands in the Greek worldview. The Apollonian, based on dream visions, was harmonious, orderly, well proportioned, lucid, and spiritual; the Dionysian, based on ecstatic trance, was chaotic, disorderly, unpredictable, enthusiastic, and wild. He thought that the complementary coexistence and dynamic tension of these two strands of thought—one rational/mental and the other irrational/emotional—was responsible for the particular genius of Greek culture. This distinction has had great intuitive appeal and is consistent with the image of Dionysus as the god who brings ecstatic revelation through ingestion of visionary plants.

One important aspect of the Dionysus cult that Nietzsche overlooked, however, was the fact that it was primarily a woman's rite in a patriarchal society. Ancient Greek city culture, which some have called a "phallocracy," was a society in which women were basically household and breeding slaves, and the highest ideal of erotic love was pederasty. For Greek women, imprisoned in their houses, the week-long Dionysian festival was the one time of the year when they were permitted to leave the rigid patriarchal control of their fathers and husbands and follow the intoxicating sound of Dionysus's band of musicians for a wild night of singing and dancing in the woods.[8] Thus, it represented the ecstatic liberation of women and the celebration of primordial feminine goddess energies.

Shiva

In India, the deity that most closely resembles Dionysus is Shiva. Alain Daniélou has pointed out the many parallels between these two gods. He argues that Shiva was, in fact, the nature deity, the androgynous god of ecstatic and erotic energy, among the Dravidians who lived in India before the Aryan invasions.[9] In the post-Vedic literature, Shiva becomes the god of transcendence-seeking, ascetic yogis, who meditates for ten thousand years in the solitude of the Himalayas. Like Dionysus, he is associated with the bull and with serpents and also with trees, plants, and the hallucinogenic-aphrodisiac hemp *(Cannabis indica)*. His preeminent icon is the *lingam* (phallus) united with the *yoni* (vulva). In the Tantric yoga tradition, the ancient cult of Shiva was revived, and the image of Shiva and Shakti in ecstatic embrace became the prototype of transcendence *through,* rather than away from, erotic union. Tantric yogis smoking cannabis sit in the burning *ghats* of Calcutta and Benares, meditating on the transience of life and death.

Demeter

The goddess counterpart to the Dionysian wine cult in ancient Greece was the Demeter-Persephone grain cult celebrated in the Mysteries of Eleusis. As Dionysus taught humans the cultivation of the vine, so Demeter, whom the Romans called Ceres, taught humans the cultivation of grain. The Dionysian and Eleusinian Mysteries were the two most widespread religions of the ancient world. An Orphic hymn to Demeter addresses her: "Divine mother of all, goddess of many names, . . . you nourish the ears of grain, O giver of all, and you delight in peace and toilsome labor. . . . You give sustenance to all mortals, and you were the

Demeter the grain goddess and Dionysus the wine god, meeting and exchanging gifts and offerings. (Votive tablet from Lokri, Italy, 460 B.C.E.; Museo Nazionale, Reggio Calabria)

first to yoke the ploughing ox and to send up from below a rich and lovely harvest. . . . Through you there is growth and blossoming."[10]

Demeter was probably a Cretan form of the Great Goddess, and the historical reality is that the Aryan Hellenes did learn the cultivation of both grain and the vine from the indigenous Mediterranean agrarian cultures they invaded. The grain mysteries of Eleusis also included a visionary experience through ingestion of the hallucinogenic rye fungus ergot, known as "mother grain" (Mutterkorn) in German.[11] The Eleusinian Mysteries reminded the initiates of the story of the conflict between the Olympians and Demeter, who is at first aggrieved and then appeased. Thus, they represented a ritual of reconciliation between the peaceful, agrarian Goddess culture of Minoan Crete and the predatory invading Hellenes, who at first suppressed and then were obliged to acknowledge the divinity of the Earth Goddess.

Osiris

In Egyptian mythology, the god who corresponds to Dionysus and the Green Man is the green-skinned Osiris, known as the "Great Green One," who is sometimes shown lying with stalks of corn growing out of his body. He was also sometimes depicted as white, wrapped in mummy cloths, as befits the Lord of the Underworld, or black, as befits the god of the Nile, whose waters fertilize the rich soil of the Black Earth Land (Kamia), as the ancient Egyptians called their country. Osiris and his sister-consort, Isis, brought the arts of civilization to humans; Isis was the life-giving mother, healer, and magician, and Osiris brought plant growth, wine culture, and regeneration. One of his names was Wennefer, "the eternally good being." Osiris is also associated with the treelike *djed* pillar; when a person died, the priests prayed for the *djed* to be "straight," so that the soul could leave the body unhindered.[12]

According to the most ancient Egyptian creation myth, Isis and Osiris are two of the five children of the Earth god Geb and the sky goddess Nut, the other three being Seth, Nephthys, and Horus. Nephthys is sister and companion to Isis, and Horus also often appears as the son of Isis and Osiris; he continues his father's struggle against Seth when Osiris becomes ruler of the Underworld. Osiris embodies the fertilizing waters of the Nile and Seth the searing, violent heat of the desert. Egyptian myth is pervaded by the image of the struggle between these two figures,

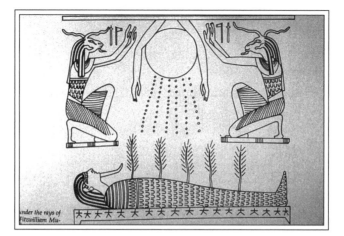

Plants sprout from the dead body of Osiris as the rays of the sun god Re shine down from above. (Coffin painting from the 21st Dynasty, 1000 B.C.E.)

which represents the ever changing dynamics at the edge of these opposite ecosystems and climate zones.

In a famous myth, Seth imprisons Osiris in a wooden coffin, which becomes a tree, which, in turn, is used in a building—until Isis releases him by her magical healing arts. This could be seen as a metaphor for the magical productive and transformative capacity of plant life. Seth then cuts Osiris into fourteen pieces, which Isis searches for and finds, all except the male member, which was thrown into the Nile and devoured by a fish or a crocodile. The goddess reconstitutes her consort's body, fashions a replica of his member, and impregnates herself. This could be seen as a metaphor for the plant's ability to be "killed" and still regenerate and produce new life out of itself, with the healing power of the Goddess. After this "death," Osiris descends into the Underworld, where he becomes the judge of souls. The falcon-headed Horus continues the struggle against Seth and, with his mother, Isis, becomes the protector of pharaohs and ordinary mortals.

The myths and cults of Isis, Osiris, and Horus were adopted into first the Greek and later the Roman world. The Green God (Osiris) is the consort of the Black Goddess (Isis). The mysteries of Isis were, as we have seen, the most widespread religion in the Roman Empire at the time of the birth of Christianity. The healing black goddess Isis became the prototype for the compassionate and comforting Mother of God. The image of Isis with the child Horus on her lap was transformed into the Christian image of the Madonna and Christ child. In Einsiedeln, Switzerland, the image of the Black Madonna has six or seven magnificent baroque robes of different colors, with elaborate plantlike gold brocade: one is ruby red, another white, one blue, one turquoise—and one a superb emerald green. Here is the perfect fusion in Christian iconography of the green and the black divinity!

Xochipilli

In the pre-Columbian Aztecan culture, there is also a deity corresponding to Dionysus and Shiva. His name is Xochipilli, the "Prince of Flowers." There are statues of this god seated in an ecstatic posture, his legs crossed, toes curled, and masked face rapturously turned upward. Designs of flowers and plants, including the hallucinogenic morning glory and mushrooms, are curling around his limbs and pedestal. R. Gordon Wasson, the ethnomycologist who has made the most intensive study of the hallucinogenic mushroom cult of ancient Mexico, writes: "Here is the carving of man in the midst of an unearthly experience, the formal hieratic effigy of the God of Rapture, the God of 'Flowers': the god of youth, of light, of the dance and music and games, of poetry and art; the Child God, the god of the rising sun, of summer and warmth, of flowers and butterflies, of the 'Tree-in-Flower' that the Nahuatl poets frequently invoke, of the inebriating mushrooms, the miraculous plants that transport one to a heavenly Paradise."[13]

Kokopelli

The similarity in the name alone suggests that there may be an affinity, or even a cultural diffusion, between Xochipilli and Kokopelli, the humpbacked flute-player whose image is painted or carved on thousands of cave walls in the American Southwest, many of them dating to pre-Columbian times. Among the Hopi, he was the kachina called Kokopilau, identified with the locust or grasshopper, who accompanied the people on their migrations with his song. The horns on his head are insect antennae, and the long "flute" is a proboscis. The Indians say the hump on his back is actually a bag in which he carries seeds—of corn, squash, and beans as well as flowers. Thus, he is a spirit who embodies insects and

Xochipilli—Aztec "Prince of Flowers,"
god of ecstasy, vision, and poetry.
(Museo Nacional de Anthropologia,
Mexico)

their role in pollination as well as bringing seeds for the growth of nourishing plants in the dry deserts of the Southwest. Among the Navaho
and elsewhere he is sometimes called "Water Sprinkler"—invoked for
rain and fertility. His power to impart fertility is also evident in the images often found among the petroglyphs, which show Kokopelli with
protruding phallus—much to the embarrassment of the early mission-
aries. In the stories and dances, he acquired the characteristics of a sexual
trickster and seducer: barren women sought his company, while unmar-
ried maidens fled from him in dismay and laughter.[14]

Ossaím

Ossaím, or Osaín, is one of the deities, known as *orixas,* who were brought
to Brazil by the West African Yoruba people. These gods and goddesses
now play a major role in the Afro-Brazilian syncretic religious cults,

Ossaím—the one-legged, one-eyed Afro-Brazilian orixa of herbalists, doctors, alchemists, and magicians. (Painting by Nelso Boera Faedrich)

including Candomblé and Santeria. The sixteen or more deities, male and female, figure in numerous popular myths, and people identify themselves as the "sons" or "daughters" of one or the other of these orixas, depending on their personal characteristics and spiritual inclinations. Ossaím is the one-legged god of magical herbs and plants who lives alone in the forest and is described as having a reserved, saturnine, and mysterious character. The symbolism of having only one leg is the clue to his identity as a vegetation or plant god: trees and plants usually have just one main trunk or stalk. His color also is green, and he is very much respected and sought after, by both other deities and humans, for his unsurpassed and secret knowledge of medicinal and magical plants. He is the guardian deity of healers, herbalists, chemists, botanists, and pharmacists.[15]

ANIMAL DEITIES AND WILD HUMANS

The plant realm and the animal realm are the two main trunks of the evolutionary tree of life with which we humans are connected. Whereas the plant kingdom provided our pagan ancestors with nourishing food, healing medicines, and visionary sacraments, the animals were our direct ancestors and relatives, the guardian spirits, totems, and allies of shamanic traditions. The spiritual intelligences of the plant realm were personified in the ancient vegetation deities, such as Dionysus, the god of the vine; Osiris, the green-skinned river god; and Demeter, the grain goddess—and in folkloric images, such as the Green Man, or Leafy Face.

The ancestral wisdom of the animal realm is embodied in such animal deities as the Greek Pan and Artemis and the Celtic Cernunnos and in folkloric conceptions of wild men and wild women and the legendary Sasquatch, or Big Foot. We were all wild humans before we became civilized in that peculiar process of self-domestication known as the Neolithic agricultural revolution. The word "wild" is related to the word "will"; the wild creature is self-willed, autonomous, not domesticated, living by nature's ways not the laws of human beings.

Greek and Roman mythology is filled with beings part human and part animal that represent totemic identity and shamanic alliances, such as the goat-bodied satyrs, the horse-bodied centaurs, and the dolphin-bodied mermaids. The ancient Egyptians had numerous deities with animal heads, such as the ibis-headed Thoth, the jackal-headed Anubis, and the falcon-headed Horus. The oldest images of the Great Goddess, dating from the fifth and sixth millennia B.C.E. in the cultures of Old Europe, are composites of a human torso with bird head, or snake feet, or features of a bear, or the horns of a bull—often associated with a vulva triangle and with rounded and voluptuous female body parts, such as breasts, buttocks, and swelling abdomen.[16]

The Wild Man has long hair or fur all over his body, horns on his head, hooves for feet, and a tail. The oldest prototype we know is Enkidu, in the Gilgamesh epic, who has hair all over his body, and lives and hunts with the animals, whom he helps escape the hunters' snares. He has been created by the ancient creator goddess to be an even match for the tyrannical and arrogant warrior-king Gilgamesh. A priestess of the love-goddess Ishtar seduces him into the ways of civilization. He and

Gilgamesh become inseparable companions. This story could be seen as a metaphor for the transition of the human from the wild state of the roaming hunter-gatherers to the domesticated condition of living in city-states under the rule of patriarchal kings. In the epic, Enkidu the Wild Man is psychically more sensitive than Gilgamesh; he can interpret prophetic dreams, and he has more respect for the power of the great divinities of nature, such as Humbaba, the forest guardian.[17]

In Greek myth the god of wild animals is Pan, the goat-legged satyr from Arcadia renowned for his libidinous nature, whom the Romans called Faunus and whom Christianity turned into the image of the Devil. Satyrs were a strong presence in the Dionysian revels as well and are shown in art pursuing the maenads with obvious erotic intent, although usually unsuccessfully. There are also the hairy woodland spirits, *sileni*, led by the venerable and wise Silenus, and the horse-bodied centaurs,

Pan—Arcadian god of nature, lord of the animals, with goat-body and playing the pan flute. (18th century German engraving)

Pan demonized as the Devil, chaining and separating the lovers. (From the Medieval Tarot, the Waite deck)

led by the teacher-healer Chiron. All these beings represent a shamanic and totemic symbiosis with particular animal species. The dancing ithyphallic satyrs, led by Pan, can be seen as paying erotic homage to the goddess and the androgynous god. Far from being the embodiment of evil and deceit, among the Greeks, Pan was a good-natured, highly charged sexual being who loved dancing and cavorting in the woods and meadows with nymphs, animals, and children.

Like the Dionysus cult, the Pan cult was associated with dance and music, and the panpipes made from reeds are an invention of the woodland god. At the processions and revels of the satyrs and maenads, there was loud singing or even howling, perhaps in imitation of the howling of such animals as wolves. Although generally easygoing, Pan could terrify through the suddenness of an unpredictable appearance or the eerie sound of his conch shell. He helped the Olympians in their battle against the Titans by blowing his conch and throwing them into a "panic" at the stunningly loud sound. Thus, the violence and fierceness of animals, when provoked, are also part of Pan's domain.

The name Pan is usually derived from *paein*, meaning "to pasture," although it is interesting that "pan" in Greek also means "all," as in *panacea*, the "cure-all," and *pandemonium*, the congregation of "all the demons." This universality of the animal-god was incorporated into his myth and cult. He was the Master of Animals, the Lord of Nature, who ruled over all the smaller nature spirits, such as nymphs, elves, fairies, undines, dwarves, gnomes, salamanders, and the like. An Orphic hymn addresses Pan as follows:

> O great Pan the strong I call, the shepherd god, the wholeness of all—the sky, the ocean, great queen of earth, and the immortal fire as well, for all these are Friend of all enthusiastic souls, ecstatic one, living in caves, you play the harmonies of the world, with the joyous song of your flute. You inspire us with images and terrify us with your force.[18]

Pan's feminine counterpart was the Lady of the Beasts, whom the Greeks called Artemis and the Romans named Diana. Diana, in turn, became the chosen protectress deity of the medieval and modern witches, the wise and healing women of the woods.

The zoological name for the chimpanzee, our closest genetic relative among the primates, is *Pan troglodytes*, which literally means "Pan the cave-dweller." Here myth, natural history, and science converge to remind us that the anthropoid apes and human beings share a common ancestor, who was a hairy hominid. It was only about twelve thousand years ago that hunters gradually became herders and gatherers became gardeners and farmers. Humans became the primate species who domesticated themselves. Before that, for hundreds of thousands of years— perhaps a couple of million—wild hairy men and women roamed the savannas and forests, living in symbiotic mutuality with animals. The wild humans, Cro-Magnons and Neanderthals, had a social order, a sustainable lifestyle, an instinctual mystical connectedness with living nature, communication, art, ritual, and shamanistic practices. All these are qualities and functions that have degenerated or atrophied completely as we have moved first into villages and then cities and, finally, industrial nation-states.

Some believe that a line of anthropoid apes or large protohominids may have survived in remote corners of the planet, keeping themselves in isolation from the encroachments of civilization. This is the being the Himalayan natives call the Yeti and the Indians of the Pacific Northwest call Sasquatch, or Big Foot. I once dreamed I was a Big Foot: a large, lumbering hairy creature of great strength and agility, but shy and not at all aggressive. I felt secure in the knowledge of our long survival and our separateness from "civilization." I liked this dream much better than the one where I was a two-legged ape in a cage, an image of wildness neurotically domesticated.

In Celtic mythology, the deity that is the Pan-like master of animals is called Cernunnos, the Horned God or Lord of the Stags. Whereas Pan is the god of goat-shamans (satyrs), Cernunnos is more closely identified with the deer. He is shown on the silver Gundestrup cauldron, found in Denmark and dating from the first century B.C.E., with magnificent, multipronged deer antlers on his head, emblems of his visionary shamanic gifts, sitting in a lotus posture and surrounded by animals. In his right hand he holds a Celtic torque and in his left, a huge serpent with the head of a ram. His eyes are closed as if in trance. The animals include a deer, a dog, two antelopes, two lions fighting, and a boy riding on a dolphin. This image is reminiscent of several Ice Age cave paintings,

Celtic horned god Cernunnos, in meditative absorption, surrounded by animals; from the silver Gundestrop cauldron, 100 B.C.E., Denmark. (The National Museum, Copenhagen)

Dancing deer-shaman, wearing antlered mask and animal skin. (Siberian Tungus shaman, from an 18th century engraving made by a Dutch diplomat at the Tsar's court)

particularly the one of the "dancing sorcerer" found in the Trois Frères cave, dating from 14,000 B.C.E., who also has deer antlers on his head and seems to be wearing a deerskin. Wearing an animal's skin, whether wolf, bear, or deer, is a widespread practice in shamanic societies the world over, when the shaman wishes to identify with the hunting prowess, strength, or perception of that animal. Wearing the animal pelt also serves to disguise the scent of the hunter.

Stone Age animal spirit, called "Dancing Sorcerer":
a composite of deer antlers, wolf ears, lion beard,
bear paws, and horse tail. (Paleolithic cave paint-
ing; from Les Trois Frères cave, France; 15,000 B.C.E.)

Mimir's Well

In Nordic-Germanic mythology, which is replete with nature spirits of all kinds—giants, dwarves, and elves, as well as sky gods and Earth goddesses—it is the shamanic knowledge-seeking god Odin, or Wodan, who embodies some of the qualities of the ecstatic visionary Dionysus and the all-comprehending master-sorcerer Pan. The root word *od* means something like "ecstasy" or "frenzy." The Odin mythic complex is filled with references to magical herbs and visionary mead (fermented honey beer). He is also associated with several shamanic power animals, including ravens, wolves, and bears: he is the god of the *berserker,* bearskin-wearing warriors. But the story that best expresses the kind of evolutionary remembering we have been describing is the story of Odin and Mimir's well, the Well of Remembrance.

Mimir, whose name is related to the Latin *memor,* was a wise giant who guarded the well at the foot of the great World Tree Yggdrasil. It was said that to drink from this well would give one knowledge of the beginnings and origins of things—of humans, of life, of the worlds. Odin the knowledge-seeker naturally wanted to drink from this well but knew also that he had to pay a price to do so. True knowledge is earned, through disciplined learning; it is not given away. The price the god paid was one of his eyes. He became known as the One-Eyed God and always wore a wide-brimmed slouch hat to disguise this telltale sign when he wandered among humans. When the giant Mimir, or other gods or knowledge-seeking shamans, drank mead from the well, they would see Odin's eye looking back at them according to one of the ancient songs of the Eddas.

In German translations, the term used to describe Mimir's well is *märchenreich,* "filled with stories"—a clue that to drink from the well was an experience that involved both visioning and storytelling. Stories tell us about our past, and visions tell us about our future. We know that the Odin cult of seers and poets involved the pursuit of ecstatic states of heightened consciousness, comparable to Asiatic shamanic practices that include incantations, fasting, ordeals, and hallucinogens. We also know that professional seeresses *(völvas),* who were followers of Freyja, had their own traditional methods of gaining access to past and future knowledge, using special states of consciousness and a question-and-answer format. In Celtic mythology, too, there are references to seers and poets drinking from a special magical well to obtain knowledge. Drinking a hallucinogenic beverage may release a flood of images from the personal, ancestral, and evolutionary layers of the subconscious mind and can well be represented by the metaphor of drinking from the well of memory.

What is the meaning of this image of the well? Odin the sorcerer willingly gives up one of his eyes, which sees externals, to be able to obtain clairvoyant inner vision and memory. This is the kind of perception that yogis call the "third eye" and shamans the "strong eye." The Scots people term it "second sight"; others refer to it as the "sixth sense," the sense that perceives the inner meaning of events. With this kind of vision, the shaman-sorcerer can look into the origins of things to understand the present and anticipate the future. To drink from Mimir's Well, then, is to enter into a state of consciousness of recollection, where we can remember our evolutionary origins, our relatedness to the realms of animals and plants, and our primordial nature as children of Earth.

Reunification of the Sacred and the Natural

Over the past two millennia Western civilization has increasingly developed patterns of domination based on the assumption of human superiority. The dominator pattern has involved the gradual desecration, objectification, and exploitation of all nonhuman nature. Alternative patterns of culture survived, however, among indigenous peoples, who preserved animistic belief systems and shamanic practices from the most ancient times. The current intense revival of interest in shamanism, including the intentional use of entheogenic plant sacraments, is among the hopeful signs that the split between the sacred and the natural can be healed again.[1]

As a psychologist, I have been involved in the field of consciousness studies, including altered states induced by drugs, plants, and other means, for more than thirty-five years. In the 1960s I worked at Harvard University with Timothy Leary and Richard Alpert, conducting research on the possible therapeutic applications of psychedelic drugs, such as LSD and psilocybin.[2] During the 1970s the focus of my work shifted to the exploration of nondrug methods for the transformation of consciousness, such as are found in Eastern and Western traditions of yoga, meditation, and alchemy and new psychotherapeutic methods using deep altered states. During the 1980s I came into contact with the work of Michael Harner and others, who have studied shamanic teachings and practices around the globe, involving nonordinary states of consciousness induced by drumming, hallucinogenic plants, fasting, wilderness vision questing, sweat lodges, and other practices. Realizing that there were traditions reaching into prehistoric times of the respectful use of hallucinogens for shamanic purposes, I became much more interested in plants and mushrooms that have a history of such use, rather than the newly discovered powerful drugs, the use of which often involves unknown risks. I have come to see the revival of interest in shamanism and sacred plants as part of the worldwide seeking for a renewal of the spiritual relationship with the natural world.

A recognition of the spiritual essences inherent in nature is basic to the worldview of indigenous peoples, as it was for our own ancestors in preindustrial societies. In shamanistic societies, people have always devoted considerable attention to cultivating a direct perceptual and spiritual relationship with animals, plants, and Earth itself, with all its magnificent diversity of life. Our modern materialist worldview, obsessively focused on technological progress and on the control and exploitation of what are arrogantly called "natural resources," has become more or less completely dissociated from such a spiritual awareness of nature. This split between human spirituality and nature has some roots in the ancient past, but a major source of it was the rise of mechanistic paradigms in science in the sixteenth and seventeenth centuries, as discussed in chapter 7, "Historical Roots of the Split Between Humans and Nature."

As a result of the conflict between the Christian Church and the new experimental science of Newton, Galileo, Descartes, and others, a dualistic worldview was created. On the one hand was science, which confined itself to material objects and measurable forces. Anything having to do with purpose, value, morality, subjectivity, psyche, or spirit was the domain of religion, and science stayed out of it. Inner experiences, subtle perceptions, and spiritual values were not considered amenable to scientific study and came to be regarded, therefore, as inferior forms of reality, "merely subjective," as we say. This encouraged a purely mechanistic and myopically detached attitude toward the natural world. Perception of and communication with the spiritual essences and intelligences inherent in nature have regularly been regarded with suspicion or ridiculed as misguided "enthusiasm" or "mysticism."[3]

This strange course of events has resulted in a tremendously distorted situation in the modern world, since our own experience, as well as common sense, tells us that the subjective realm of spirit and value is equally real and important as the realm of material objects. The revival of animistic, neopagan, and shamanic beliefs and practices, including the sacramental use of hallucinogenic or entheogenic plants, represents a reunification of science and spirituality, which have been divorced since the rise of mechanistic science in the seventeenth century.[4] I believe spiritual values can again become the primary motivation for scientists. It should be obvious that this direction for science would be a lot healthier for all of us, and for the planet, than science directed, as it is now, primarily toward generating weaponry and profit.

COMMON ELEMENTS OF SHAMANIC/HALLUCINOGENIC EXPERIENCE

To provide an example of an experience induced by hallucinogenic plant sacraments, I will begin by quoting from the account of an American psychologist concerning his experience with the hallucinogen ayahuasca. Here is the account:

> My initiation to ayahuasca occurred by way of an ethnobotanist friend who had spent considerable time in South America, studying with mestizo *ayahuasceros* in Peru. He had learned how to grow the two plants that enter into the medicine in Hawaii, and had prepared the brew according to the traditional recipe. The setting was a spacious house set among trees, in a rural area of Northern California. The attitude was open and respectful, treating the medicine as a sacrament. We drank the brew, which has a taste that is a strange mixture of bitterness and syrupy sweetness, in almost total darkness, with only a candle or two. We listened to the Mayan music of *Xochimoci*. I began to feel very relaxed, heavy and soft, but also as if my head were expanding.

A swaying tapestry of visions comes into view, at first mostly geometric patterns. I experience these geometric patterns with distaste verging on disgust: they seem tacky, plastic and artificial, like the décor of a shopping mall or a Las Vegas casino. As I search for the meaning of my reaction, I am shown how this is the human technocultural overlay on the natural world: I am looking at the human world! As I accept that, with some regret, I am able to see through it to the pulsating energies of the real world of underlying nature, but permeated by spiritual or astral beings and forms. There are shapes and forms of plants, animals, humans, ethereal temples and cities, flying craft and floating structures. Particular images from time to time emerge out of the continuous flux, and then are reabsorbed back into it. As the images of forms and objects recede back into the swaying fabric of visions, I realize that I am seeing them as if projected on the twisting coils of an enormous serpent, with glittering silvery and green designs on its skin. I cannot see either head or tail of the serpent, which gives me a rough sense of its size: it encompasses the entire two-story building. Curiously, the sight of this gigantic serpent does not evoke the slightest fear; on the contrary, my emotional response is one of awe and humility at the magnificence of this being and its spiritual power. Pablo Amaringo's ayahuasca paintings depict this giant serpent seen in the visions as the "mother spirit," on which other smaller spirits ride and travel; in the Amazon region they see three different serpent *mamas*—of the air, of the river, and of the forest.

Then I meet another serpent, more "normal" in its dimensions: in fact it is about the same size as me. It enters my body through my mouth and starts to slowly wind its way through my stomach and intestines over the next two or three hours. When it gets to the gut, there is some cramping, and incredibly loud sounds of gurgling and digesting are coming from my viscera. I become aware of a morphic resonance between serpent and intestines: the form of the snake is more or less a long intestinal tract, with a head and a tail end; and conversely, our gut is serpentine, with its twists and turns and its peristaltic movement. So the serpent, in winding its way through my intestinal tract is "teaching" my intestines how to be more powerful and effective—certainly a gut-level experience!

Then I see several black-skinned people, dancing as they come toward me and recede away. They are always in pairs, like twins, moving in parallel fashion: I wonder whether they represent the spirits of the two paired plants of the ayahuasca tea. Then, as I'm lying sideways on a couch, a jaguar suddenly comes into me. It is an enormous black male, and he enters my body assuming the same semi-reclining position I was in. Shortly after I notice it, the jaguar is gone. Another time, as I am on my hands and knees, I distinctly feel a bird landing on my back. I am being briefly introduced to some of the different spirits that the ayahuasca medicine can access. The realization grows within me that with practice and increased concentration, I would be able to hold the encounters with the different animal spirits for longer—and then be able to question them for divination. Don Fidel, one of the old ayahuasceros, says: "the visions come into you and heal you."

Many images of old Mayan gods and Underworld demons dancing: skeletal, crippled, diseased, skin flapping, blood dripping, pustular, bulbous, with gaping wounds and cut-off heads, toads on their necks, pierced with thorns. Their message, repeated several times, is: "*you* don't have to *do* anything." By incorporating death, decay and disease and other unimaginable horrors into their dance of transformation, a deep inner healing takes place, seemingly independent of any personal involvement on my part. I am astonished at being initiated into this ancient lineage of visionary healers.

It is late in the evening, and I am again on my hands and knees, feeling overwhelmed and exhausted by this gut-wrenching, yet soul-refreshing journey through the netherworlds of jungle, river and serpents. I lower my forehead to touch the ground: then I realize I am falling slowly through the earth, through soil and rock, moving faster and faster, and then dropping out the other side into deep space, vast in its darkness, exhilarating, filled with countless points of light, *scintillae,* luminous streaks and stars of the universe.[5]

This account exemplifies several of the common elements that can be found in the anthropological literature on shamanism and the use of hallucinogenic plants and that also tend to show up in the experiences of people taking such medicines in a religious or therapeutic context. I will simply list these features, since there is not the space here to document them extensively:

First, there is the *importance of set and setting*, or intention and context, in determining the nature of the experience. This was perhaps the key finding that came out of the psychedelic research in the 1960s.[6]

Second, the experience can be *healing on physical, psychic, and spiritual levels.* Such healing may involve the subjective experience of being first dismembered, destroyed, or "killed" and then reconstituted with a healthier, stronger "body." The experience of dismemberment is a classic feature of shamanic healing worldwide. It should be noted that the "levels" referred to are analytical concepts; during the actual experience they are not separate, but simultaneous and coexistent.

Third, the experience can provide *access to hidden or new knowledge*— this is the aspect of diagnosis, divination, intuition, or visioning. There is a sense of an intelligence associated with the plant medicine, an intelligence that communicates in an interior way to the person who has ingested the medicine. People have come to refer to these plants as "plant teachers."

Fourth, there is a feeling and perception of *access to one or more non-physical realms or worlds.* Such realms have traditionally been referred to variously as inner world, spirit world, fairy world, dreamtime, or otherworld; modern researchers may call them "nonordinary reality" or even "hyperspace." The access to the otherworld may come through a kind of journey to that world, or the spirit beings of that other world may appear in our world. In any event, the usual boundaries between the worlds seem to become more permeable.

Fifth, the experience may involve the *perception of nonmaterial, normally invisible spirit beings or entities.* Such spirits are recognized as being associated with particular animals (for example, serpent, jaguar); certain plants, trees, or fungi; certain places (for example, river, rain forest); deceased ancestors; and other nonordinary entities (for example, extraterrestrials, elves). It can include the experiences of actually becoming or identifying with that spirit (for example, the experience of becoming the jaguar). The healing and visioning is experienced as being done by or with the assistance of such spirits.

Sixth, listening to *music or singing*, or singing oneself, is an essential ingredient for productive hallucinogenic experiences. The rhythmic drive of the *icaros* (chants) in ayahuasca ceremonies, like the rhythmic pulse of the drumming in drumming journeys, gives support for moving through the flow of visions and prevents one from becoming "stuck" or "hung up" in frightening or seductive experiences.

Last, the traditional ceremonies are almost always conducted in darkness or low light; this apparently facilitates the emergence of visions. The exception is the peyote ceremony, celebrated around a fire (though at night); here participants may see visions as they stare into the fire.

Some Classic Ritual Forms of Hallucinogen Use

If we accept the idea, growing out of scientific research, that set and setting are the crucial determinants of the content of a hallucinogenic experience, then the use of these substances in a ritual setting, with careful attention paid to conscious intention, is in fact the logical as well as the traditional approach. Shamanic rituals using hallucinogens are the intentional arrangement of the set and the setting for purposes of healing and divination.

The traditional *shamanic ceremonial* form using hallucinogenic plants is a carefully structured experience, in which a small group of people (six to twelve) come together with a respectful, spiritual attitude to share a profound inner journey of healing and transformation, facilitated by these powerful catalysts. Music and/or singing is invariably a part of such rituals. There is a significant role and function of the guide, or medicine person, who conducts the ceremony. The traditional shamanic rituals involve very little or no talking among the participants, except perhaps during a preparatory phase or after the experience, to evaluate the teachings or visions received.

A second kind of ceremonial form has evolved in the Brazilian *syncretic religious* movements that use ayahuasca or *hoasca*. There are three such ayahuasca cults that have arisen in Brazil since the 1950s: Uniao de Vegetal, Santo Daime, and Barquinia. These differ considerably but share several common features: they typically comprise large groups of people, from about thirty or forty to several hundred, and they all use some kind of rhythmic chanting or singing, and some include dancing as well. Like the shamanic ceremonies, there is little or no overt discussion or description of experiences or of psychological issues.[7]

Both of these kinds of ceremonies—the shamanic and the syncretic religious—are quite different from the psychotherapy rituals involving hallucinogens, group or individual, that have arisen in the West and that represent a kind of hybrid of psychotherapeutic and shamanic ritual forms.[8] From an anthropological point of view, it is perfectly appropriate to call psychotherapy a kind of ritual—a purposive, intentional structuring of a state of consciousness. Psychoanalysis (originally called the "talking cure") and most forms of psychotherapy use verbal dialogue as the means for exploring consciousness. In recent times, more "experiential" forms have arisen that may use breathing methods, movement, bodily contact, music, or hypnotic regression to induce profoundly altered states of consciousness. The use of psychedelics or empathogens (such as MDMA) in individual or group psychotherapy can be considered in that context. Their use in structured ritualistic experiences represents a radical departure from conventional psychiatric practice with psychotropic medications, where drugs are simply given to the patient and assumed to work without the conscious participation of the patient or the doctor.[9]

I will briefly mention some of the variations on the traditional rituals using hallucinogens. In the peyote ceremonies of the Native American Church, in North America, participants sit in a circle, in a tepee, on the ground around a blazing central fire. The ceremony goes on all night and is conducted by a "road man," with the assistance of a drummer, a firekeeper, and a cedar man (for purification). A staff and a rattle are passed around, and participants sing the peyote songs, which have a rapid, rhythmic beat. The peyote ceremonies of the Huichol Indians of northern Mexico also take place around a fire, with much singing and storytelling, after the long group pilgrimage to find the rare cactus.

The ceremonies of the San Pedro cactus, in the Andean regions, are sometimes also held around a fire with singing, but occasionally the *curandero* (healer) sets up an altar on which are placed different symbolic figurines and objects, representing the light and dark spirits that one is likely to encounter. In the mushroom ceremonies *(velada)* of the Mazatec Indians of Mexico, the participants sit or lie in a very dark room with only a small candle. The healer, who may be a woman or a man, sings almost uninterruptedly throughout the night, weaving into her chants the names of Christian saints, spirit allies, and the spirits of Earth—the elements, animals, plants, the sky, the waters, and the fire.

In traditional Amazonian Indian ceremonies with ayahuasca, a small group sits in a circle in semidarkness while the initiated healers sing the songs *(icaros)* through which the healing and/or diagnosis takes place. These songs also have a fairly rapid rhythmic pulse, which keeps the flow of the experience moving along. Shamanic "sucking" methods of extracting toxic psychic residues or poisonous implants are sometimes used.[10] The ceremonies involving the African iboga plant, used by the Bwiti cult in Gabon, are also conducted around an altar with ancestral and deity images, and people sit on the floor and chant or sometimes get up to dance.

Ceremonies in North America and Europe in which I have been a participant-observer have combined certain elements from the shamanic ritual form while keeping intact the basic essentials: the structure of the circle; the dedication of sacred ritual space with the invocation of protective and teaching spirit allies; the cultivation of a respectful, spiritual attitude; the semidarkness; the use of music, singing, rattling, and drumming; and the presence of a more experienced elder or guide. Some variation of the *talking staff* or *singing staff* is often used: with this practice, which orginated among the Indians of the Pacific Northwest, only the person who has the staff sings or speaks, and there is no discussion, questioning, or analysis (as there might be in the therapeutic formats involving psychedelics).

While there are numerous other kinds of set-and-setting rituals using hallucinogens in the modern West, ranging from the casual, recreational "tripping" of a few friends to "rave" events of hundreds or thousands, combining Ecstasy (MDMA) with the continuous rhythmic pulse of "technomusic," my research has focused on the traditional and neoshamanic "medicine circles" and the kind of transformations that are undergone by participants in such circles.

Basic Features of the Worldview
Associated with Shamanic-Hallucinogenic Practices

If we inquire into the basic model of reality, the worldview or cosmology that is revealed by such hallucinogenic experiences, we find that it is essentially similar to that shared by indigenous shamanistic cultures—and radically different from the prevailing Western paradigm associated with mechanistic science. (Many features of the traditional shamanic worldview overlap to a considerable degree, however, with the most recent and growing edge theories and findings of postmodern science.) Since there is no space here to document these basic ideas or to present the evidence for them, I will merely state them, at the risk of oversimplification. I believe that if one were to question a number of long-term shamanic practitioners—both those who do and those who do not use hallucinogens—in traditional and modern societies, something like this worldview would be shared by most of them.

- The fundamental reality of the universe is a continuum, a unitive field or fabric of energy and consciousness that goes beyond time, space, and all forms and yet lies within them.
- In traditional Asian religions, this unitive field is variously referred to as Tao or Brahman. Some Native North Americans refer to it as Wakan-Tanka, the all-pervading Creator Spirit. The pre-Christian Anglo-Saxons of the British Isles called it the Wyrd.[11] In the systems language of postmodern science, it is seen as an infinitely complex system of interrelationships or a "web of life."[12]
- The world, or cosmos, is multidimensional, a spectrum of many worlds. In most shamanic traditions we have the upper, middle, and lower worlds. In some mythic-shamanic traditions we have five, seven, nine, or more worlds, often arrayed around a central tree or axis, the *axis mundi*. In esoteric and theosophical traditions we hear of seven levels of consciousness, such as the etheric, the astral, the mental, and so forth. In modern systems theory, we speak of the multiple levels of wholes and parts: clusters of galaxies, galaxies, solar systems, and planets; biosphere, ecosystems, populations, and species; societies, subcultures, organizations, tribes, and families; organisms, organ systems, cells, molecules, atoms, and subatomic particles.
- The universal unitive field, or cosmic continuum, has a basic symmetrical polarity, referred to by such names as yin and yang, light and dark, positive and negative charge, male and female, electric and magnetic, Father Sky and Mother Earth, and numerous others. These polarities can be observed and experienced at all levels of reality, from the macrocosmic to the microscopic.

- The symmetrically polarized basic continuum differentiates, at all levels, into an infinite variety of names and forms, images and objects, identities and beings. We can recognize this multiplicity at the level of galaxies, stars, and planets; in the biological diversity of plant and animal species on Earth; in the cultural diversity of human societies; and in the psychic multiplicity of our inner lives.

- Since we are part of the unified system of interdependence, just like every other being, we can never actually be outside it, as a detached, "objective" observer. Because the unified field is *energy*, however, we are energetically connected to every other form and being in the universe. And since the field is also *consciousness*, we can, as human beings, attune to, identify with, and communicate with any and every other life-form, object, or being in the universe, from the macrocosmic to the microscopic.

- It can be seen that this characterization is a restatement of the belief system of *animism*, which sees all material and biological forms as animated by life and consciousness, and of *shamanism*, which practices methods of intentionally attuning to and identifying with all kinds of forms and beings via the unifying field of consciousness that links us all.

- Whereas the so-called "higher religions" associated with literate, urban, industrial civilization tend to be monotheistic, with a single (usually male) deity, the theology of animistic-shamanistic cultures is polytheistic, with an enormous variety in the names and forms of gods and goddesses, particularized for each culture and its mythic tradition. It is not uncommon for participants in ceremonies using hallucinogenic plants to perceive or feel the presence of deities or spirits from many different cultures, including some with whom they have no prior cultural or biographical connection.

Significance of the Animistic-Shamanistic Revival in the Present World Situation

Having presented a few of the fundamental features of the animistic, indigenous worldview that is associated with the revival of interest in shamanic practices, including the use of hallucinogens or entheogens, I now want to address the question of what it means in the context of the present world situation. What does it signify that people in large numbers are returning to these ancient traditions of spiritual and healing practice in our world of multinational industrial corporations, of computers and electronic networks?

To return to my earlier argument, I am saying that the unprecedented industrial-technological assault on the biosphere we are witnessing in our time is rooted in the mechanistic science of the modern world, which deliberately divorced itself from spirituality, values, and consciousness. There exists a vast gulf in common understanding between what we regard as sacred and what we regard as natural. And yet, out of the experiences of millions of individuals in the Western world with hallucinogenic sacraments as well as other shamanic practices, we are seeing the reemergence of the ancient integrative worldview that views all of life as an interdependent web of relationships that needs to be carefully protected and preserved.

If we look at the history of the animistic-shamanistic revival, there are remarkable synchronicities (in the Jungian sense) associate with the (re-)introduction of hallucinogens into our culture. First, there is the following eerie "coincidence." In 1942, at the height of World War II, the Italian physicist Enrico Fermi, working at the University of Chicago, succeeded in triggering the first nuclear chain reaction, thereby setting the stage for the construction of the first atomic bombs. The power of these bombs exceeded existing explosives by a factor of one thousand. In 1943 the Swiss chemist Albert Hofmann, working with ergot derivatives at Sandoz Laboratories in Basel to find treatments for migraine, first accidentally absorbed a tiny amount of lysergic acid diethylamide (LSD). He then tested the drug and found it to be the most potent hallucinogenic substance ever known, exceeding mescaline, the best-known psychoactive drug at that time, by a factor of one thousand in potency. Thus, in the 1940s we saw the simultaneous development of atomic energy and a psychoactive drug that acts like an atomic explosion on the human mind, changing forever the worldview and basic life orientation of all who experience it.

As the second note in a Gurdjieffian octave of cultural transformations, the decade of the 1950s saw the introduction into the culture of several mind-expanding plant-based shamanic spiritual movements. In 1957 the American banker and mycologist Robert Gordon Wasson rediscovered the sacred mushroom ceremony of the Aztecs under the guidance of the Mazatecan *curandera* Maria Sabina. The publication of his observations in *Life* magazine triggered a surge of activity in which tens of thousands of young North Americans and Europeans started experimenting with hallucinogenic mushrooms, both in Mexico and elsewhere. In 1959 a Brazilian rubber tapper named Gabriel de Costa, having experienced the hallucinogenic potion ayahuasca, received a vision that he was to start a church in which this "tea" was the central sacrament, the Uniao de Vegetal (UDV), now probably the largest and most tightly organized of the three Brazilian ayahuasca churches. The other two—Santo Daime and Barquinia—also grew and attracted increasing numbers of followers during this period. While they remain separate from the shamanic rituals, the Brazilian ayahuasca churches maintain a respectful and spiritual attitude toward the use of the visionary plant medicines and a strong feeling of connection to their indigenous roots in shamanic healing practices. The spread of hallucinogenic mushroom use and cultivation connected the psychedelic movement to age-old animistic-shamanistic traditions.

In the 1960s experiences with consciousness-expanding drugs and plants moved out of the psychiatric clinics and laboratories and gave rise to a series of profound cultural transformations the dimensions of which have yet to be fully appreciated. In the early 1960s Timothy Leary and his associates began their research with psychedelics at Harvard University, and, in 1963, Leary, Richard Alpert, and I published *The Psychedelic Experience: A Manual Based on the Tibetan Book of the Dead*. At about the same time, in California, novelist Ken Kesey and his associates, called the Merry Pranksters, staged a series of rock concerts, called "acid tests," in which thousands of people took LSD while listening to music and watching light shows. Thus was born a revolution in collective consciousness, in which hundreds of thousands of people, perhaps millions, had one or more profound, life-changing psychedelic experiences.

Along with this transformation of collective consciousness, the 1960s saw the beginnings or the vitalization of several other sociocultural-change movements (often joined by the same people who had experienced psychedelics) with profound and lasting impact: the ecology and environmental movement (for which Rachel Carson's book *Silent Spring,* published in 1962, was a major catalyst); an upsurge of creative innovation in music, the arts, fashion, and literature; the women's liberation movement, with its "consciousness-raising" circles (for which Betty Friedan's book *The Feminine Mystique,* from 1963, was a major catalyst); the sexual revolution and increased freedom of sexual expression, brought about by the contraceptive pill; the civil rights, antidiscrimination movement, inspired by Martin Luther King; and the antiwar movement, galvanized by the televised horrors of Vietnam.

In each of these movements, which started in the United States and spread from there throughout the Western-influenced world, there was a transcending, a breaking of what were perceived as the restrictive conventions and social norms of the 1950s and earlier. This kind of transcending of conventions, the going beyond the hitherto accepted paradigms of reality and identity that we see in each of these social movements, is basically characteristic of psychedelic and hallucinogenic experiences. It is tempting to speculate whether the introduction of powerful mind-expanding agents, both drug and plant, into the culture might somehow relate, at some deeper cosmic and karmic level, to the mounting crisis in world civilization.

Certainly, it is not difficult to see the parallels in several cultural movements that seek to correct the dangerous imbalance in humanity's relationship to nature: in deep ecology and ecofeminism, which call for a respectful, egalitarian, ecocentric attitude toward the natural world; in the organic gardening and farming movements, which seek to return to traditional methods that avoid chemical fertilizers and pesticides; in the movement to increase use of herbal, nutritional, and complementary healing methods, with less reliance on high-tech interventions; and in several other philosophical, scientific, and religious movements, including bioregionalism, ecopsychology, living systems theory, creation spirituality, ecotheology, and others.[13] In these diverse movements, from many disciplines, to transform our human perceptions, attitudes, and practices in relation to Earth toward a healthier, nonexploitative, nondominating recognition of interrelatedness, the respectful use of entheogenic plant medicines in spiritual/therapeutic contexts may yet come to play a highly significant role.

Transition to an Ecological Worldview

In the late twentieth century we are living in a time of tumultuous cultural upheaval in which the dominant worldview of our time, variously called the scientific or modern or industrial, is undergoing a profound reappraisal. In this essay, I try to summarize as succinctly as possible the dimensions of the transition to an ecological worldview, whose emergence I both perceive and advocate.[1]

The global environmental crisis is serving as a catalyst for far-reaching reexaminations of basic values and assumptions in every area of human knowledge and inquiry. This offers both a challenge and an opportunity for all the disciplines to reformulate the fundamental questions and issues in each field. The theologian and ecophilosopher Thomas Berry has often said that the time has come to "re-invent the human at the species level." I take this to mean that the existing cultural paradigms cannot deal adequately with the issues we are now facing and that we need to draw on the evolutionary wisdom of the human species in its interrelationships with all other species and ecosystems. The viability of the human species and its mode of adaptation to the natural world is now called into question. Indeed, we have brought conditions on the entire biospheric life system to a dangerous impasse.

It is not necessary to belabor the well-known parameters of the ecological catastrophe we are facing, since these are well documented in such publications as the annual *State of the World* reports issued by the Worldwatch Institute. The issues and problems of environmental pollution and degradation have passed from the literature of the scientific communities into the mainstream media. Because pollution does not respect national boundaries, its proliferation lends momentum to efforts at international, even global, cooperation. Since ecosystem destruction likewise does not respect sociopolitical boundaries, we are witnessing new calls for social and environmental accountability from all levels of government and the professions, including law, business, medicine, and education.

The analysis of environmental degradation and of the need for restoration cuts across the paradigm boundaries of the traditional knowledge disciplines. Whereas older definitions of ecology spoke of the relationship of organisms to their environment, a systems approach goes beyond this dualistic conception, defining it as the study of the complex webs of interdependent relationships in ecosystems. For this reason, ecology, owing to its necessarily interdisplinary character, has been called the "subversive science."[2] The transition to an ecological way of thinking, systemic relationship thinking, truly involves revolutionary change.

A growing chorus of voices is acknowledging that the fundamental roots of the environmental disaster lie in the attitudes, values, perceptions, and basic worldview that we humans of the industrial-technological global society have come to hold. Many now understand that the worldview and associated attitudes and values of the industrial age have permitted and driven us to pursue expoitative, destructive, and wasteful applications of technology. The modern, industrial worldview was shaped by the scientific revolution of the sixteenth and seventeenth centuries and the Industrial Revolution of the eighteenth and nineteenth centuries. The outlines of an ecological worldview are being articulated in the natural sciences, the social sciences, and philosophy and religious thought. The main features of the emerging worldview are summarized and contrasted with those of the currently dominant industrial worldview in the tables included in this chapter.

I would like to briefly mention some alternative analyses of the transformation that Western society is presently undergoing. Many social thinkers state that the crucial transition taking place now is from the *industrial* era to the *information* or *electronic* era. While it is true that the advent of personal computers and electronics represents a qualitative shift in technology, with far-reaching effects on the economy, culture, and human relationships, it is, in my view, only a continuation of the mechanistic, technological mind-set. Cyberculture and "virtual reality" do not represent a real shift in values, such as is demanded by the environmental crisis.

Other social critics argue that we are moving out of the *modern* age of rationalism and positivism, which began in the eighteenth-century Enlightenment period, into a *postmodern* age of deconstructionist relativism. In the deconstructionist view, all theories and models of reality are socially and historically determined "texts" and as such are accorded equal validity. None, including the theories of science, can claim "privileged access" to truth or validity. In contrast to this view, I concur with those who believe it is possible to do more than just critique the modern view. A constructive ecological or systems postmodernism is possible, in which we can recognize consistent features of the newly emerging worldview. These features can be recognized as those that contribute to sustainability, preservation, and restoration of all life-forms and habitats on Earth, not just those of humans or of one group of humans.[3]

In the natural sciences, several new paradigm transitions can be discerned. The "mechanical philosophy" of Newton, Galileo, and Descartes, which began by devising quantitative, mechanical models of physical processes, developed in the course of three centuries into a *mechanomorphic* worldview, in which the universe is erroneously identified with the analogical models originally designed to explain it. This mechanistic worldview is giving way in many circles to an *organismic* view, which sees the universe as an evolving process, a "story" in Thomas Berry's terms. Instead of seeing life as biochemical machinery somehow derived from random molecular combinations, the new biology defines life as a self-generating *(autopoietic)*, genetically coded process adaptively coupled with the environment.

Earth, instead of an inert body of dead matter, is seen in the Gaia theory of James Lovelock and Lynn Margulis as a kind of superorganism, evolving in homeostatic reciprocal interaction between living organisms and the physicochemical environment. Some critics intially found fault with the Gaia theory for not offering any "new mechanism" and instead just changing the metaphor. This statement ignores the fact that "mechanism" is itself a metaphor. The currently accepted mechanomorphic worldview is usually not recognized as a metaphor. The psychic fixation of scientific thinking on the machine metaphor is demonstrated in even so eminent an ecologist as Paul Ehrlich, who can write a textbook with the title *The Machinery of Nature.*

SCIENTIFIC PARADIGMS

INDUSTRIAL AGE	ECOLOGICAL AGE
Mechanomorphic	Organismic
Universe as machine	Universe as process or story
Earth as inert matter	Gaia: Earth as super-organism
Life as random chemistry	Life as autopoiesis
Determinism	Indeterminacy, probability
Linear causality	Chaos: nonlinear dynamics
Atomism	Holism and systems theory

Quantum physics, with its uncertainty principle, has challenged the old deterministic model of a predictable clockwork universe. Traditional concepts of linear causality and mechanical forces acting on material objects are being superseded by chaos theory, nonlinear dynamics, and dissipative structures. The notion of chaos as the epitome of unpredictable disorder has been transformed by new mathematical approaches that yield unexpected orderliness in complex dynamical systems. The atomistic, or "billiard ball" conception of ultimate reality is giving way to a holistic view, in which reality is analyzed as a *holarchy* (nested hierarchy) of systems with complex, multilevel interactions of phenomena, from subatomic wave/particles and atoms to galactic clusters and the universe itself.

In epistemology, the older, conventional view was that of logical positivism, according to which only sense observations can be meaningful statements. Along with that view was the doctrine of operationalism, according to which the meaning of variables lies in the experimental operations. These views have given way to more open-ended approaches that recognize the possible validity of different perspectives (critical realism) and that take into account the fact that theories and models are mental constructions (constructivism). The reductive-analytic strategy of conducting scientific research, which looks for explanations "from below," has led in the conventional paradigm to a reductionist ontology, in which all the sciences are supposedly ultimately reducible to the physics of elementary particles. In the postmodern philosophy of science, the reductionist orientation is complemented by integrative, systemic perspectives, including the possibility of causation "from above."[4]

EPISTEMOLOGY

INDUSTRIAL AGE	ECOLOGICAL AGE
Logical positivism	Critical realism
Operationalism	Constructivism
Reductionism	Reduction and integration

The emerging ecological worldview calls for a very different perception of the role of the human being in the scheme of things. For thousands of years, since the beginnings of the Neolithic domestication, the human being has tended to assume a dominating and exploitative attitude toward nature. Judaeo-Christian theology has taught that humans were created in God's image and put on Earth to "subdue" and "have dominion" over the plants and animals. Heroic individualism and patrilineal property control have been our dominant value systems, and our self-appointed task has been the "conquest of nature." This anthropocentric attitude assumes that nature is an unlimited repository of resources, to be exploited for our benefit. Even the conservation movement is largely based on an ethic that assumes that natural resources should be conserved or managed for our own future uses.

In contrast, the influence of ecological concepts of co-evolution and symbiosis has led to an awareness of the evolutionary importance of protecting ecosystem integrity and preserving the diversity of species. The philosophy of deep ecology teaches biocentric or ecocentric values, in which humans are seen as part of nature, not set over or against it. The philosopher Arne Naess suggests that we have the potential for extending our sense of identity (identification) to include animals, plants, biotic communities, ecosystems, the entire Earth. The destiny of humankind is seen not in the domination and control of nature, but in the special quality of human consciousness, its unique reflectivity and tool-making creativity. Living systems of all kinds are valued intrinsically, in and for themselves—not instrumentally, as resources to be exploited, managed, or conserved.

The Role of the Human

INDUSTRIAL AGE	ECOLOGICAL AGE
Conquest of nature	Living as part of nature
Dominion, control	Co-evolution, symbiosis
Heroic individualism	Ecological consciousness
Exploitation and management	Stewardship, restoration
Anthropocentric and humanist	Biocentric or ecocentric
Nature has instrumental value	Nature has intrinsic value

In relation to the land, the Western industrial-technological worldview is fundamentally based on the notion of property and ownership. Land exists to be used and developed, for farming, herding, building, and so on. Since the beginning of the Kurgan invasions of Europe and the Mediterranean by nomadic pastoralist warrior tribes from Central Asia about six thousand years ago, the competing tribes have been fighting for territories and for the herds and slaves that went with them. Indigenous cultures, such as the Native Americans, have had a very different relationship to the land—more akin to stewardship, with a profound respect for place and the sacredness of particular sites of power. Similarly, the American ecologist Aldo Leopold spoke of a "land ethic" that would require us to learn to "think like a mountain." Today, the bioregional movement advocates a return to an appreciation of the natural (for example, watershed) boundaries of a given region, optimally with decentralized self-sufficiency. The task of the human is then to "reinhabit" the place, to really know it and dwell in it.[5]

HUMAN RELATIONSHIP TO LAND

INDUSTRIAL AGE	ECOLOGICAL AGE
Land use: farming, herding	Land ethic: thinking like a mountain
Competing for territory	Dwelling in place
Owning "real estate"	Reinhabiting the bioregion

The value systems governing human social relationships are also changing under the impact of the global transition to an ecological worldview. Feminists and ecofeminists have cogently argued that the domination of nature is inseparable from the domination of women. Under patriarchy, which has come to be the accepted social norm almost the world over, women were regarded as possessions, along with the children, the herds, and the slaves of conquered peoples. Partnership, or "gylany," is the term used by Riane Eisler to indicate the balanced male-female relationship pattern that needs to be reintroduced.[6] Value divisions based on racial or ethnic differences will increasingly give way to a new planetary culture that respects and celebrates qualitative differences. Its beginnings can already be seen in the worldwide "fusion" of diverse styles in fashion, music, cuisine, and lifestyle, facilitated by the global media networks. The position of the social ecologist Murray Bookchin argues that class domination patterns must be corrected simultaneously with the patterns of our relationship with nature.[7]

HUMAN SOCIAL RELATIONS

INDUSTRIAL AGE	ECOLOGICAL AGE
Sexism, patriarchy	Ecofeminism, partnership
Racism, ethnocentrism	Multiculturalism, diversity
Hierarchies of class and caste	Social ecology, ecojustice

Several religious and theological scholars have pointed out that in the three great monotheistic religions, God (always masculine) is a transcendent creator and lawgiver deity. In such religions there is an inseparable gulf between God and humans, whose only recourse is to obey the law and support the priesthood or Church. In the animistic religious view of primordial peoples, all of nature—animals, plants, mountains, forests, streams, landscapes—is animated by living intelligences (called "spirits"), with which both shamans and ordinary people could be in communication. The monotheistic religions altered this relationship entirely: nature, the world, was the creation of a remote and transcendent deity and was inherently corrupt, tainted by original sin, dark, nonsacred, and, finally, demonic and frightening (which fit in well with the command to dominate and conquer). By destroying pagan animism and the shamanic traditions preserved in witchcraft, Christianity drastically severed itself from the roots of a regenerative spirituality grounded in the natural world.[8] Protestantism, which, as Max Weber pointed out, furthered the development of exploitative capitalism by focusing on the value of work in the material world, completed the profanation of the natural world. In the modern atheistic, materialist worldview, there is no spiritual being anywhere, either in this life or after death, either in nature or above it—but control, use, and exploitation are still the norm.

Although their environmental record is not above reproach, the polytheistic, animistic religions that preceded Judaism and Christianity still had at least a conception of spirituality as immanent within nature. Pantheism ("everything is divine") or panentheism ("the divine is in everything") was the theology of the original Europeans and of the Jewish and Christian mystics (such as Francis of Assisi and Hildegard von Bingen) as well. The "creation spirituality" concept of the theologian Matthew Fox as well as the work of Teilhard de Chardin and Alfred North Whitehead are modern examples of theology that incorporates the insights of ecology.

THEOLOGY AND RELIGION

INDUSTRIAL AGE	ECOLOGICAL AGE
Nature as background	Animism
Nature as demonic	Nature as sacred
Transcendent divinity	Immanent divinity
Creation as fallen, corrupt	Creation spirituality
Monotheism, atheism	Polytheism, panentheism

EDUCATION AND RESEARCH

INDUSTRIAL AGE	ECOLOGICAL AGE
Specialized disciplines	Integrative disciplines
"Value-free knowledge" pursued	Unconscious values explicated
Science/humanities split	Unified worldview

In education and research we have come to see, in the modern era, the ever narrower specialization of disciplines and an unbridgeable gap between the "two cultures" of science and the humanities. The mechanistic paradigm of classical physics, which has been adopted by the life sciences and the social sciences, assumes that its method attains to "objective" knowledge, to "facts" free of values. Beginning with the work of Thomas Kuhn in the 1960s, historians and philosophers of science have long since established that the pursuit of scientific knowledge is anything but free of values or metaphysical assumptions. In actuality, the underlying value systems presupposed by science are congruent with the domination and exploitation agenda of the patriarchal mind-set. Prediction and control are the stated objectives of research, and the results of research are fed into technology for "man's benefit" (read: profit and capital accumulation) and "security" (read: militarism). In the emerging ecological worldview, with ecology instead of physics as the model discipline, education and the pursuit of knowledge would of necessity be multidisciplinary and integrative. Unconscious values and hidden agendas will need to be brought into the light of critical review. Global citizens of a unified world in catastrophic transition cannot afford to hang on to the fragmented paradigms of European industrial culture.

In the political arena, the industrial-technological culture has crystallized around the nation-state. During the modern era, the concept of nation-state sovereignty and centralized authority emerged out of the monarchic, feudal, and ecclesiastical forms of the medieval period. Patriarchal power groups, organized to protect patrilineal property and ownership "rights," imposed a gradually increasing stranglehold of industrial and militaristic cultural uniformity on their subject populations. The propagandistic use of mass-psychological processes of scapegoating and enemy-making culminated in the fascist, genocidal, totalitarian holocausts that European "civilization" inflicted upon the world in the twentieth century. In departing from these suicidal and ecocidal patterns, the kinds of political forms that are emerging are various forms of federations and confederations, a decentralization of the nation-state into pluralistic societies of ethnic and national groupings, increased reliance on self-sufficient and self-maintaining bioregions, and a shift of values and priorities away from military to human and environmental concerns.

POLITICAL SYSTEMS

INDUSTRIAL AGE	ECOLOGICAL AGE
Nation-state sovereignty	Multinational federations
Centralized national authority	Decentralized bioregions
Patriarchal oligarchies	Egalitarian democracies
Cultural homogeneity	Pluralistic societies
National security focus	Humans and environment focus
Militarism	Commitment to nonviolence

ECONOMIC SYSTEMS

INDUSTRIAL AGE	ECOLOGICAL AGE
Multinational corporations	Community-based economies
Assume scarcity	Assume interdependence
Competition	Cooperation and competition
Limitless economic growth	Limits to growth
Economic "development"	Steady state, sustainability
No accounting of nature	Economics based on ecology

The prevailing economic systems, both capitalist and socialist, are based on the illusion that unlimited material progress can be achieved by further industrialization. Natural capital is relegated to "externalities" in current accounting, and pollution, toxic waste, and adverse health impacts are counted as contributing to "growth" if money is spent on them. Under the impact of an avalanche of feedback that humans are exceeding the carrying capacity (the "limits to growth") of the biosphere, while destroying habitats and causing the extinction of countless species of plants and animals whose existence is vital to the regenerative capacity of the biosphere, these assumptions and policies will need to be revised in favor of cooperative, community-based, steady-state, sustainable economies that recognize the prime and ultimate dependence of all human economic activity as well as all nonhuman life-forms on the integrity of the biosphere and the local ecosystems.[9]

TECHNOLOGY

INDUSTRIAL AGE	ECOLOGICAL AGE
Addiction to fossil fuels	Reliance on renewables
Profit-driven technologies	Appropriate technologies
Waste overload	Recycling, reusing
Exploitation, consumerism	Protect and restore ecosystems

Profit-driven technologies that pollute the global elemental energy cycles and generate catastrophic amounts of toxic and nonrecyclable wastes will have to be replaced by appropriate technologies, also called "soft energy paths" by Amory Lovins, and a massive conversion of the entire industrial infrastructure to reusable and recyclable materials and products.[10] Technology, instead of being used to feed a runaway cycle of exploitation and consumerism ("more and more goods for more and more people"), will need to be redirected toward the protection and restoration of damaged ecosystems. In agriculture in the industrialized nations, excessive reliance on chemical fertilizers and pesticides, combined with monoculture using artificially produced hybrids has led to disastrous loss of topsoil, genetic erosion, and decreasing yields for increasing populations. The way out of this dilemma, as propounded by the organic farming movement and such thinkers as Wes Jackson and Wendell Berry, is to return to traditional, small- and medium-scale farming methods that use crop rotation and biological methods of pest control and achieve thereby a truly sustainable agriculture.[11]

AGRICULTURE

INDUSTRIAL AGE	ECOLOGICAL AGE
Monoculture farming	Poly- and permaculture
Agribusiness, factory farms	Community and family farms
Chemical fertilizers and pesticides	Biological pest control
Vulnerable high-yield hybrids	Preservation of genetic diversity

In reflecting on the ecological worldview outlined here, it would appear that there is actually a remarkable degree of congruence and agreement, if not consensus, even among people working in quite different areas. The disastrous features of our present policies and practices seem to flow from a few widely shared basic assumptions and value systems. These assumptions and values have no inherent staying power: they are cultural, not biological givens. The alternate attitudes and values now being advocated in many circles are unconventional but not unnatural. Indeed, they seem to resonate to the most ancient human longings for exuberant life, freedom to grow, the recognition of spirit, the appreciation of differences, the delight in creativity. The pathways into the ecological age have been and are being convincingly articulated by many pioneers. It remains for us to muster the personal and political will to walk these paths.

If a cultural transition to an ecological worldview does take place somewhat as outlined, it may be that the long-range vision of the theologian Thomas Berry is also on target. Looking at an evolutionary timescale, Berry has proposed that we are coming to the end of the Cenozoic (the age of mammals and flowering plants), which began sixty-five million years ago, and moving into an Ecozoic era.[12] According to Berry, we will then realize that we live in a world that is a "communion of subjects," not just a "collection of objects." In such a world, humans will be able to find their rightful place not as rulers, but as participants in the integral and interdependent community of all life.

The Place and the Story

Ecopsychology and bioregionalism are two fields of the emerging new eco-logical worldview. Both are concerned with revisioning our understanding of human identity in relationship to place, to ecosystem, and to nature. Tra-ditional people had a much closer relationship to place. We need to learn to understand ourselves in relationship to a place, and to the story of that place.[1]

Ecopsychology may be defined as the expansion and re-envisioning of psychology to take the ecological context of human life into account.[2] It is *not* a variation of environmental psychology, which deals mostly with the impact of institutional environments on psychological states. It offers a critique of all existing schools of psychology—including the psychodynamic, object relations, cognitive, behaviorist, humanistic, and transpersonal—for focusing their research solely on the intrapsychic, interpersonal, and social dimensions of human life and ignoring the ecological foundation. The most basic facts of our existence on this Earth—that we live in these particular kinds of ecosystems, in biotic communities with these species of animals and plants, in these par-ticular kinds of geographical and climatological surroundings—appears to be irrelevant to our psychology and yet our personal experience as well as common sense contradict this self-imposed limitation.

In that regard, ecopsychology parallels similar re-envisionings taking place in other knowledge disciplines: philosophy is being challenged by environmental ethics and deep ecology, economics by green or ecological economics, religion and theology by the concept of creation spirituality and other ecotheological formulations, and sociology and history by new ecological perspectives.[3–6] All of these foundational revisions may be seen as part of an emerging ecological or systems worldview, a worldview that can also be called ecological postmodernism.[7]

Underlying these fundamental revisions of our systems of knowledge is a major paradigm shift in the natural sciences, a shift from physics to ecology and evolution as the foundational or model science.[8] Ecology has been called the "subversive science" because it deals with systemic interrelationships and is therefore, in essence, transdisciplinary and subversive of academic specialization. Ecological concepts are ideally suited for helping the knowledge disciplines transcend their specialized blinders to consider the wider contexts of ecosystem and Gaia.

Bioregionalism is one of four sociophilosophical movements that could be characterized as "radical ecology," the other three being deep ecology, ecofeminism, and social ecology (with socialist ecology a possible fifth). These movements are radical, and even revolutionary, in that they are not limited to advocating conservation or antipollution legislation. They challenge the very foundations of the modernist industrial worldview, its most cherished value systems and deeply engrained attitudes and habits of thought. The focus of the deep ecology critique is what is called "anthropocentrism," but it can more accurately be described as a humanist superiority complex. The ecofeminist diagnosis of our ecocultural malaise is that it is based on patriarchal "androcentrism" rather than anthropocentrism. The social ecology movement critiques all social structures of hierarchy and domination, whether toward ethnic groups, the poor, women, or nature. For socialist ecologists, the crucial diagnosis is via the analysis of capitalist class oppression, which includes the domination and exploitation of nature.[9]

Bioregionalism offers a radical critique of the conventional approach to *place,* revolving around the idea of ownership of land and the attendant right to develop and exploit. Political control over the ecology and economy of local regions rests with the nation-state government, which is generally allied with and supportive of the interests of large industrial corporations. The bioregional approach advocates replacing the man-made, historically arbitrary political boundaries of nations, states, and counties. It suggests, instead, using natural ecosystem features, such as watersheds, mountain ranges, and entire biotic communities (human and nonhuman) as the defining features of a given region. The primary values, from a bioregional perspective, are not "property rights" and "development" but preservation of the integrity of the regional ecosystem and maximization of economic self-sufficiency within the region. Political control would thus rest with the community of people actually living in the region: this is the concept of "reinhabitation."[10]

The bioregional movement, like the other radical ecology movements, contains within it a challenge to change our perception and understanding of the human role in the natural world. It encourages us to become aware of native plants and animals in the region where we live so that we can feel and experience our actual place in the natural order. It encourages us to learn about the historical and present-day indigenous peoples of that region and how they sustained themselves before the arrival of European culture with its industry and technology. It thus forges an explicit connection and solidarity with existing native peoples, their cultures, and their struggle for autonomy. These cultures are clearly bioregional in their explicit sense of rootedness in the land and have been gently offering a radical critique of Eurocentric arrogance ever since the time of Columbus and the Conquest.[11]

Bioregionalism also involves something like a consciousness-raising practice or, we might say, an ecopsychological practice. Such a practice can affect our sense of identity, our self-image. By creating bioregional maps that depict watersheds, rivers, forests, and mountain ranges, rather than roads and cities, we come to a renewed appreciation of the ecological complexity of the place we inhabit. There is a bioregional self-questionnaire that tests our knowledge of the place where we live. My favorite consciousness-expanding question on it is: "Could you direct someone to the house you live in without using any human-made buildings or signs?" When I first attempted to do this, it led me to notice much more of the landscape through which I was driving mindlessly every day.

Another principal question is whether you can identify the four directions in the place where you live or where your are. This is reminiscent of the Native American practice (also found in other parts of the world) of beginning every meeting, whether a political council or a religious ceremony, with a prayer in the four directions. What better way to come into communion with the natural energies and features of a place or region than by tuning in to the four directions? Here in California, for example, it is difficult to escape the dominant presence of the Pacific Ocean in the west, even when you can't see it.

The native practice of aligning ourselves with the four directions coincides with the bioregional practice of attaining a deeper sense of the place. It reminds us of ancient, pre-Christian European concepts of the "spirit of place," the genius loci. Surely the spirit of a place is constituted by the whole system of interdependent relations in the bioregion. The biotic community is also a spiritual community—if we approach it from the intuitive, perceptual, subjective standpoint and do not confine our observations to those that can be quantified.

In doing so, we are back in the realm of polytheistic animism, a worldview in which all of nature is respected as imbued with conscious intelligence. This was the religion of our ancestors in the ancient world, before the ascendancy of transcendental monotheism. William Blake described the suppression of polytheistic animism as follows, in his visionary prose poem *The Marriage of Heaven and Hell:*

> The ancient Poets animated all sensible objects with Gods and Geniuses, calling them by the names and adorning them with the properties of woods, rivers, mountains, lakes, cities, nations, and whatever their enlarged and numerous senses could perceive. And particularly they studied the genius of each city & country, placing it under its mental deity. Till a system was formed, which some took advantage of & enslaved the vulgar by attempting to realize or abstract mental deities from their objects: thus began Priesthood. Choosing forms of worship from poetic tales. And at length they pronounced that the Gods had ordered such things.[12]

Here we have a convergence of the ancient and indigenous spirit of place with ecological consciousness and a bioregional orientation. We also see how understanding the story of our religious beliefs can help us gain fresh perspective.

We can now use the combined perspectives of bioregionalism and ecopsychology to come to a deeper understanding of the nature and meaning of "place." What is a place, and how does it relate to and differ from the concept of space? Moreover, since time and space are the fundamental organizing categories of our knowledge of the external world, how does time relate to space and to place?

The koan or question I would like to pose is: *What is related to time the way place is related to space?*

AS SPACE IS TO PLACE

A place is a localized, particular region, whereas space is abstract and infinite. A place can be defined and delimited, mapped and described. In the unfathomable vastness of macrocosmic space, a galaxy, a solar system, a planet are localized, identifiable places. On the continental landmasses of planet Earth, we can map and identify local places of different size: deserts, mountains, lakes, plains, forests, cities, houses, trees, rocks, caves (which open into interior space). Speaking geographically or topographically, a place always has *boundaries*. They may be very definite or fuzzy and indistinct; certain boundary regions or borderlands are themselves identifiable places, often of special significance. A key aspect of the bioregional agenda is to change the way we define the boundaries of a place.

Places always have a certain *size* or *extension*. A place of particular extent always forms the background for the Cartesian *res extensa*, the "extended substance." Surveyors and cartographers measure and map the size of the place with all its details and features. The size of a place may be large, medium, or small. From the perspective of size, we could say that the bioregion is intermediate between the global and the local. If we are to think globally and act locally, should we perhaps learn to feel bioregionally?

There is another kind of space that is less abstract, more psychological or psychic. For example, an individual may say to a partner, "I need more space in this relationship." Or we may feel our "personal space" intruded upon in a crowded elevator. There is also the psychological notion of an "altered state of consciousness," in which one may experience traveling, or being "on a trip" or a journey, traversing a kind of inner landscape. In traditional cultures such experiences are referred to as a "shamanic journey" or an "otherworld journey," which clearly implies that consciousness is regarded as analogous to some kind of terrain or territory. In this interior world, the space of our subjective experience, there are also four directions in which attention can move: forward and backward, left and right. One may contrast these with the four directions of objective space: east, south, west, and north. The two coordinate systems, inner and outer, change in relationship to each other as our orientation changes.

A particular place always has *internal divisions* and structural features in which it resembles and differs from other places in a variety of ways. These internal features and divisions can also be mapped, described, and named. The exception to the principle of internal divisions occurs with the oceans (and, to some extent, certain deserts). The vast, undifferentiated expanse of oceans is often disorienting to land dwellers such as humans, precisely because we cannot find landmarks or other distinctive structural features. Scientists can map the ocean floor, with its ridges and troughs, and sailors can learn to navigate by the stars and instruments to traverse the ocean. But "being at sea" is similar to being lost, and even the sailor has to "come home from the sea."

Most places, at least on land, also have a *center:* this is the fulcrum or hub around which the events and activities in the place organize themselves. Ayers Rock is dead in the center of Australia, and the Black Hills of South Dakota are exactly in the middle of North America. Both places have an undeniable magnetic power, and the native people have long regarded them as sacred and performed rituals there. Towns and cities have centers, often marked by a plaza or other public structure, where people tend to congregate for trade and entertainment. In older towns the center of community life is usually marked by a church, cathedral, temple, or shrine. In a dwelling, the center of family life is usually the living room, perhaps with a fireplace; in some dwellings it might be the kitchen and eating area.

A place may also be said to have *inhabitants,* dwellers, those who are "from there." Both human and nonhuman dwellers make up the community of that place, whether or not the human beings recognize it. Inhabitants might be natives (humans, plants, animals) or immigrants or invaders. Part of the bioregional agenda is to raise consciousness about plants and animals that are native and therefore sustainably adapted to the regional environment. With this comes the recognition that non-native plants and animals can sometimes be invasive and destructive to the ecosystem. It might be thought that this approach translates to anti-immigrant policies at the human political level. But it is just the opposite. In the Americas, white Europeans and their descendants were the immigrants and invaders, and it is they who have had devastating effects on the land and native peoples. The bioregional philosophy advocates that we should learn from the surviving native people in a given bioregion how to live sustainably and in balance in that area. This is the project of *reinhabitation:* learning the *habits* of living that will enable us to survive sustainably in the *habitat.*

Places have *names.* This allows us to talk about them and to talk about the spirits of that place and about our own relatedness to that named place. In ancient times, the name of a place was related to the spirit of that place, the genius loci. As Blake pointed out, our ancestors associated spirits, gods, and goddesses with particular places, such as "woods, rivers, mountains, lakes, cities, nations." Indeed, the whole planet Earth was the home of the goddess named Gaia or Gaea, from which our words "geology" and "geography" are derived. The Sun, the Moon, and the planets each were given the names of gods and goddesses.

In indigenous societies, such as the First Americans and the Australian Aborigines, great importance attaches to the relatedness of a person to a particular named place. Such a person might introduce him- or herself by saying: "I am from this place, and my father's family comes from these mountains, and my mother's from this river." It is only after describing in some detail their relationship to a certain place, a land, that indigenous people can proceed with the business at hand. In Euro-American society, we are much more likely to introduce ourselves and friends by saying what we "do," our profession, accomplishments, and the like. We don't know where we are from very often. Even if we own a house somewhere, we might not really be "inhabiting" that place with consciousness or feel at home and rooted there. The Indo-European tribes have always been nomads, wanderers, emigrants, and invaders. They invaded Europe, conquering and dominating the aboriginal civilization known as Old Europe thousands of years before they set sail for the so-called New World. It has been aptly said that as the Euro-American descendants of the European invaders and colonizers begin to understand the true story of what happened, perhaps the time for the real discovery of America has come.

So Time Is to Story

Time, like space, is an abstraction of the philosophers and scientists. If we want to localize and identify a particular segment of time, we do so by *telling a story.* "Once upon a time" begins the fairy tale. "What happened here before, what took place here?" we ask when we want to find out about a place. "What's your story?" we ask when we want to get to know someone. Or we might say, metaphorically, "Where are you coming from with that attitude, or that point of view?" Just as time and space are really a continuum, rather than separate categories, so place and story are intimately and mutually related. Wallace Stegner, that great interpreter of the American West, has written: "No place is a place until things that have happened in it are remembered in history, ballads, yarns, legends or monuments."[13]

Thus we study the history and mythology of our ancestors, our people and the places they inhabited, and what happened there to understand how we have become who we are. Biologists study the evolution of species, the story of life on this planet, how species have adapted to changing environments and habitats. Cosmologists now speak of the "universe story," the story of cosmic evolution starting with the "Big Bang" or the "Primordial Flaring Forth."[14] As every place is defined by its boundaries, *every story is bounded* by its beginning and ending. Every life story is bounded by a birthing and a dying. Creation myths start with "in the beginning" and end with eschatological visions of the end times.

Just as every place has a certain size or extension that can be measured and mapped, so does every story, every temporal process, every developmental sequence have a certain *extended duration* that can be measured and recorded using clocks and chronographs. Time on planet Earth is measured by reference to the orbit of Earth around the Sun and by the rotation of Earth itself, in other words, by the movements of planetary bodies through space. Some people and cultures have conceptions of time as a cyclical, recurring process, probably based on their perception of the rotations of planets and the recurrence of seasons. Others, impressed by such irreversible events as birthing and dying, have thought of time as a linear vector, like a stream, moving ineluctably in one direction only. When Heraclitus said, "We can step into the same river," he was speaking about a place with boundaries; when he added "it is always different water flowing past," he was describing the irreversible stream of temporal process.

There is also a psychic experience of time, just as there is psychic space. In altered states of consciousness, such as dreams and visions, time can seem to be shortened or lengthened or seemingly bypassed altogether. Everyone knows that when we are excited and stimulated time passes quickly; when we are bored or burdened, it crawls at a snail's pace. In near-death and other extreme situations, people may have the experience of being suspended outside time, of having ample time to make complex decisions, even though only seconds may have elapsed in clock time. In the inner worlds of dreaming and shamanic out-of-body journeys, time is different: we can travel instantaneously across the globe, as well as backward and forward in time, on the wings of thought and desire.

Like places, stories, too, have *internal divisions*, structural features and parts. Every developmental sequence, for example, in the growth and maturation of animals and plants, has its definite stages. The grand universe story contains nested within it innumerable other stories: the story of the galaxy, the story of the solar system, the story of planet Earth, the story of life on Earth, the story of animal and human life, the story of human culture. Continuing the lineage, we then come to the story of our ethnic group, the story of our ancestors and family, and our personal story. This personal story, too, has its subdivisions: the story of my childhood, youth, work, relationships, children, and so forth. Every story line or narrative has endless permutations of plot and subplot. Every cyclic process, too, has its crests and troughs: the seasonal cycle, the sleep and wakefulness cycle, hormonal cycles, the swings of mood between elation and depression, and many others.

And stories have *centers,* the core issue or central theme around which the whole story is organized. One central theme in a person's life story is often the midlife crisis or transition. The central theme in the Darwinian story of evolution is the principle of *natural selection*. When bioregionalists and deep ecologists advocate abandoning a homocentric perspective, where everything is seen from our hopelessly muddled and arrogant human perspective, they advocate an ecocentric (ecosystem-centered) or biocentric (life-centered) perspective instead. Of course, in one sense, we are always and inevitably looking at life and the world from the human-centered perspective—just as dogs have a canocentric and cows a bovicentric point of view. Perhaps this perspective need not remain as fixed as we think. Using empathy and identification, we can perhaps learn to transcend our homocentric prejudice and understand the life story of another animal from the inside. Certainly, this is what numerous myths and legends of native peoples seem to suggest; in ancient times humans and animals could understand each other's language and maybe even marry each other on occasion.

As a place has its *inhabitants,* so does a story have its characters, actors, heroes and antagonists, role-players, and support crew. They are the agents in the dramatic action, performing the story or play as scripted by the laws of nature, the genetic code, the cultural tradition, family upbringing, karmic predispositions, traits of character and temperament, our thoughts and our intentions. According to Rupert Sheldrake's theory of morphogenesis, the laws of nature are really more like *habits* that have developed over time than they are abstract principles existing in a timeless dimension.[15] The forms of the cosmos and nature develop the way they do by resonant similarity to previous forms. Thus, organisms of different species inhabit the niches and habitats for which their ancestors have developed the habits of adaptation. The ecological crisis shows us that the human species has learned some extremely maladaptive and destructive habits in relation to the natural environment. The bioregional vision is that humans need to humbly learn *reinhabitation*—dwelling in a place in a balanced way, with respect for the stories of the other inhabitants.

Places have *names,* and so do stories. Indeed, the name of a place is inextricably connected to the story of "what took place there." We think of a place, say, Egypt or Rome, and myriad images crowd our minds—the images of the history and peoples of those places. The life story of an animal or a plant cannot be told or even imagined separately from the place it inhabits. In the life story of humans, too, biography and geography are intimately interwoven. The story of a city dweller is different in spirit from that of a country dweller. In medieval times, the difference was thought to be so significant that Church-dominated city dwellers asserted that country dwellers, *pagani* or heathens, had no religion. For indigenous people, the name of the place often *is* the story, as in these lines from a poem by Kim Stafford called "There Are No Names But Stories."[16]

> *When the anthropologist asked the Kwakiutl*
> *for a map of their coast, they told him*
> *stories: Here? Salmon gather. Here?*
> *Sea otter camps. Here seal sleep.*
> *Here we say body covered with mouths.*
>
> *How can a place have a name? A man,*
> *a woman may have a name, but they die.*
> *We are a story until we die.*
> *Then our names are very dangerous.*
> *A place is a story happening many times.*

Just as particular places each had a deity or genius associated with it, so did the divisions of time. The Babylonian calendar, which the West has inherited, invented the weekly cycle of seven days, each associated with the deity of one of the planets (for example, Saturday with Saturn, Monday with Moon). The ancient science of astrology was based on the view that the spirit of the time and place of a person's birth can be determined by the pattern of the planetary positions at that moment. The rising or culminating of a given planet at the time of birth symbolically indicated something of that person's character and spirit. For instance, a person born when the planet Mars was rising might have a "martial" temperament; those born when Saturn was prominent were said to have a disposition to melancholia. During a given era, a whole society may be permeated by a certain mood or feeling or "spirit of the time," the zeitgeist.

Every person's life story begins at a certain moment in time in a particular place, and it ends at a certain time, also in a particular place. In the worldview and mythologies of many cultures, the life story is thought of as a journey to and through a series of places. It might be a hero's journey of transformation, or the mystical path to enlightenment, or an exploration of hidden worlds, or the quest for vision in the wilderness.

The very word "destiny" betrays its metaphoric kinship with the destination of the journey of our life. Ancient traditions tell us that as we come closer to the end of our life, we begin to gather the wisdom of old age, the understanding that comes from having dwelled fully in those places. As T. S. Eliot wrote,

> *We shall not cease from exploration*
> *And the end of all our exploring*
> *Will be to arrive where we started*
> *And know the place for the first time.*[17]

Epilogue

John Seed

*Cofounder of the Rainforest Information Centre, Australia,
and coauthor of* Thinking Like a Mountain

IN THE TWELFTH CENTURY the Abbess Hildegard von Bingen prophesied: "Now in the people that were meant to be green there is no more life of any kind. There is only shriveled barrenness. The winds are burdened with the utterly awful stink of evil, selfish goings-on. Thunderstorms menace. The air belches out the filthy uncleanliness of the peoples. The earth should not be injured! The earth must not be destroyed!"[1]

In 1996 the Swiss-based World Conservation Union (IUCN), in collaboration with over six hundred scientists, found that 25 percent of mammal and amphibian species, 11 percent of birds, 20 percent of reptiles, and 34 percent of fish species studied so far are threatened with extinction.

In May 1998 the Worldwatch Institute announced that world extinction rates for mammals, fish, birds, amphibians and reptiles were one hundred to one thousand times greater than normal and rising sharply. Today, one in four vertebrates is endangered and nearly half of the world's 233 primate species are now threatened.

In October 1998 World Wide Fund for Nature reported on the world's resource binge over the past three decades, during which it is estimated that a third of the world's natural resources have been consumed.

How are we to understand our predicament? Is humankind really going to extinguish itself—and so much else—for want of a mote of understanding? Where are we to find the roots of our malady, the key to our   helplessness?

According to a Sufi tale, the wise fool Nasrudin was once on his hands and knees, searching in a pool of light beneath a street lamp when a friend came by and asked what he was doing. Nasrudin said that he had lost his key and so the friend joined him in his search. After a while the friend said, "We've looked everywhere, are you sure that this is where you lost your key?"

"Actually, I lost it over there," Nasrudin replied, pointing in another direction. But over there it's too dark to see a thing."

Ecophilosopher Theodore Roszak, in the foreword to this volume, muses on how "cultures keep secrets; they illuminate some things and suppress others." He points to the mainstream exclusion of the natural environment from psychological theory.

How can we be so stupid? Are we suffering from some spiritual or psychological disease? In this volume Ralph Metzner has searched among our individual distresses for clues to our collective distress that now, wedded to awesome technology, threatens us with oblivion. He rummages among the diagnostic categories—autism, dissociation, addiction—in search of a key to our planetary healing.

Metzner stays resolutely in this realm of psychological darkness, restlessly searching. He is not afraid of dark and secret and forbidden places. He walks out of the reassuring light of civilization, past the outposts where societies' brutal watchdogs piss their warnings, and into the darkness, searching for the key.

Where shall we find the key? Will it be in the smiting of the earth goddess by the sky gods? Or in the shadows of our more recent history? Or with Goethe and Hildegard von Bingen, alchemists and the other traditions obscured in the shadows cast by the flames of enlightenment, burning with the faggots and the witches?

Perhaps the ancient shamanic, pagan, animistic roots, so brutally severed in humankind's recent history, may still have life enough to graft our spirits on to them and through them, to the living Earth. Perhaps unearthing these roots may reveal a lifeline back to the source from which we have strayed and without which our continued existence will not be supported.

The spry old shaman conjures the ancient deities forth from his

European tribes and also from the Americas, from Africa, from Asia, as if beseeching them to forgive the insults, to return into our lives and awaken us from the vicious and deadly dream of human superiority and separation.

We remember this man.

Thirty-five years ago, he coauthored *The Psychedelic Experience* with Timothy Leary and Richard Alpert.

Allen Ginsberg says, "It would be natural (in fact déjà vu) that the very technology stereotyping our consciousness and desensitizing our perceptions should throw up it's own antidote, an antidote synthetic synchronous with mythic tribal soma and peyote."[2]

They guided a generation through death and darkness and a rebirth into love of nature. Now, Timothy is gloriously dead, Richard is Ram Dass and, wedded to an ancient spiritual tradition, has found some answers. Ralph visits the descendants of the Maya in Chiapas, drinking their sacramental potions, lamenting for a vision, asking questions.

Thirty-five years later and Metzner continues to claim that the emperor wears no clothing. He continues to speak for the primal peoples and primal nature and the primal sacraments that may free us yet to participate in humility with Earth again.

Nasrudin reminds us that we continue searching in the foolish pool of light only because the dark is so scary. He points out that it was not so long ago that astronomers were burnt at the stake for staring too hard at the darkness and daring to suggest that we were not at the center of the universe.

And more recently, that Leary became Public Enemy Number One for maintaining, even unto his death, that "DNA did not work for fifty million years to produce a brain with all those receptor sites to have the government come along and say they're illegal—you can't activate those circuits of the brain."[3]

And they say, "Who's Moloch? Never heard of him"
as out in the dark Moloch belches
and grows redder and redder
and fatter and fatter
as he eats the children.[4]
Who dares to leave the pool of light?

Notes

Chapter 1: The True, Original First World

1. A version of this article was first published under the title "Where Is the First World?" in *Resurgence*, no. 172 (Sept./Oct. 1955). It was also published in the *Sun* no. 240 (Dec. 1955), as "The True, Original First World" and in *Yearbook for Ethnomedicine and the Study of Consciousness*, edited by Christian Rätsch and John Baker (Berlin: VWB-Verlag, 1955: 231–44).

2. For information about the Botanical Preservation Corps and their seminar programs, write to BPC, P.O. Box 1368, Sebastopol, CA 95473.

3. Dunlap, Riley, and Angela Mertig, eds. *American Environmentalism: The U.S. Environmental Movement 1970–1990.*

4. The evidence for this awareness is regularly published by the Worldwatch Institute in Washington, D.C., in the form of their annual *State of the World* reports, edited and produced by Lester Brown and his team of researchers.

5. Jerry Mander and Edward Goldsmith, eds. *The Case Against the Global Economy.*

6. Alan Thein Durning. *Guardians of the Land: Indigenous Peoples and the Health of the Earth.* Durning writes that indigenous people have "in their ecological knowledge . . . a map to the biological diversity of

the earth on which all life depends" (p. 7). The statement about the miner's canary is quoted by Durning from the Guajiro Indian writer Jose Barreiro.

7. Vandana Shiva. *Monocultures of the Mind: Perspectives on Biodiversity and Biotechnology.*

8. Christian Rätsch. "Their Word for World is Forest: Cultural Ecology and Religion among the Lacandon Maya Indians of South Mexico." *Yearbook for Ethnomedicine and the Study of Consciousness*, vol. 1. Berlin: VWB-Verlag, 1992: 17–32. See also C. Rätsch, *The Dictionary of Sacred and Magical Plants.*

9. Sophia Adamson, ed. *Through the Gateway of the Heart: Accounts of Experiences with MDMA and Other Empathogenic Substances.* See also R. Metzner and S. Adamson, "The Nature of the MDMA Experience and Its Role in Healing, Psychotherapy and Spiritual Practice." *ReVision* 10, no. 4 (spring, 1988): 59–72.

10. Ralph Metzner. *The Well of Remembrance: Rediscovering the Earth Wisdom Mythology of Northern Europe.*

11. John Bellamy Foster. *The Vulnerable Planet: A Short Economic History of the Environment.*

12. *Akwekon: A Journal of Indigenous Issues* 11, no. 2 (summer 1994). Special Issue "Chiapas: Challenging History." Cornell University: Akwekon Press, 1994.

Chapter 2: Gaia's Alchemy: Ruin and Renewal of the Earth

1. This essay was first published under the title "Gaia's Alchemy: Ruin and Renewal of the Elements" in *ReVision*, 9, no. 2 (1987: 41–51). Reprinted in *The Sacred Landscape*, edited by Frederick Lehrman.

2. Gregory Bateson. *Mind and Nature: A Necessary Unity*, pp. 142–43. Gregory Bateson referred to this analogical mode of thought as *abduction*, borrowing the term from C. S. Pierce. "The lateral extension of abstract compounds of description is called abduction. . . . Metaphor, dream, parable, allegory, the whole of art, the whole of science, the whole of poetry, totemism, the organization of facts in comparative anatomy . . . all are instances of abduction." Bateson comments that "the very possibility of abduction is a little uncanny" and that the phenomenon is enormously more widespread than one would suppose.

3. Carolyn Merchant. *The Death of Nature: Women, Ecology and the Scientific Revolution*, p. 104. In many ways, the Gaia hypothesis was anticipated in the organismic philosophies that flourished during the

Renaissance, in the works of Vaughan, della Porta, Campanella, Giordano Bruno, and others. Common to all was the notion that the parts of the cosmos are connected and interrelated in a living unity. As Carolyn Merchant writes, "The organic unity of the cosmos derived from its conception as living animal: a vast organism, everywhere quick and vital, its body, soul, and spirit held tightly together."

4. George Lakoff and Mark Johnson. *Metaphors We Live By.*

5. Theodore Roszak. *Person/Planet*, p. 54.

6. Robert O. Becker and Gary Selden. *The Body Electric: Electromagneticsm and the Foundation of Life.*

7. For a more detailed discussion of alchemical symbolism in relation to states of consciousness, see the chapter on alchemy in my book *Maps of Consciousness.* For a discussion of elemental symbolism in relation to the Jungian personality typology and astrology, see my book *Know Your Type.* For a modern scientific cosmology formulated in the symbolic language of the elements, see *The Universe Is a Green Dragon* by Brian Swimme.

8. Some ecofeminists have critiqued the Earthmother image as being an inappropriate basis for an ecological ethic. The argument is that the cultural associations with "mother," as the one who "takes care of problems," tends to diminish the taking of personal responsibility. See Carolyn Merchant, *Radical Ecology: The Search for a Livable World.*

9. For a more detailed discussion of the World Tree metaphor, see the chapter "Unfolding the Tree of Our Life" in my book *The Unfolding Self.* The World Tree image has also been used as a basis for ecological consciousness by the ecophilosopher Warwick Fox, in his book *Toward a Transpersonal Ecology.*

10. James Lovelock. *Healing Gaia: Practical Medicine for the Planet.*

11. James Lovelock. *GAIA: A New Look at Life on Earth*, p. 147.

12. Peter Russell. *The Global Brain.*

13. The ecophilosopher J. Baird Callicott, in an essay "Genesis and John Muir," *ReVision* 12, no. 3 (winter 1990), shows how these two instructions come from two different historical strands of the Genesis text. The famous command to "subdue" the earth and "have dominion" over the animals (Gen. 1:28) occurs in the Priestly ("P") segment of the many-layered text, which is now believed by scholars to have been composed in the fifth century B.C.E. and to be the work of the Levite priests who were seeking to consolidate their dogmatic and ritualistic control over the religious life of the people. The dominion theme is repeated in another portion of the P text, in the story of God's

covenant with Noah, after the flood (Gen. 9:13). The second set of instructions from God is found in the Yahwist ("J") text, which comes later in Genesis but is now known to be the earliest account, probably composed in the tenth century B.C.E. The J account contains no mention of the themes of dominion, subduing, or being fruitful. Instead, there is a reference to gardening and stewardship ("the Lord God took the man, and put him into the garden of Eden to till it and to keep it"—Gen. 2:15); and there is the story about naming the creatures. The Lord brought the animals "unto Adam to see what he would call them: and whatsoever Adam called every living creature, that was the name" (Gen. 2:19). See also the excellent discussion of the Judeo-Christian teachings concerning the human relationship to the environment in J. Baird Callicott's book *Earth's Insights.*

14. See my essay "Psychopathology of the Human-Nature Relationship" in this volume (chapter 6).

15. For a fascinating discussion of how an overcontrolling brain-mind can lead to psychosomatic disorders, see A. T. W. Simeons, *Man's Presumptuous Brain.*

16. I came to understand such practices as equivalent to what the alchemical philosophers called the operation of *separatio,* the conscious differentiation of aspects of experience, using discriminative awareness and heightened perception. For the alchemists, *separatio* was the necessary precursor to integration and synthesis, which they called *coniunctio.* For a superb and detailed discussion of the depth psychological meaning of *separatio* and other alchemical operations, see Edward Edinger's *Anatomy of the Psyche: Alchemical Symbolism in Psychotherapy.*

17. For a particularly graphic and detailed example of such eschatological visions, one might consider the Nordic myth of the "twilight of the gods" (the *ragnarök*). See the chapter on it in my book *The Well of Remembrance,* pp. 244–66.

18. Although this perception of humanity's war against nature shocked me with the force of a revelation, it is not, of course, original. One of the strongest modern statements I found was in Andrew B. Schmookler's remarkable book *The Parable of the Tribes,* which delineates a basic historical pattern of the abuse of power in human social relations. Its thesis is that Earth has become a place where no one (tribe) is free to choose peace as long as anyone (tribe) chooses to impose a competitive struggle for power upon all. In a chapter entitled "Man's Dominion: Power and the Degradation of the Ecosystem," Schmookler describes how "regimes based on power injure the

natural order of living systems. . . . Civilized man has exploited and wounded the natural order. . . . Man is a tyrant in the regime of nature. . . . Power corrupts through its workings between people and the other elements of the ecosystem" (pp. 245–50).

19. In the visionary writings of Hildegard von Bingen, the twelfth-century Rhineland seeress, abbess, poet, composer, scientist, and healer, there are views that are highly consonant with the theme of human beings at war with the elements and the injustice and imbalance involved in this condition. Whether Hildegard was prophesying future events or seeing trends and patterns in her time that would later become even more magnified, we cannot tell. See the chapter on Hildegard in the present volume (chapter 4).

20. For further consideration of this important topic, see the chapter "Reconciling with the Inner Enemy" in my book *The Unfolding Self*, pp. 114–35. See also John Mack, "The Enemy System" in *The Psychodynamics of International Relationships*, vol. 1: *Concepts and Theories*, edited by V. D. Volkan, D. A. Julius, and J. V. Montville, Lexington, Mass.: Lexington Books, 1990; Ofer Zur, "The Psychohistory of Warfare: The Co-Evolution of Culture, Psyche and Enemy" in *Journal of Peace Research* , 24, no. 2 (1987): 125–34; and Sam Keen, *Faces of the Enemy: Reflections of the Hostile Imagination*, San Francisco: Harper & Row, 1986.

Chapter 3: A Vision Quest Experience

1. This poem was previously published in E. Roberts and E. Amidon, eds. *Earth Prayers*, pp. 134–36.

Chapter 4: Mystical Greenness: The Visions of Hildegard von Bingen

1. An earlier version of this essay, under the title "The Mystical Symbolic Psychology of Hildegard von Bingen," was first published in *ReVision* 11, no. 2 (fall, 1988).

2. Hildegard von Bingen. *Wisse die Wege: Scivias*. German translation (from the Latin) by Maura Bockeler, p. 89. This edition features magnificent color plate reproductions of the illuminated Rupertsberger Codex. The English versions are translated by the present author.

3. Several recordings exist of Hildegard's musical works, among them, *A Feather on the Breath of God*, performed by Gothic Voices, with Emma Kirby, soprano, on the Hyperion label; *Ordo Virtutum*, performed by Sequentia, Ensemble für Musik des Mittelalters, Harmonia Mundi label; *Diadema*, performed by Vox, Erdenklang label; *Symphoniae:*

Spiritual Songs, performed by Sequentia, Harmonia Mundi label; and *Canticles of Ecstasy,* performed by Sequentia, BMG Music label.

4. *Wisse die Wege,* p. 85.

5. From a letter of Hildegard's, quoted in *Quellen des Heils,* a selection of her works in German translated by the present author, p. 84.

6. *Wisse die Wege,* p. 84.

7. John Neihardt. *Black Elk Speaks.*

8. *Illuminations of Hildegard von Bingen,* commentary by Matthew Fox, p. 32. Matthew Fox, the founder of the Center for Creation-Centered Spirituality, must be given the credit for generating a revival of public interest in the works of Hildegard. I cannot agree, however, with Fox's designation of Hildegard's theology as "creation-centered," since it seems unmistakeably Creator-centered to me—although it is, of course, creation-affirming. This volume of extracts from Hildegard's books and commentaries by Fox also contains color reproductions of some of the illuminations.

9. From a collection of Hildegard's songs privately copied. I acknowledge the cooperation of Zoë Klippert, a professional singer of medieval music who is an enthusiast of Hildegard's work, for providing me access to these poems.

10. Abbott Ildefons Herwegen, in the preface to *Wisse die Wege: Scivias,* p. 11.

11. From the *Liber Divinorum Operum* ("Book of Divine Works"), cited in *Quellen des Heils,* p. 45.

12. Matthew Fox. *Illuminations of Hildegard von Bingen,* p. 19.

13. *Wisse die Wege,* p. 133.

14. *Wisse die Wege,* p. 131.

15. *Quellen des Heils,* p. 48.

16. *Wisse die Wege,* pp. 345–50.

17. *Wisse die Wege,* pp. 346.

18. *Wisse die Wege,* pp. 349–50.

Chapter 5: The Role of Psychoactive Plant Medicines

1. This essay was originally published as "Molecular Mysticism: The Role of Psychoactive Substances in Transformations of Consciousness," in *Shaman's Drum,* no. 12 (spring, 1988): 15–21. It also appeared as part of a *Festschrift* for Albert Hofmann, in Christian Rätsch, ed., *The Gateway to Inner Space,* pp. 73–88.

2. Albert Hofmann. *LSD—My Problem Child,* translated by Jonathan Ott.

3. Andrew Weil. Talk at Second Esalen ARUPA Conference, June 1985.

4. Francis Robicsek. *The Smoking Gods: Tobacco in Maya Art, History, and Religion.*

5. William Emboden. *Narcotic Plants;* Weil, Andrew, *From Chocolate to Morphine.*

6. Bruce Eisner. *Ecstasy: The MDMA Story*, Adamson, Sophia, ed., *Through the Gateway of the Heart.*

7. R. Gordon Wasson, Carl A. P. Ruck, Albert Hofmann. *The Road to Eleusis: Unveiling the Secret of the Mysteries.*

8. Rupert Sheldrake. *A New Science of Life.*

9. Ralph Metzner. "On the Evolutionary Signficance of Psychedelics." *Main Currents of Modern Thought* 25, no. 1 (1968): 20–25. The possible evolutionary significance of psychedelic drugs, or mushrooms specifically, has been brilliantly elucidated by Terence McKenna in his book *Food of the Gods.*

10. Ralph Metzner. "States of Consciousness and Transpersonal Psychology," in Ronald Vallee and Steen Halling eds., *Existential and Phenomenological Perspectives in Psychology,* pp. 329–38.

11. Elsewhere, I have made the argument that shamanism, alchemy, and yoga are the three historically most prominent systems of transformation of consciousness, with many parallels in the underlying processes, intentions, and methods used. See "Transformation Processes in Shamanism, Alchemy and Yoga," in Shirley Nicholson, ed., *Shamanism: An Expanded View of Reality,* pp. 233–52.

12. R. Gordon Wasson, *The Wondrous Mushroom: Mycolatry in Mesoamerica*; R. E. Schultes and A. Hofmann, *Plants of the Gods: Origins of Hallucinogenic Use;* Michael Harner, ed., *Hallucinogens and Shamanism;* Peter T. Furst, *Hallucinogens and Culture*; Joan Halifax, *Shaman: The Wounded Healer;* Luis Eduardo Luna, and Pablo Amaringo *Ayahuasca Visions;* Terence K. McKenna, and Dennis J. McKenna, *The Invisible Landscape;* Florinda Donner, *Shabono;* F. Bruce Lamb, *Wizard of the Upper Amazon;* Andrew Weil, *The Marriage of the Sun and the Moon;* Claudio Naranjo, *The Healing Journey.*

13. Michael Harner. "The Role of Hallucinogenic Plants in European Witchcraft." In *Hallucinogens and Shamanism*, edited by M. Harner. See also my *Maps of Consciousness*, where, in the chapter on alchemy, possible alchemical psychedelics are mentioned.

14. Michel Strickmann. "On the Alchemy of T'ao Hung-ching." In *Facets of Taoism,* edited by Holmes Welch, and Anna Seidel, pp. 123–92.

15. Mircea Eliade. *The Forge and the Crucible: The Origins and Structures of Alchemy.*

16. R. J. Stewart. *The Underworld Initiation: A Journey Towards Psychic Transformation.*

17. Mircea Eliade. *Yoga: Immortality and Freedom.*

18. R. Gordon Wasson. *Soma: Divine Mushroom of Immortality.*

19. Michael Aldrich. "Tantric Cannabis Use in India." *Journal of Psychedelic Drugs* 9, no. 3 (July–Sept. 1977), pp. 227–33.

20. Ralph Metzner. *Maps of Consciousness,* especially the chapters on Tantra and Actualism (Agni Yoga). See also the chapter "Purification by Inner Fire" in my book *The Unfolding Self.*

21. Mircea Eliade. *Yoga: Immortality and Freedom,* pp. 278–84. "We may say that the physicochemical processess of the *rasayana* serve as the vehicle for psychic and spiritual operations. The elixir obtained by alchemy corresponds to the 'immortality' pursued by tantric yoga" (p. 283).

22. Lama Anagarika Govinda. *Foundations of Tibetan Mysticism.*

23. See Stanislav Grof, *Beyond the Brain: Birth, Death and Transcendence in Psychotherapy,* and Lester Grinspoon and James B. Bakalar, *Psychedelic Drugs Reconsidered.*

Chapter 6: Psychopathology of the Human-Nature Relationship

1. An earlier version of this essay was published in *Ecopsychology,* edited by T. Roszak, M. Gomes, and A. Kanner, pp. 55–67, and also in *The Company of Others: Essays in Celebration of Paul Shepard,* edited by M. Oelschlaeger, pp. 197–211.

2. Wilhelm Reich. *The Mass Psychology of Fascism,* translated by Theodore Wolff; Lloyd deMause, *The Foundations of Psychohistory.*

3. Warren M. Hern. "Why Are There So Many of Us? Description and Diagnosis of a Planetary Ecopathological Process." *Population and Environment* 12, no. 1 (1990): 9–39.

4. Theodore Roszak. *The Voice of the Earth,* pp. 215–18.

5. Al Gore. *Earth in the Balance: Ecology and the Human Spirit,* p. 217. Gore also erroneously attributes the disease metaphor to deep ecology, although it is clearly not part of the deep ecology platform.

6. James Lovelock. *Healing Gaia: Practical Medicine for the Planet,* p. 154.

7. George Sessions. "Ecocentrism and the Anthropocentric Detour." *ReVision* 13, no. 1 (winter 1991): 109–15.

8. Ralph Metzner. "Psychologizing Deep Ecology: A Review Essay." *ReVision* 13, no. 3 (winter 1991): 147–52.

9. Ralph Metzner. "Pride, Prejudice and Paranoia: Dismantling the Ideology of Domination." *World Futures* 51 (1998): 239–67.

10. David Ehrenfeld. *The Arrogance of Humanism.*

11. Paul Shepard. "A Post-Historic Primitivism." In *The Wilderness Condition,* edited by Max Oelschlaeger, p. 85.

12. Paul Shepard. *Nature and Madness,* p. 40.

13. Erik Erikson. *Identity and the Life Cycle,* p. 97. Erikson pointed out how totalitarian doctrines have a special appeal to youths looking for solid identity structures: "The tempestuous adolescence lived through in patriarchal and agrarian countries . . . explains the fact that their young people find convincing and satisfactory identities in the simple totalitarian doctrines of race, class or nation" (p. 98).

14. Jean Liedloff. *The Continuum Concept.*

15. Paul Shepard. *Nature and Madness,* p. 124.

16. Ibid., p. 128.

17. Thomas Berry. "The Ecozoic Era." *Eleventh Annual E. F. Schumacher Lectures.* Great Barrington, Mass.: E. F. Schumacher Society, 1991.

18. American Psychiatric Association. *Diagnostic and Statistical Manual of Mental Disorders (DSM-IV),* 4th ed. Washington, D.C.: American Psychiatric Association, 1994, pp. 70–71.

19. Dolores LaChapelle. *Sacred Land, Sacred Sex: Rapture of the Deep,* p. 48.

20. Chellis Glendinning. *My Name Is Chellis and I'm in Recovery from Western Civilization.* Glendinning actually uses the diagnosis of posttraumatic stress disorder as well, in her insightful analysis of the malaise of civilization.

21. Quoted in A. Kanner and M. Gomes. "The All-Consuming Self." In *Ecopsychology,* p. 79.

22. Ibid., p. 89.

23. Paul Devereux. *Earthmind,* pp. 2–3.

24. Charles Pellegrino. *Unearthing Atlantis.*

25. T. Roszak. *The Voice of the Earth,* p. 320.

26. Ibid., p. 291.

27. Ernest Hilgard. *Divided Consciousness,* p. 26.

28. Robert J. Lifton. *The Nazi Doctors.*

Chapter 7: Historical Roots of the Split Between Humans and Nature

1. This essay, under the title "The Split Between Spirit and Nature in European (Western) Consciousness," was first published in the *Noetic Sciences Review* no. 25 (spring 1993): pp. 4–9; in *The Trumpeter* 10, no. 2 (winter 1993): pp. 2–9; and in *ReVision* 15, no. 4 (spring 1993): pp. 177–84. It has been completely revised for this volume.

2. Richard Leaky and Roger Lewin. *The Sixth Extinction*, p. 45. "The Big Five interrupted that rise (in diversity) dramatically, periodically plunging diversity to dangerously low levels. . . . This handful of major events, from oldest to most recent, are: the end-Ordovician (440 million years ago), the Late Devonian (365 million years ago), the end-Permian (225 million years ago), the end-Triassic (210 million years ago), and the end-Cretaceous (65 million years ago)."

3. Evelyn Fox Keller. *Reflections on Gender and Science;* Carolyn Merchant, *The Death of Nature: Women, Ecology and the Scientific Revolution.*

4. B. Vickers, ed. *Occult and Scientific Mentalities in the Renaissance;* and B. J. T. Dobbs, *The Foundations of Newton's Alchemy.*

5. Morris Berman. *The Reenchantment of the World;* Rupert Sheldrake, *The Rebirth of Nature: The Greening of Science and God.*

6. Robert Augros and George Stanciu. *The New Biology.*

7. Stephen Jay Gould. *Wonderful Life: The Burgess Shale and the Nature of History.*

8. Lynn Margulis and Dorion Sagan. *Microcosm: Four Billion Years of Microbial Evolution.*

9. David Ehrenfeld. *The Arrogance of Humanism.*

10. Rupert Sheldrake. *The Rebirth of Nature.* pp. 28–31.

11. Jack Weatherford. *Indian Givers.*

12. Alfred W. Crosby. *Ecological Imperialism: The Biological Expansion of Europe, 900–1900;* Kirkpatrick Sale, *The Conquest of Paradise: Christopher Columbus and the Columbian Legacy.*

13. Hans Koning, *The Conquest of America: How the Indian Nations Lost Their Continent;* Jerry Mander, *In the Absence of the Sacred: The Failure of Technology and the Survival of the Indian Nations.*

14. Lynn White Jr. "Historical Roots of Our Ecologic Crisis." *Science* 155 (March 1967): 1203–07.

15. Thomas Berry. *The Dream of the Earth*, p. 113.

16. J. W. Goethe. *Faust I* lines 1112–16. Translation by the present author.

17. Ralph Metzner. *The Well of Remembrance.*

18. Matthew Fox. *Illuminations of Hildegard of Bingen.* "Creation spirituality" is contrasted with mainstream Christian tradition, which has taught a spirituality concerned with the Fall and Redemption. See also the chapter on Hildegard in this volume.

19. William Blake. *The Marriage of Heaven and Hell*, Plate 11.

20. J. Donald Hughes. *American Indian Ecology.*

21. The Greek word *daimon* originally meant "spirit" in the sense of guardian spirit, or guiding spirit. Socrates was said to have consulted

with his *daimon*. It was the early church fathers who argued that intermediate spirits could not possibly be divine, since God was far removed
in a transcendental heaven. They therefore had to be in league with
the Devil, hence, demonic in the sense of evil. See Marie-Louise von
Franz, *Projection and Re-Collection in Jungian Psychology*, pp. 143–59.

Chapter 8: Sky Gods and Earth Deities

1. This essay was previously published under the title "Clashing Cultures
   and Hybrid Mythologies" in *From the Realm of the Ancestors: Essays in
   Honor of Marija Gimbutas*, edited by Joan Marler, pp. 262–77.
2. Marija Gimbutas. *The Civilization of the Goddess*, p. 401.
3. Robert Graves, in his *Greek Myths*, writes: "A study of Greek mythology should begin with a consideration of what political and religious
   systems existed in Europe before the arrival of the Aryan invaders
   from the distant North and East. The whole of Neolithic Europe, to
   judge from surviving artifacts and myths, had a remarkably homoge-
   neous system of religious ideas, based on worship of the many-titled
   Mother-goddess (p. 13). . . . All early myths about the gods' seduction
   of nymphs refer apparently to marriages between Hellenic chieftains
   and local Moon-priestesses; bitterly opposed by Hera, which means
   by conservative religious feeling (p. 18). . . . The familiar Olympian
   system was then agreed upon as a compromise between Hellenic and
   pre-Hellenic views: a divine family of six gods and goddesses, headed
   by the co-sovereigns Zeus and Hera and forming a Council of Gods
   in Babylonian style" (p.19). See also Merlin Stone, *When God Was a
   Woman*; Charlene Spretnak, *Lost Goddesses of Early Greece*; and Elinor
   Gadon, *The Once and Future Goddess*.
4. Arthur Evans. *The God of Ecstasy: Sex Roles and the Madness of Dionysus.*
5. William Anderson. *The Green Man: Archetype of Our Oneness with the
   Earth.*
6. M. W. Meyer, ed. *The Ancient Mysteries: A Sourcebook*, p. 168.
7. Alain Daniélou. *Shiva and Dionysus.*
8. I have made an audiotape of the Gilgamesh story along these lines:
   The Hero, the Wildman and the Goddess (available from the Green
   Earth Foundation, P.O. Box 327, El Verano, CA 95433).
9. For a detailed reexamination and interpretation of the Nordic-
   Germanic myths, including the conflicts between the Aesir and Vanir
   deities, in the light of Marija Gimbutas's concept of hybrid mythologies, see my *Well of Remembrance: Rediscovering the Earth Wisdom
   Mythology of Northern Europe.*

10. Snorri Sturluson, the Icelandic author who, in the thirteenth century, compiled the *Prose Edda* (also called *Younger Edda*), one of our main sources for Germanic myth, himself stated in his introduction that the Aesir were the (human) leaders of warrior bands who came from Asia. The etymological connection he made between "Aesir" and "Asia" is, however, regarded as spurious by contemporary scholars. See Rudolf Simek, *Lexikon der Germanischen Mythologie*, pp. 460–61. See also *The Well of Remembrance*, pp. 165–72.

11. Mircea Eliade. *A History of Religious Ideas*, vol. 2, p. 159.

12. J. P. Malory. *In Search of the Indo-Europeans*, pp. 137–38.

13. Merlin Stone. *When God Was a Woman.* "The image of Eve as the sexually tempting but God-defying seductress was surely intended as a warning to all Hebrew men to stay away from the sacred women of the temples, for if they succumbed to the temptations of these women, they simultaneously accepted the female deity—Her fruit, Her sexuality and, perhaps most important, the resulting matrilineal identity for any children who might be conceived in this manner. . . . The Hebrew creation myth, which blamed the female of the species for initial sexual consciousness in order to suppress the worship of the Queen of Heaven, Her sacred women and matrilineal customs, from that time on assigned women the role of sexual temptress" (pp. 221–22). See also Gerda Lerner, *The Creation of the Patriarchy;* Elinor Gadon, *The Once and Future Goddess;* Carol Ochs, *Behind the Sex of God;* and John A. Phillips, *Eve: The History of an Idea.*

14. See Ralph Metzner, *The Well of Remembrance*, pp. 165–72, for further elaboration on this fascinating myth.

15. Ibid., pp. 219–28.

16. It is interesting that according to James Lovelock's "Gaia theory"— that Earth is one vast unitary living organism—the atmosphere is, in fact, produced (outgassed) by the living matter of Earth. Thus, both ancient myth and twentieth-century science tell us that the air/sky is produced by, or born from, the living Earth.

17. Mary Condren. *The Serpent and the Goddess: Women, Religion and Power in Celtic Ireland.* See, particularly, chapter 2, "Crushing the Serpent: The End of Matricentered Ireland and the Curse of the Goddess Macha." "In the Macha story, the Irish warriors saw their period of hibernation in their 'pangs' as a curse, just as the fall from grace in the Garden of Eden was part of the curse of Yahweh. . . . The life of the warrior, under the rule of the king rather than the clan collective, would be bloody and brutal. They were indeed cursed and cast out of the

Garden of Paradise.... The Irish story has, therefore, preserved for us the true nature of the event: the matricide that lies at the heart of patriarchal culture and the Fall into patriarchal time and space that would have devastating consequences for the banished children of Eve" (p. 43).

18. Ibid., pp. 209–10.
19. R. Gordon Wasson, Carl A. P. Ruck, and Albert Hofmann. *The Road to Eleusis.*
20. Mary Condren. *The Serpent and the Goddess,* p. 26.
21. Ralph Metzner. *The Well of Remembrance,* pp. 230–38.
22. William Blake. *The Marriage of Heaven and Hell,* Plate 14.

Chapter 9: The Black Goddess, the Green God, and the Wild Human

1. This essay was originally published in *The Green Man: Magazine for Pagan Men,* 1, no. 1 and no. 2 (spring and fall, 1993); also published in C. Rätsch, ed., *Naturverehrung und Heilkunst,* Südergellesen: Verlag Bruno Martin, 1993: 37–63.
2. Ralph Metzner. *The Well of Remembrance: Rediscovering the Earth Wisdom Myths of Northern Europe.*
3. Ean Begg. *The Cult of the Black Virgin.*
4. Ibid., p. 61.
5. See the chapter in this volume on Hildegard von Bingen (chapter 4).
6. M. W. Meyer, ed. *The Ancient Mysteries. A Source Book,* p. 105.
7. Robert Graves, *Greek Myths,* 3rd ed. London: Cassell, 1960; Terence McKenna, *Food of the Gods: The Search for the Original Tree of Knowledge.*
8. Arthur Evans. *The God of Ecstasy: Sex Roles and the Madness of Dionysus.*
9. Alain Daniélou. *Shiva and Dionysus.*
10. J. O. Plassman, ed. *Orpheus: Altgriechische Mysterien,* p. 78 (English translation by the present author).
11. R. Gordon Wasson, Carl A. P. Ruck, and Albert Hofmann. *The Road to Eleusis.*
12. Ralph Metzner. *The Unfolding Self,* pp. 208–10.
13. R. Gordon Wasson. *The Wondrous Mushroom: Mycolatry in Meso-america,* p. 58.
14. J. V. Young. *Kokopelli: Casanova of the Cliff Dwellers;* Dennis Slifer, and James Duffield. *Kokopelli: Flute Player in Rock Art.*
15. Edmundo Barbosa, *Afro-Brazilian Rituals: Altered States and Healing Manifestations,* M.A. thesis, California Institute of Integral Studies, 1985; Migene Gonzales Wippler, *Tales of the Orishas.*
16. Marija Gimbutas. *The Civilization of the Goddess.*

17. Ralph Metzner. *The Unfolding Self*, pp. 190–94.

18. J. O. Plassmann, ed. *Orpheus: Altgriechische Mysterien*, p. 3.

Chapter 10: Reunification of the Sacred and the Natural

1. This essay is based in part on a presentation made at the conference of the International Transpersonal Association (ITA), May 1996, in Manaus, Brazil; an earlier version was published, in Italian and English, in the journal *Eleusis: Bulletin of the Italian Society for the Study of States of Consciousness* no. 8 (August 1997): 3–13.

2. For an account of the Harvard psychedelic research project, see my chapter "From Harvard to Zihuatanejo" in *Timothy Leary: Outside Looking In*, edited by Robert Forte.

3. As ever, language encodes historical-cultural changes and paradox. "Enthusiasm," the term of scorn used by the followers of experimental science toward the adherents of medieval alchemy and magic, is based on the Greek *entheos*, "inspired by a god." In our day, the Gaia theory of Lovelock and Margulis, which on strictly scientific grounds regards Earth as a kind of living organism, was at first attacked as being "mystical." The dictionary defines *mysticism* both as "direct, intuitive knowing of divine reality" and as "confused and groundless speculation."

4. A further note on terminology: I use "psychedelic," "hallucinogenic," and "entheogenic" interchangeably. "Psychedelic," coined by Humphrey Osmond and Aldous Huxley and popularized by Leary and the Harvard group, means "mind-manifesting." "Hallucinogenic" is the word most often used in the psychiatric research literature for these substances. The main objection to "hallucinogenic" is that these drugs and plants do not in fact induce hallucinations, in the sense of "illusory perceptions." The term *hallucinogen* deserves to be rehabilitated, however. The original meaning of the Latin *alucinare* is to "wander in one's mind," and traveling, or journeying, in inner space is actually quite an appropriate descriptive metaphor for such experiences, also referred to colloquially as "trips." The term *entheogen*, proposed by R. Gordon Wasson and Jonathan Ott, has the same root as "enthusiasm" and means "releasing the god within." See Jonathan Ott, *The Age of Entheogens and The Angels' Dictionary*.

5. Quoted from the forthcoming volume *Ayahuasca: Human Consciousness and the Spirits of Nature*, edited by Ralph Metzner.

6. For a comprehensive scientific review of psychedelic research, see Lester Grinspoon and James Bakalar, *Psychedelic Drugs Reconsidered*.

7. See *Ayahuasca*, edited by Ralph Metzner.

8. Ralph Metzner. "Hallucinogenic Drugs and Plants in Psychotherapy and Shamanism." *Journal of Psychoactive Drugs* vol. 30 (4), 1998.

9. See *Through the Gateway of the Heart: Accounts of Experiences with MDMA and Other Empathogenic Substances,* edited by Sophia Adamson; and Stanislav Grof, *LSD Psychotherapy.*

10. See Luis Eduardo Luna and Pablo Amaringo. *Ayahuasca Visions: The Religious Iconography of a Peruvian Shaman.*

11. Brian Bates. *The Wisdom of the Wyrd.*

12. See Fritjof Capra, *The Web of Life,* and Edward Goldsmith, *The Way: An Ecological Worldview.*

13. See Rosemay Radford Ruether, *Gaia and God: An Ecofeminist Theology of Earth Healing;* Charlene Spretnak, *States of Grace: The Recovery of Meaning in the Postmodern Age;* and Andrew Weil, *Natural Health, Natural Medicine.*

Chapter 11: Transition to an Ecological Worldview

1. This essay was originally published as "Age of Ecology" in *Resurgence* no. 149 (Nov/Dec 1991), and as "The Emerging Ecological Worldview" in *Worldviews and Ecology,* edited by Mary Evelyn Tucker and John Grim, pp. 163–74.

2. See *The Subversive Science: Essays Toward an Ecology of Man,* edited by Paul Shepard and Daniel McKinley.

3. See David Ray Griffin, ed., *The Reenchantment of Science: Postmodern Proposals* (SUNY Series in Constructive Postmodern Thought); see also Charlene Spretnak, *States of Grace: The Recovery of Meaning in the Postmodern Age.*

4. Willis Harman. *Global Mind Change.*

5. See Aldo Leopold, *A Sand County Almanac;* see also Van Andruss et al. *Home! A Bioregional Reader.*

6. Riane Eisler. *The Chalice and the Blade: Our History, Our Future.*

7. Murray Bookchin. *Remaking Society: Pathways to a Green Future.*

8. See Mary Evelyn Tucker and John Grim, eds., *Worldviews and Ecology;* Thomas Berry, *The Dream of the Earth.*

9. See William R. Catton, *Overshoot: The Ecological Basis of Revolutionary Change;* Hazel Henderson, *Paradigms in Progress: Life Beyond Economics.*

10. Amory Lovins. *Soft Energy Paths.*

11. See Wes Jackson, *Altars of Unhewn Stone;* Wendell Berry, *A Continuous Harmony: Essays Cultural and Agricultural.*

12. Brian Swimme and Thomas Berry. *The Universe Story.*

Chapter 12: The Place and the Story

1. This essay was first published in the *Trumpeter* 12, no. 3, (summer 1995): 119–23.
2. T. Roszak, M. Gomes, and A. Kanner, eds. *Ecopsychology: Restoring the Earth, Healing the Mind.*
3. Michael Zimmerman, et al. *Environmental Philosophy: From Animal Rights to Radical Ecology.*
4. P. Ekins. *The Gaia Atlas of Green Economics.*
5. M. E. Tucker and J. A. Grim, eds. *Worldviews and Ecology.*
6. William R. Catton, *Overshoot: The Ecological Basis of Revolutionary Change;* Clive Ponting, *A Green History of the World.*
7. C. Spretnak. *States of Grace: The Recovery of Meaning in the Postmodern Age.*
8. E. Goldsmith. *The Way: An Ecological World-view;* and Fritjof Capra, *The Web of Life.*
9. Carolyn Merchant. *Radical Ecology: The Search for a Livable World.* This book is a good overview of these movements, though bioregionalism is actually not included among them. I believe that it should be.
10. Kirkpatrick Sale. *Dwellers in the Land: The Bioregional Vision;* Van Andruss, et al., *Home! A Bioregional Reader.*
11. Jerry Mander. *In the Absence of the Sacred: The Failure of Technology and the Survival of the Indian Nations.*
12. William Blake. *The Marriage of Heaven and Hell,* Plate 11.
13. Wallace Stegner. *Where the Bluebird Sings to the Lemonade Springs,* p. 202.
14. Brian Swimme and Thomas Berry. *The Universe Story: From the Primordial Flaring Forth to the Ecozoic Era.*
15. Rupert Sheldrake. *The Presence of the Past: Morphic Resonance and the Habits of Nature.*
16. Kim Stafford. *Places and Stories,* p. 11.
17. T. S. Eliot. "Little Gidding" from *Four Quartets.*

Epilogue

1. Quoted in Matthew Fox, *Original Blessings.*
2. Allen Ginsberg in *Beyond Life.*
3. Timothy Leary in *Beyond Life.*
4. "Working for Moloch after reading Adrienne Rich," by Mary McCann.

Bibliography

Adamson, Sophia, ed. *Through the Gateway of the Heart: Accounts of Experiences with MDMA and Other Empathogenic Substances.* San Francisco: Four Trees Publications, 1985.

American Psychiatric Association. *Diagnostic and Statistical Manual of Mental Disorders (DSM-IV)* 4th edition. Washington, D.C.: American Psychiatric Association, 1994.

Anderson, William. *The Green Man: Archetype of Our Oneness with the Earth.* New York: HarperCollins, 1990.

Andruss, Van, et al. *Home! A Bioregional Reader.* Philadelphia: New Society Publishers, 1990.

Augros, Robert, and George Stanciu. *The New Biology.* Boston: Shambhala, 1988.

Bates, Brian. *The Wisdom of the Wyrd.* London: Rider & Co., 1996.

Bateson, Gregory. *Mind and Nature: A Necessary Unity.* New York: E. P. Dutton, 1979.

Becker, Robert O., and Gary Selden. *The Body Electric: Electromagneticsm and the Foundation of Life.* New York: William Morrow, 1985.

Begg, Ean. *The Cult of the Black Virgin.* London: Routledge & Kegan Paul, 1985.

Berman, Morris. *The Reenchantment of the World.* Ithaca, N.Y.: Cornell University Press, 1989.

Berry, Thomas. *The Dream of the Earth.* San Francisco: Sierra Club Books, 1988.

Berry, Wendell. *A Continuous Harmony: Essays Cultural and Agricultural.* San Diego: Harcourt, Brace, Jovanovich, 1970.

Bingen, Hildegard von. *Wisse die Wege: Scivias.* Translated into German from the Latin by Maura Bockeler. Salzburg: Otto Muller Verlag, 1954.

————. *Quellen des Heils.* Salzburg: Otto Muller Verlag, 1982.

Blake, William. *The Marriage of Heaven and Hell.* Oxford: Oxford University Press facsimile edition, 1975. (Originally published in 1789.)

Bookchin, Murray. *Remaking Society: Pathways to a Green Future.* Boston: South End Press, 1990.

Brown, Lester, et al. *State of the World: 1998.* New York: W.W. Norton & Co., 1998.

Callicott, J. Baird. *Earth's Insights.* Berkeley: University of California Press, 1994.

Capra, Fritjof. *The Web of Life.* New York: Doubleday Anchor Books, 1996.

Catton, William R. *Overshoot: The Ecological Basis of Revolutionary Change.* Urbana: University of Illinois Press, 1980.

Condren, Mary. *The Serpent and the Goddess: Women, Religion and Power in Celtic Ireland.* New York: HarperCollins, 1989.

Crosby, Alfred W. *Ecological Imperialism: The Biological Expansion of Europe, 900–1900.* Cambridge: Cambridge University Press, 1986.

Daniélou, Alain. *Shiva and Dionysus.* London: East-West Publications, 1982.

deMause, Lloyd. *The Foundations of Psychohistory.* New York: Creative Roots, Inc., 1982.

Devereux, Paul. *Earthmind.* San Francisco: Harper & Row, 1989.

Dobbs, B. J. T. *The Foundations of Newton's Alchemy.* Cambridge: Cambridge University Press, 1975.

Donner, Florinda. *Shabono.* New York: Delacorte Press, 1982.

Dunlap, Riley, and Angela Mertig, eds. *American Environmentalism: The U.S. Environmental Movement 1970–1990.* Philadelphia: Taylor & Francis, 1992.

Durning, Alan Thein. *Guardians of the Land: Indigenous Peoples and the Health of the Earth.* Washington D.C.: Worldwatch Institute, 1992. (Worldwatch Paper 112.)

Edinger, Edward. *Anatomy of the Psyche: Alchemical Symbolism in Psychotherapy.* La Salle, Ill.: Open Court Publishing Co., 1985.

Ehrenfeld, David. *The Arrogance of Humanism.* Oxford: Oxford University Press, 1978.

Eisler, Riane. *The Chalice and the Blade: Our History, Our Future.* San Francisco: Harper & Row, 1987.

Eisner, Bruce. *Ecstasy: The MDMA Story.* Berkeley, Calif.: Ronin Publishing, 1989.

Ekins, Paul. *The Gaia Atlas of Green Economics.* New York: Doubleday Anchor Books, 1992.

Eliade, Mircea. *Yoga: Immortality and Freedom*. Princeton, N.J.: Pantheon Books, 1958.

———. *The Forge and the Crucible: The Origins and Structures of Alchemy*. New York: Harper & Row, 1962.

———. *A History of Religious Ideas*, vol. 2. Chicago: University of Chicago Press, 1982.

Eliot, T. S. *Four Quartets*. London: Faber & Faber, 1944.

Emboden, William. *Narcotic Plants*. London: Studio Vista, 1972.

Erikson, Erik. *Identity and the Life Cycle*. New York: Norton & Co., 1980. (1959).

Evans, Arthur. *The God of Ecstasy: Sex Roles and the Madness of Dionysos*. New York: Saint Martin's Press, 1988.

Forte, Robert, ed. *Timothy Leary: Outside Looking In*. Rochester, Vt.: Inner Traditions International, 1999.

Foster, John Bellamy. *The Vulnerable Planet: A Short Economic History of the Environment*. New York: Monthly Review Press, 1994.

Fox, Matthew. *Illuminations of Hildegard von Bingen*. Santa Fe: Bear & Co., 1985.

Fox, Warwick. *Toward a Transpersonal Ecology*. Boston: Shambhala, 1990.

Furst, Peter T. *Hallucinogens and Culture*. San Francisco: Chandler & Sharp, 1976.

Gadon, Elinor. *The Once and Future Goddess*. San Francisco: Harper & Row, 1989.

Gimbutas, Marija. *The Civilization of the Goddess*. San Francisco: HarperCollins, 1991.

Glendinning, Chellis. *My Name Is Chellis and I'm in Recovery from Western Civilization*. Boston: Shambhala, 1994.

Goldsmith, Edward. *The Way: An Ecological World-view*. Boston: Shambhala, 1993.

Gore, Al. *Earth in the Balance: Ecology and the Human Spirit*. Boston: Houghton Mifflin Co., 1992.

Gould, Stephen Jay. *Wonderful Life: The Burgess Shale and the Nature of History*. New York: W.W. Norton & Co., 1989.

Govinda, Lama Anagarika. *Foundations of Tibetan Mysticism*. New York: Samuel Weiser, 1960.

Graves, Robert. *Greek Myths*. London: Penguin Books, 1955.

Griffin, David Ray, ed. *The Reenchantment of Science: Postmodern Proposals*. Albany: State University of New York Press, 1988.

Grinspoon, Lester, and James B. Bakalar. *Psychedelic Drugs Reconsidered*. New York: Basic Books, 1979.

Grof, Stanislav. *LSD Psychotherapy*. Pomona, Calif.: Hunter House, 1980.

———. *Beyond the Brain: Birth, Death and Transcendence in Psychotherapy*. Albany: State University of New York Press, 1985.

Halifax, Joan. *Shaman: The Wounded Healer.* New York: Crossroad, 1982.

Harman, Willis. *Global Mind Change.* Indianapolis: IONS & Knowledge Systems, 1988.

Harner, Michael, ed. *Hallucinogens and Shamanism.* Oxford: Oxford University Press, 1973.

Henderson, Hazel. *Paradigms in Progress: Life Beyond Economics.* Indianopolis: Knowledge Systems, 1991.

Hilgard, Ernest. *Divided Consciousness.* New York: John Wiley & Sons, 1986.

Hofmann, Albert. *LSD: My Problem Child.* Translated by Jonathan Ott. Los Angeles: Jeremy P. Tarcher, 1983.

Holy Bible. George M. Larnsa translation from the Aramaic of the Peshitta. San Francisco: Harper & Row, 1957.

Hughes, J. Donald. *American Indian Ecology.* El Paso: University of Texas Press, 1983.

Jackson, Wes. *Altars of Unhewn Stone.* Berkeley, Calif.: North Point Press, 1987.

Keller, Evelyn Fox. *Reflections on Gender and Science.* New Haven, Conn.: Yale University Press, 1985.

Koning, Hans. *The Conquest of America: How the Indian Nations Lost Their Continent.* New York: Monthly Review Press, 1993.

LaChapelle, Dolores. *Sacred Land, Sacred Sex: Rapture of the Deep.* Silverton, Colo.: Fine Hill Arts, 1988.

Lakoff, George, and Mark Johnson. *Metaphors We Live By.* Chicago: University of Chicago Press, 1980.

Lamb, F. Bruce. *Wizard of the Upper Amazon.* New York: Houghton Mifflin, 1971.

Leaky, Richard, and Roger Lewin. *The Sixth Extinction.* New York: Doubleday, 1995.

Lehrman, Frederick, ed. *The Sacred Landscape.* San Rafael, Calif.: Celestial Arts, 1988.

Leopold, Aldo. *A Sand County Almanac.* Oxford: Oxford University Press, 1949.

Lerner, Gerda. *The Creation of the Patriarchy.* Oxford: Oxford University Press, 1986.

Liedloff, Jean. *The Continuum Concept.* Reading, Mass.: Addison-Wesley, 1977.

Lifton, Robert J. *The Nazi Doctors: Medical Killing and the Psychology of Genocide.* New York: Basic Books, 1988.

Lovelock, James. *GAIA: A New Look at Life on Earth.* Oxford: Oxford University Press, 1979.

———. *Healing Gaia: Practical Medicine for the Planet.* New York: Harmony Books, 1991.

Lovins, Amory. *Soft Energy Paths.* Cambridge, Mass.: Ballinger, 1977.

Luna, Luis Eduardo, and Pablo Amaringo. *Ayahuasca Visions: The Religious*

Iconography of a Peruvian Shaman. Berkeley, Calif.: North Atlantic Books, 1991.

Malory, J. P. *In Search of the Indo-Europeans*. London; Thames & Hudson, 1989.

Mander, Jerry. *In the Absence of the Sacred: The Failure of Technology and the Survival of the Indian Nations*. San Francisco: Sierra Club Books, 1991.

Mander, Jerry, and Edward Goldsmith, eds. *The Case Against the Global Economy*. San Francisco: Sierra Club Books, 1996.

Margulis, Lynn, and Dorion Sagan. *Microcosm: Four Billion Years of Microbial Evolution*. New York: Summit Books, 1986.

Marler, Joan, ed. *From the Realm of the Ancestors: Essays in Honor of Marija Gimbutas*. Manchester, Conn: Knowledge, Ideas and Trends, 1997.

McKenna, Terence. *Food of the Gods: The Search for the Original Tree of Knowledge*. New York: Bantam Books, 1992.

McKenna, Terence K., and Dennis J. McKenna. *The Invisible Landscape*. New York: The Seabury Press, 1975.

Merchant, Carolyn. *The Death of Nature: Women, Ecology and the Scientific Revolution*. San Francisco: Harper & Row, 1980.

————. *Radical Ecology: The Search for a Livable World*. New York: Routledge, 1992.

Metzner, Ralph. *Maps of Consciousness*. New York: Collier-Macmillan, 1971.

————. *Know Your Type*. Garden City, N.Y.: Doubleday Anchor Press, 1978.

————. *The Well of Remembrance: Rediscovering the Earth Wisdom Mythology of Northern Europe*. Boston: Shambhala, 1994.

————. *The Unfolding Self: Varieties of Transformative Experience*. Novato, Calif.: Origin Press, 1997.

————, ed. *Ayahuasca: Human Consciousness and the Spirits of Nature*. New York: Thunder's Mouth Press, 1999.

Meyer, M. W., ed. *The Ancient Mysteries: A Sourcebook*. San Francisco: Harper & Row, 1987.

Naranjo, Claudio. *The Healing Journey*. New York: Ballantine Books, 1973.

Neihardt, John. *Black Elk Speaks*. Lincoln: University of Nebraska Press, 1961.

Nicholson, Shirley, ed. *Shamanism: An Expanded View of Reality*, Wheaton, Ill.: Theosophical Publishing House, 1987.

Ochs, Carol. *Behind the Sex of God*. Boston: Beacon Press, 1977.

Oelschlaeger, Max, ed. *The Wilderness Condition*. San Francisco: Sierra Club Books, 1992.

————, ed. *The Company of Others: Essays in Celebration of Paul Shepard*. Durango, Colo.: Kivakí Press, 1995.

Ott, Jonathan. *The Age of Entheogens and The Angels' Dictionary*. Kennewick, Wash.: Natural Products Co., 1995.

Pellegrino, Charles. *Unearthing Atlantis*. New York: Random House, 1991.

Phillips, John A. *Eve: The History of an Idea*. San Francisco: Harper & Row, 1984.

Plassman, J. O., ed. *Orpheus: Altgriechische Mysterien*. Köln: Eugen Diederichs Verlag, 1982.

Ponting, Clive. *A Green History of the World*. New York: Saint Martin's Press, 1991.

Rätsch, Christian, ed. *The Gateway to Inner Space*. Garden City Park, N.Y.: Avery Publishing, 1989.

————. *The Dictionary of Sacred and Magical Plants*. Santa Barbara: ABC-Clio, 1992.

————, ed. *Naturverehrung und Heilkunst*. Südergellesen: Verlag Bruno Martin, 1993.

Reich, Wilhelm. *The Mass Psychology of Fascism*. New York: Orgone Institute Press, 1946.

Roberts, Elizabeth, and Elias Amidon, eds. *Earth Prayers*. San Fransisco: HarperSanFrancisco, 1991.

Robicsek, Francis. *The Smoking Gods. Tobacco in Maya Art, History, and Religion*. Norman: University of Oklahoma Press, 1978.

Roszak, Theodore. *Person/Planet*. Garden City, N.Y.: Anchor Press, Doubleday, 1979.

Roszak, Theodore. *The Voice of the Earth*. New York: Simon & Schuster, 1992.

————, Mary Gomes, and Allen Kanner, eds. *Ecopsychology: Restoring the Earth, Healing the Mind*. San Francisco: Sierra Club Books, 1995.

Ruether, Rosemay Radford. *Gaia and God: An Ecofeminist Theology of Earth Healing*. San Fransisco: HarperSanFrancisco, 1992.

Russell, Peter. *The Global Brain*. Los Angeles: Jeremy P. Tarcher, 1983.

Sale, Kirkpatrick. *Dwellers in the Land: The Bioregional Vision*. San Francisco: Sierra Club Books, 1985.

————. *The Conquest of Paradise: Christopher Columbus and the Columbian Legacy*. New York: Alfred A. Knopf, 1990.

Schmookler, A. B. *The Parable of the Tribes*. Berkeley: University of California Press, 1984.

Schultes, R. E. and A. Hofmann. *Plants of the Gods: Origins of Hallucinogenic Use*. New York: McGraw-Hill, 1979.

Sheldrake, Rupert. *A New Science of Life*. Los Angeles: Jeremy P. Tarcher, 1981.

————. *The Presence of the Past: Morphic Resonance and the Habits of Nature*. New York: Times Books, 1988.

————. *The Rebirth of Nature: The Greening of Science and God*. New York: Bantam Books, 1991.

Shepard, Paul. *Nature and Madness*. San Francisco: Sierra Club Books, 1982.

Shepard, Paul, and Donald McKinley, eds. *The Subversive Science: Essays Toward an Ecology of Man.* Boston: Houghton-Mifflin, 1967.

Shiva, Vandana. *Monocultures of the Mind: Perspectives on Biodiversity and Biotechnology.* London: Zed Books, 1993.

Simek, Rudolf. *Lexikon der Germanischen Mythologie.* Stuttgart: Alfred Kröner Verlag, 1984.

Simeons, A. T. W. *Man's Presumptuous Brain.* New York: E. P. Dutton, 1961.

Slifer, Dennis, and James Duffield. *Kokopelli: Flute Player in Rock Art.* Santa Fe: Ancient City Press, 1994.

Spretnak, Charlene. *Lost Goddesses of Early Greece.* Boston: Beacon Press, 1978.

———. *States of Grace: The Recovery of Meaning in the Postmodern Age.* San Fransisco: HarperSanFrancisco, 1992.

Stafford, Kim. *Places and Stories.* Pittsburgh: Carnegie Mellon University Press, 1987.

Stegner, Wallace. *Where the Bluebird Sings to the Lemonade Springs.* New York: Penguin Books, 1993.

Stewart, R. J. *The Underworld Initiation. A Journey Towards Psychic Transformation.* Wellingborough, England: The Aquarian Press, 1985.

Stone, Merlin. *When God Was a Woman.* New York: Harcourt, Brace, Jovanovich, 1976.

Swimme, Brian. *The Universe Is a Green Dragon.* Santa Fe: Bear & Co., 1985.

Swimme, Brian, and Thomas Berry. *The Universe Story: From the Primordial Flaring Forth to the Ecozoic Era.* San Fransisco: HarperSanFrancisco, 1993.

Tucker, Mary Evelyn, and John Grim, eds. *Worldviews and Ecology.* Lewisburg, Pa.: Bucknell University Press, 1993.

Vallee, Ronald, and Steen Halling, eds. *Existential and Phenomenological Perspectives in Psychology.* New York: Plenum Press, 1988.

Velikovsky, Immanuel. *Mankind in Amnesia.* Garden City, N.Y.: Doubleday & Co., 1982.

Vickers, B., ed. *Occult and Scientific Mentalities in the Renaissance.* Cambridge: Cambridge University Press, 1984.

von Franz, Marie-Louise. *Projection and Re-Collection in Jungian Psychology.* La Salle, Ill: Open Court Publishing, 1980.

Wasson, R. Gordon. *Soma: Divine Mushroom of Immortality.* New York: Harcourt, Brace, Jovanovich, 1971.

———. *The Wondrous Mushroom: Mycolatry in Mesoamerica.* New York: McGraw-Hill, 1980.

Wasson, R. Gordon, Carl A. P. Ruck, and Albert Hofmann. *The Road to Eleusis: Unveiling the Secret of the Mysteries.* New York: Harcourt, Brace, Jovanovich, 1978.

Weatherford, Jack. *Indian Givers*. New York: Fawcett Columbine-Ballantine Books, 1988.

Weil, Andrew. *The Marriage of the Sun and the Moon*. New York: Houghton Mifflin, 1980.

——. *From Chocolate to Morphine*. New York: Houghton Mifflin, 1983.

——. *Natural Health, Natural Medicine*. Boston: Houghton Mifflin, 1990.

Welch, Holmes, and Anna Seidel, eds. *Facets of Taoism*. New Haven, Conn.: Yale University Press, 1979.

Wippler, Migene Gonzales. *Tales of the Orishas*. New York: Original Publications, 1985.

Young, J. V. *Kokopelli: Casanova of the Cliff Dwellers*. Palmer Lake, Colo.: Filter Press, 1990.

Zimmerman, Michael, et al. *Environmental Philosophy: From Animal Rights to Radical Ecology*. Englewood Cliffs, N.J.: Prentice Hall, 1993.

Index

BOOKS OF RELATED INTEREST

THE UNIVERSE IS A GREEN DRAGON
A Cosmic Creation Story
by Brian Swimme, Ph.D.

CATASTROPHOBIA
The Truth Behind Earth Changes in the Coming Age of Light
by Barbara Hand Clow

ORIGINAL WISDOM
Stories of an Ancient Way of Knowing
by Robert Wolff

THE WORLD IS AS YOU DREAM IT
Shamanic Teachings from the Amazon and Andes
by John Perkins

WALKING ON THE WIND
Cherokee Teachings for Harmony and Balance
by Michael Garrett

PASSION FOR CREATION
The Earth-Honoring Spirituality of Meister Eckhart
by Matthew Fox

A SPIRITUALITY NAMED COMPASSION
Uniting Mystical Awareness with Social Justice
by Matthew Fox

SACRED PLACES
How the Living Earth Seeks Our Friendship
by James Swan

Inner Traditions • Bear & Company
P.O. Box 388 • Rochester, VT 05767
1-800-246-8648 • www.InnerTraditions.com
Or contact your local bookseller